THE MUELLER PAPERS

Compiled by Strong Arm Press with an Introduction by Ryan Grim

WASHINGTON D.C.

Editors: Ryan Grim & Peter James Callahan

Cover Design: Paige Kelly

Copy Editor: Alex Abbott

Managing Editor: Troy N. Miller

Requests for permission to reproduce selections from this book should be mailed to: Strong Arm Press, 1440 G St NW, Washington, D.C. 20005

Published in the United States by Strong Arm Press, 2019

www.strongarmpress.com

ISBN-13: 978-1-947492-30-1

Contents

INTRODUCTION BY RYAN GRIM

It was the firing heard round the world. With one move, on the advice of his son-in-law Jared Kushner, Donald Trump fired James Comey on May 9, 2017. It would change the course of the Trump presidency.

Comey, delivering a speech in California, learned of his termination when it flashed across cable news. Trump, under pressure to explain his decision, blamed a Justice Department official named Rod Rosenstein, a man Trump himself had appointed to his position. In explaining the firing, Trump released a memo Rosenstein had written, at Trump's request, that listed Comey's failures over the years.

It was Trump's second impulsive move, and it may have been his most consequential. Attorney General Jeff Sessions, much to Trump's dismay, had recused himself from oversight of the probe into Russian interference in the 2016 election. That meant the authority fell to Rosenstein, the next-highest ranking official in the Department of Justice. Infuriated by Trump's attempt to pin the blame for Comey's firing on him, Rosenstein used the power he had at his unilateral disposal to do the one thing that could cause Trump more damage than anything else: He created the position of Special Counsel, and filled it with former FBI director Robert Mueller.

"Bob Mueller is one of the country's great, great pros," Comey said during his 2017 Senate testimony.

The product of Mueller's year and a half of investigation may never be made public, but the investigation has already produced some of the most extraordinary documents made public by a prosecutor in the United States, opening a rare window into the world of big money, high-stakes politics and foreign lobbying, a world that normally operates in dim Georgetown restaurants or in hotel bars in exotic locales.

Those documents are to be found in Mueller's legal filings. "Mueller has spoken loudly, if indirectly, in court — indictment by indictment, guilty plea by guilty plea. In doing so, he tracked an elaborate Russian operation that injected chaos into a U.S. presidential election and tried to help Trump win the White House. He followed a GOP campaign that embraced the Kremlin's help and championed stolen material to hurt a political foe. And ultimately, he revealed layers of lies, deception, self-enrichment and hubris that followed. Woven through thousands of court papers, the special counsel has made his public report," wrote Chad Day and

Eric Tucker of The Associated Press, after an exhaustive review of his filings.

President Trump repeatedly dubbed the Mueller probe a "Witch Hunt" propelled forward by a "Fake News Media" and a Deep State hellbent on undermining his administration. Readers can decide for themselves how legitimate the inquiry was.

As it relates to the Trump presidency specifically, the mandate of the investigation related to whether he or senior members of his campaign actively colluded with the Russian government's attempts to undermine Hillary Clinton, and whether Trump or his associates tried to cover up such activity and obstruct the investigation into it. If they did, what did they have to gain from it? No charges have been filed against anyone in the Trump orbit for colluding with Russian government officials.

Of more general importance is the integrity of our elections themselves. The peaceful transfer of power, an underappreciated innovation of our politics, rests on faith in the fairness of democracy and of our elections. Mueller's filings, if heeded by lawmakers typically bored by the issue of election security, may be the first step toward earning back that trust.

CHAPTER 1: GEORGE PAPADOPOULOS, OCT. 5, 2017

UNITED STATES v. GEORGE PAPADOPOULOS

FILED: October 5, 2017 in the U.S. District Court for the District of Columbia

Editor's Note: On July 27, 2017, former Trump campaign aide George Papadopoulos stepped off a flight at Dulles International airport and was arrested by federal agents before he reached customs. He was charged with lying to the FBI, and would eventually become a cooperating witness for Special Counsel Robert Mueller.

Timeline of Events

March 2016: PAPADOPOULOS joins the Trump campaign as a London-based foreign policy advisor.

March 14, 2016 - April 2016: PAPADOPOULOS (as a representative of the campaign's relatively small team of foreign policy advisors) seeks out meetings and maintains correspondence with various individuals connected to the Russian government in an attempt to begin discussions on how U.S.-Russian relations might improve if Trump were to become president and to facilitate a possible meeting between Putin and Trump - or other representatives of the Russian government and the Trump campaign - before the election.

April 26, 2016: PAPADOPOULOS is told by one of his main Russian contacts that Moscow is in possession of a large trove of potentially damaging emails connected to the Clinton campaign. PAPADOPOULOS will continue to work to secure a face-to-face between Trump and Putin or their representatives after learning this.

July 22, 2016: Wikileaks begins to release the emails stolen from the DNC.

On or about August 15, 2016: PAPADOPOULOS is encouraged by his supervisor to make a trip to meet with Russian officials off-the-record as a representative of the campaign but this meeting never occurs.

October 7, 2016: Wikileaks starts publishing emails stolen from Clinton's campaign chairman, John Podesta.

January 27, 2017: PAPADOPOULOS lies about his Russia contacts in an interview with the FBI.

February 16, 2017: PAPADOPOULOS is interviewed again by the FBI.

July 27, 2017: PAPADOPOULOS is arrested by the FBI at Washington-Dulles airport in Virginia while returning to the United States. Shortly after, PAPADOPOULOS begins cooperating with federal investigators.

October 5 2017: PAPADOPOULOS pleads guilty to making false statements to the FBI.

Statement of the Offense

Pursuant to Federal Rule of Criminal Procedure, the United States of America and the defendant, GEORGE PAPADOPOULOS, stipulate and agree that the following facts are true and accurate. These facts do not constitute all of the facts known to the parties concerning the charged offense; they are being submitted to demonstrate that sufficient facts exist that the defendant committed the offense to which he is pleading guilty.

I.   *Overview*

1.   The defendant, GEORGE PAPADOPOULOS, who served as a foreign policy advisor for the presidential campaign of Donald J. Trump (the "Campaign"), made material false statements and material omissions during an interview with the Federal Bureau of Investigation ("FBI") that took place on January 27, 2017. At the time of the interview, the FBI had an open investigation into the Russian government's efforts to interfere in the 2016 presidential election, including the nature of any links between individuals associated with the Campaign and the Russian government, and whether there was any coordination between the Campaign and Russia's efforts. The FBI opened and coordinated the investigation in Washington, D.C.

2.   Defendant PAPADOPOULOS made the following material false statements and material omissions to the FBI:

a.   Defendant PAPADOPOULOS claimed that his interactions with an overseas professor, who defendant PAPADOPOULOS understood to have substantial connections to Russian government officials, occurred before defendant PAPADOPOULOS became a foreign policy adviser to the Campaign. Defendant PAPADOPOULOS acknowledged that the professor had told him about the Russians possessing "dirt" on then-candidate Hillary Clinton in the form of " thousands of emails," but stated multiple times that he learned that information prior to joining the Campaign. In truth and in fact, however, defendant PAPADOPOULOS learned he would be an advisor to the Campaign in early March, and met the professor on or about March 14, 2016; the professor only took interest in defendant PAPADOPOULOS because of his status with the Campaign; and the professor told defendant PAPADOPOULOS about the "thousands of emails" on or about April 26, 2016, when defendant PAPADOPOULOS had been a foreign policy adviser to the Campaign for over a month.

b. Defendant PAPADOPOULOS further told the investigating agents that the professor was "a nothing" and "just a guy talk[ing] up connections or something." In truth and in fact, however, defendant PAPADOPOULOS understood that the professor had substantial connections to Russian government officials (and had met with some of those officials in Moscow immediately prior to telling defendant PAPADOPOULOS about the "thousands of emails") and, over a period of months, defendant PAPADOPOULOS repeatedly sought to use the professor's Russian connections in an effort to arrange a meeting between the Campaign and Russian government officials.

3. Defendant PAPADOPOULOS claimed he met a certain female Russian national before he joined the Campaign and that their communications consisted of emails such as, "Hi, how are you?" In truth and in fact, however, defendant PAPADOPOULOS met the female Russian national on or about March 24, 2016, after he had become an adviser to the Campaign; he believed that she had connections to Russian government officials; and he sought to use her Russian connections over a period of months in an effort to arrange a meeting between the Campaign and Russian government officials. Through his false statements and omissions, defendant PAPADOPOULOS impeded the FBI's ongoing investigation into the existence of any links or coordination between individuals associated with the Campaign and the Russian government's efforts to interfere with the 2016 presidential election.

II   *Timeline of Selected Events*
PAPADOPOULOS' Role on the Campaign

4. In early March 2016, defendant PAPADOPOULOS learned he would be a foreign policy advisor for the Campaign. Defendant PAPADOPOULOS was living in London, England, at the time. Based on a conversation that took place on or about March 6, 2016, with a supervisory campaign official (the "Campaign Supervisor"), defendant PAPADOPOULOS understood that a principal foreign policy focus of the Campaign was an improved U.S. relationship with Russia.

PAPADOPOULOS 's Introduction to the Professor and the Female Russian National

5. On or about March 14, 2016, while traveling in Italy, defendant PAPADOPOULOS met an individual who was a professor based in London (the "Professor"). Initially, the Professor seemed uninterested in defendant PAPADOPOULOS. However, after defendant PAPADOPOULOS informed the Professor about his joining the Campaign, the Professor appeared to take great interest in defendant PAPADOPOULOS. Defendant PAPADOPOULOS was interested in the

Professor because, among other reasons, the Professor claimed to have substantial connections with Russian government officials, which defendant PAPADOPOULOS thought could increase his importance as a policy advisor to the Campaign.

6.   On or about March 21, 2016 , the Campaign told *The Washington Post* that defendant PAPADOPOULOS was one of five named foreign policy advisors for the Campaign.

7.   On or about March 24, 2016, defendant PAPADOPOULOS met with the Professor in London. The Professor brought with him a female Russian national (the "Female Russian National"), introduced to defendant PAPADOPOULOS as a relative of Russian President Vladimir Putin with connections to senior Russian government officials.

PAPADOPOULOS Pursues His Contacts with the Professor and the Female Russian National

8.   Following his March 24, 2016 meeting with the Professor and the Female Russian National, defendant PAPADOPOULOS emailed the Campaign Supervisor and several members of the Campaign's foreign policy team and stated that he had just met with his "good friend" the Professor, who had introduced him to the Female Russian National (described by defendant PAPADOPOULOS in the email as "Putin's niece") and the Russian Ambassador in London (*Footnote 1:* Defendant PAPADOPOULOS later learned that the Female Russian National was not in fact a relative of President Putin. In addition, while defendant PAPADOPOULOS expected that the Professor and the Female Russian National would introduce him to the Russian Ambassador in London, they never did.) Defendant PAPADOPOULOS stated that the topic of their discussion was "to arrange a meeting between us and the Russian leadership to discuss U.S.-Russia ties.under President Trump." The Campaign Supervisor responded that he would "work it through the campaign," but that no commitments should be made at that point. The Campaign Supervisor added: "Great work."

9.   On or about March 31, 2016, defendant PAPADOPOULOS attended a "national security meeting" in Washington, D.C., with then-candidate Trump and other foreign policy advisors for the Campaign. When defendant PAPADOPOULOS introduced himself to the group, he stated, in sum and substance, that he had connections that could help arrange a meeting between then-candidate Trump and President Putin.

10.   After his trip to Washington, D.C., defendant PAPADOPOULOS worked with the Professor and the Female Russian National to arrange a meeting between the Campaign and the Russian government, and took steps to advise the Campaign of his progress.

a.   In early April 2016, defendant PAPADOPOULOS sent multiple emails to other members of the Campaign's foreign policy team regarding his contacts with "the Russians" and his "outreach to Russia."

    b. On or about April 10, 2016, defendant PAPADOPOULOS emailed the Female Russian National, who responded the next day, on or about April 11, 2016, that she "would be very pleased to support your initiatives between our two countries." Defendant PAPADOPOULOS then asked the Female Russian National, in an email cc'ing the Professor, about setting up "a potential foreign policy trip to Russia."

    c. The Professor responded to defendant PAPADOPOULOS' email later that day, on or about April 11, 2016: "This [has] already been agreed. I am flying to Moscow on the 18th for a Valda meeting, plus other meetings at the Duma." The Duma is a Russian government legislative assembly.

    d. The Female Russian National responded: "I have already alerted my personal links to our conversation and your request... As mentioned we are all very excited by the possibility of a good relationship with Mr. Trump. The Russian Federation would love to welcome him once his candidature would be officially announced."

The Professor Introduces PAPADOPOULOS to a Russian National Connected to the Russian Ministry of Foreign Affairs

    11. On or about April 18, 2016, the Professor introduced defendant PAPADOPOULOS over email to an individual in Moscow (the "Russian MFA Connection") who told defendant PAPADOPOULOS he had connections to the Russian Ministry of Foreign Affairs ("MFA"). The MFA is the executive entity in Russia responsible for Russian foreign relations. Over the next several weeks, defendant PAPADOPOULOS and the Russian MFA Connection had multiple conversations over Skype and email about setting "the groundwork" for a "potential" meeting between the Campaign and Russian government officials.

    12. On or about April 22, 2016, the Russian MFA Connection sent defendant PAPADOPOULOS an email thanking him "for an extensive talk" and proposing "to meet in London or in Moscow." Defendant PAPADOPOULOS replied by suggesting that "we set one up here in London with the Ambassador as well to discuss a process moving forward."

    13. On or about April 25, 2016, defendant PAPADOPOULOS emailed a senior policy advisor for the Campaign (the "Senior Policy Advisor"): "The Russian government has an open invitation by Putin for Mr. Trump to meet him when he is ready. The advantage of being in London is that these governments tend to speak a bit more openly in 'neutral' cities."

PAPADOPOULOS learns that the Russians Have "Dirt" on Clinton

14. On or about April 26, 2016, defendant PAPADOPOULOS met the Professor for breakfast at a London hotel. During this meeting, the Professor told defendant PAPADOPOULOS that he had just returned from a trip to Moscow where he had met with high- level Russian government officials. The Professor told defendant PAPADOPOULOS that on that trip he (the Professor) learned that the Russians had obtained "dirt" on then-candidate Clinton. The Professor told defendant PAPADOPOULOS, as defendant PAPADOPOULOS later described to the FBI, that "[The Russians] have dirt on her"; "the Russians had emails of Clinton"; "they have thousands of emails."

15. Following that conversation, defendant PAPADOPOULOS continued to correspond with Campaign officials, and continued to communicate with the Professor and the Russian MFA Connection, in an effort to arrange a meeting between the Campaign and the Russian government.

    a. For example, the day after his meeting at the hotel with the Professor, on or about April 27, 2016, defendant PAPADOPOULOS emailed the Senior Policy Advisor: "Have some interesting messages coming in from Moscow about a trip when the time is right."

    b. Also on or about April 27, 2016, defendant PAPADOPOULOS emailed a high-ranking official of the Campaign (the "High-Ranking Campaign Official") "to discuss Russia's interest in hosting Mr. Trump. Have been receiving a lot of calls over the last month about Putin wanting to host him and the team when the time is right."

    c. On or about April 30, 2016, defendant PAPADOPOULOS thanked the Professor for his "critical help" in arranging a meeting between the Campaign and the Russian government, and remarked: "lt's history making if it happens."

PAPADOPOULOS Shares Information .from the Russian MFA Connection

16. On or about May 4, 2016, the Russian MFA Connection sent an email (the "May 4 MFA Email") to defendant PAPADOPOULOS and the Professor that stated: "I have just talked to my colleagues from the MFA. The[y] are open for cooperation. One of the options is to make a meeting for you at the North America Desk, if you are in Moscow." Defendant PAPADOPOULOS responded that he was "[g]lad the MFA is interested." Defendant PAPADOPOULOS forwarded the May 4 MFA Email to the High-Ranking Campaign Official, adding: "What do you think? Is this something we want to move forward with?" The next day, on or about May 5, 2016, defendant PAPADOPOULOS had a phone call with the Campaign Supervisor, and then forwarded the May 4 MFA Email to him, adding to the top of the email: "Russia updates."

17.   On or about May 13, 2016, the Professor emailed defendant PAPADOPOULOS with "an update" of what they had discussed in their "recent conversations," including: "We will continue to liaise through you with the Russian counterparts in terms of what is needed for a high level meeting of Mr. Trump with the Russian Federation."

18.   The next day, on or about May 14, 2016, defendant PAPADOPOULOS emailed the High-Ranking Campaign Official and stated that the "Russian government [has] also relayed to me that they are interested in hosting Mr. Trump."

19.   On or about May 21, 2016, defendant PAPADOPOULOS emailed another high- ranking Campaign official, with the subject line "Request from Russia to meet Mr. Trump." The email included the May 4 MFA Email and added: "Russia has been eager to meet Mr. Trump for quite sometime and have been reaching out to me to discuss." (*Footnote 2*: The government notes that the official forwarded defendant PAPADOPOULOS' email to another Campaign official (without including defendant PAPADOPOULOS) and stated: "Let[']s discuss. We need someone to communicate that DT is not doing these trips. It should be someone low level in the campaign so as not to send any signal.")

20.   On or about June 1, 2016, defendant PAPADOPOULOS emailed the High-Ranking Campaign Official and asked about Russia. The High-Ranking Campaign Official referred him to the Campaign Supervisor because "[he] is running point." Defendant PAPADOPOULOS then emailed the Campaign Supervisor, with the subject line "Re: Messages from Russia": "I have the Russian MFA asking me if Mr. Trump is interested in visiting Russia at some point. Wanted to pass this info along to you for you to decide what's best to do with it and what message I should send (or to ignore)."

21.   From mid-June through mid-August 2016, PAPADOPOULOS pursued an "off the record" meeting between one or more Campaign representatives and "members of president putin's office and the mfa."

a.   For example, on or about June 19, 2016, after several email and Skype exchanges with the Russian MFA Connection, defendant PAPADOPOULOS emailed the High- Ranking Campaign Official, with the subject line "New message from Russia": "The Russian ministry of foreign affairs messaged and said that if Mr. Trump is unable to make it to Russia, if a campaign rep (me or someone else) can make it for meetings? I am willing to make the trip off the record if it's in the interest of Mr. Trump and the campaign to meet specific people."

b.   After several weeks of further communications regarding a potential "off the record" meeting with Russian officials, on or about August 15, 2016, the Campaign Supervisor told defendant PAPADOPOULOS that "I would encourage you" and another foreign policy advisor to the Campaign to "make the trip, if it is feasible."

    c.   The trip proposed by defendant PAPADOPOULOS did not take place.

III.   *The Defendant's False Statements to the FBI*

    22.   On or about January 27, 2017, defendant PAPADOPOULOS agreed to be interviewed by agents from the FBI.

    23.   The agents informed defendant PAPADOPOULOS that the FBI was investigating interference by the Russian government in the 2016 presidential election and whether any individuals related to the Campaign were involved. The agents further informed defendant PAPADOPOULOS that he needed to be truthful and warned that he could get "in trouble" if he lied. The agents also advised him that lying to them "is a federal offense." They confirmed that the interview was "completely voluntary."

    24.   During the course of the interview, defendant PAPADOPOULOS made numerous false statements and omitted material facts regarding the conduct and communications described above, and, in particular, lied about the extent, timing, and nature of his communications with the Professor, the Female Russian National, and the Russian MFA Connection.

False Statement: PAPADOPOULOS Met the Professor and Learned About Russian "Dirt" Before He Joined the Campaign

    25.   During his interview with the FBI, defendant PAPADOPOULOS acknowledged that he met the Professor and that the Professor told him the Russians had "dirt" on then- candidate Clinton in the form of "thousands of emails," but defendant PAPADOPOULOS stated multiple times that those communications occurred prior to when he joined the Campaign. Defendant PAPADOPOULOS told the FBI: "This isn't like [the Professor]'s messaging me while I'm in April with Trump"; "I wasn't even on the Trump team, that wasn't even on the radar"; "I wasn't even on Trump's orbit [at this time]"; and "This was a year ago, this was before I even got with Trump." He also said it was a "very strange coincidence" to be told of the "dirt" before he started working for the Campaign.

    26.   In truth and in fact, however, and as set forth above, defendant PAPADOPOULOS met the Professor for the first time on or about March 14, 2016, after defendant PAPADOPOULOS had already learned he would be a foreign policy advisor for the Campaign; the Professor showed interest in defendant PAPADOPOULOS only after learning of his role on the Campaign; and the Professor told defendant PAPADOPOULOS about the Russians possessing "dirt" on then- candidate Clinton in late April 2016, more than a month after defendant

PAPADOPOULOS had joined the Campaign.

False Statement: PAPADOPOULOS' Contacts with the Professor Were Inconsequential

27.   During his interview with the FBI, defendant PAPADOPOULOS also made false statements in an effort to minimize the extent and importance of his communications with the Professor. For example defendant PAPADOPOULOS stated that "[the Professor]'s a nothing," that he thought the Professor was "just a guy talk[ing] up connections or something," and that he believed the Professor was "BS'ing to be completely honest with you."

28.   In truth and in fact, however, defendant PAPADOPOULOS understood the Professor to have substantial connections to high-level Russian government officials and that the Professor spoke with some of those officials in Moscow before telling defendant PAPADOPOULOS about the "dirt." Defendant PAPADOPOULOS also engaged in extensive communications over a period of months with the Professor regarding foreign policy issues for the Campaign, including efforts to arrange a "history making" meeting between the Campaign and Russian government officials.

29.   In addition, defendant PAPADOPOULOS failed to inform investigators that the Professor had introduced him to the Russian MFA Connection, despite being asked if he had met with Russian nationals or "[anyone] with a Russian accent" during the Campaign. Indeed, while defendant PAPADOPOULOS told the FBI that he was involved in meetings and did "shuttle diplomacy" with officials from several other countries during the Campaign, he omitted the entire course of conduct with the Professor and the Russian MFA Connection regarding his efforts to establish meetings between the Campaign and Russian government officials.

False Statement: PAPADOPOULOS Met the Female Russian National Before He Joined the Campaign, and His Contacts with Her Were Inconsequential

30.   During his interview with the FBI, defendant PAPADOPOULOS also falsely claimed that he met the Female Russian National before he joined the Campaign, and falsely told the FBI that he had "no" relationship at all with the Female Russian National. He stated that the extent of their communications was her sending emails - "Just, 'Hi, how are you?' That's it."

31.   In truth and in fact, however, defendant PAPADOPOULOS met the Female Russian National on or about March 24, 2016, after he had joined the Campaign; he believed that the Female Russian National had connections to high-level Russian government officials and could help him arrange a potential foreign policy trip to Russia; and during the Campaign he emailed and spoke over Skype on numerous occasions with the Female Russian National about the potential foreign

policy trip to Russia.

IV. Events Following PAPADOPOULOS' January 27, 2017 Interview with the FBI

32.   The FBI interviewed defendant PAPADOPOULOS again on February 16, 2017. His counsel was present for the interview. During the interview, defendant PAPADOPOULOS reiterated his purported willingness to cooperate with the FBI's investigation.

33.   The next day, on or about February 17, 2017, defendant PAPADOPOULOS deactivated his Facebook account, which he had maintained since approximately August 2005 and which contained information about communications he had with the Professor and the Russian MFA Connection. Shortly after he deactivated his account, PAPADOPOULOS created a new Facebook account that did not contain the communications with the Professor and the Russian MFA Connection.

34.   On or about February 23, 2017, defendant PAPADOPOULOS ceased using his cell phone number and began using a new number.

35.   On July 27, 2017, defendant PAPADOPOULOS was arrested upon his arrival at Dulles International Airport. Following his arrest, defendant PAPADOPOULOS met with the Government on numerous occasions to provide information and answer questions.

Plea Agreement
COUNT 1: Making False Statements to the FBI (Title 18, United States Code, Section 1001(a)(2))

On or about the 27th day of January, 2017, defendant GEORGE PAPADOPOULOS did willfully and knowingly make a materially false, fictitious, and fraudulent statement and representation in a matter within the jurisdiction of the executive branch of the Government of the United States, to wit, defendant PAPADOPOULOS lied to special agents of the Federal Bureau of Investigation, concerning a federal investigation based out of the District of Columbia, about the timing, extent, and nature of his relationships and interactions with certain foreign nationals whom he understood to have close connections with senior Russian government officials.

SENTENCE: 14 days in a federal prison camp, one year of probation, community service and a $9,500 fine.

Signed: Robert S. Mueller, III
Special Counsel

Prepared By: Jeirmie S. Rhee, Andrew D. Goldstein, Aaron S.J. Zelinsky
Senior Assistant Special Counsels

CHAPTER 2: PAUL MANAFORT & RICK GATES, OCT. 27, 2017

Part 1
UNITED STATES v. PAUL J. MANAFORT, JR. & RICHARD W. GATES III

FILED: October 27, 2017 in the U.S. District Court for the District of Columbia

Editor's Note: This was the first big indictment of Robert Mueller's Special Counsel investigation, putting the crosshairs directly on Trump's former campaign chairman, Paul Manafort and his longtime right hand, Rick Gates. However, the sins contained herein focus on the duo's past misdeeds rather than missteps that took place during the Trump campaign.

Timeline of Events

March 28, 2016: MANAFORT, long known in Republican circles as a convention savant, joins the Trump campaign as its convention manager in anticipation of a floor fight spurred on by the #NeverTrump-ers.

May 19, 2016: MANAFORT officially becomes Trump's campaign chairman and senior advisor to then candidate Trump. Trump's outgoing chair, Corey Lewandowski, declares shortly thereafter that MANAFORT had actually already been in full operational control of the campaign since April 7, 2016.

June 9, 2016: MANAFORT (along with Jared Kushner and Donald Trump, Jr.) met with Russian lawyer, Natalia Veselnitskaya, about a rumored trove of dirt on Trump's opponent, Hillary Clinton, that was said to be in the possession of the Russian government. The meeting wouldn't be made public until July 2017.

July 22, 2016: Wikileaks begins to release the emails stolen from the DNC.

August 14, 2016: The New York Times publishes a report detailing over $12 million in undisclosed payments made to MANAFORT by the pro-Russia, Ukrainian politician, Viktor Yanukovych. Between 2007 and 2012, MANAFORT helped Yanukovych's party gain and retain power, helping him win the presidency in 2010. Yanukovych, seen by most as nothing more than a puppet of Putin, was deposed in 2014 by Ukraine's Orange Revolution, setting the stage for the Russian annexation of Crimea that followed.

August 19, 2016: MANAFORT resigns from the Trump campaign citing differences in strategy between him and the candidate. Trump doesn't trash MANAFORT in the press or on twitter after his departure.

October 7, 2016: Wikileaks starts publishing emails stolen from Clinton's campaign chairman, John Podesta.

July 25, 2017: MANAFORT testifies before the U.S. Senate Intelligence Committee.

July 26, 2017: FBI agents execute a raid on MANAFORT's Northern Virginia home, leaving with a large haul of tax and banking documents as well as other evidence relating to his financial dealings.

October 27, 2017: MANAFORT and GATES are both indicted on multiple charges by a federal grand jury.

October 30, 2017: MANAFORT surrenders to the FBI.

February 23, 2018: GATES pleads guilty to one count of conspiracy against the United States and one count of making false statements to the FBI and federal prosecutors.

Indictment

I. *Introduction*

1. Defendants PAUL J. MANAFORT, JR., (MANAFORT) and RICHARD W. GATES Ill (GA TES) served for years as political consultants and lobbyists. Between at least 2006 and 2015, MANAFORT and GATES acted as unregistered agents of the Government of Ukraine, the Party of Regions (a Ukrainian political party whose leader Viktor Yanukovych was President from 2010 to 2014), Yanukovych, and the Opposition Bloc (a successor to the Party of Regions that formed in 2014 when Yanukovych fled to Russia). MANAFORT and GATES generated tens of millions of dollars in income as a result of their Ukraine work. In order to hide Ukraine payments from United States authorities, from approximately 2006 through at least 2016, MANAFORT and GATES laundered the money through scores of United States and foreign corporations, partnerships, and bank accounts.

2. In furtherance of the scheme, MANAFORT and GATES funneled millions of dollars in payments into foreign nominee companies and bank accounts, opened by them and their accomplices in nominee names and in various foreign countries, including Cyprus, Saint Vincent & the Grenadines (Grenadines), and the Seychelles. MANAFORT and GATES hid the existence of the foreign companies and bank accounts, falsely and repeatedly reporting to their tax preparers and to the United States that they had no foreign bank accounts.

3. In furtherance of the scheme, MANAFORT and GATES concealed from the United States their work as agents of, and millions of dollars in payments from, Ukraine and its political parties and leaders. Because MANAFORT and GATES, among other things, directed a campaign to lobby United States officials on behalf of the Government of Ukraine, the President of Ukraine, and Ukrainian political parties, they were required by law to report to the United States their work and fees.

MANAFORT and GATES did not do so. Instead, when the Department of Justice sent inquiries to MANAFORT and GATES in 2016 about their activities, MANAFORT and GATES responded with a series of false and misleading statements.

4.   In furtherance of the scheme, MANAFORT used his hidden overseas wealth to enjoy a lavish lifestyle in the United States, without paying taxes on that income. MANAFORT, without reporting the income to his tax preparer or the United States, spent millions of dollars on luxury goods and services for himself and his extended family through payments wired from offshore nominee accounts to United States vendors. MANAFORT also used these offshore accounts to purchase multi-million dollar properties· in the United States. MANAFORT then borrowed millions of dollars in loans using these properties as collateral, thereby obtaining cash in the United States without reporting and paying taxes on the income. In order to increase the amount of money he could access in the United States, MANAFORT defrauded the institutions that loaned money on these properties so that they would lend him more money at more favorable rates than he would otherwise be able to obtain.

5.   GATES aided MANAFORT in obtaining money from these offshore accounts, which he was instrumental in opening. Like MANAFORT, GATES used money from these offshore accounts to pay for his personal expenses, including his mortgage, children's tuition, and interior decorating of his Virginia residence.

6.   In total, more than $75,000,000 flowed through the offshore accounts. MANAFORT laundered more than $18,000,000, which was used by him to buy property, goods, and services in the United States, income that he concealed from the United States Treasury, the Department of Justice, and others. GATES transferred more than $3,000,000 from the offshore accounts to other accounts that he controlled.

II.   *Relevant Individuals And Entities*

7.   MANAFORT was a United States citizen. He resided in homes in Virginia, Florida, and Long Island, New York.

8.   GATES was a United States citizen. He resided in Virginia.

9.   In 2005, MANAFORT and another partner created Davis Manafort Partners, Inc. (DMP) to engage principally in political consulting. DMP had staff in the United States, Ukraine, and Russia. In 2011, MANAFORT created DMP International, LLC (DMI) to engage in work for foreign clients, in particular political consulting, lobbying, and public relations for the Government of Ukraine, the Party of Regions, and members of the Party of Regions. DMI was a partnership solely owned by MANAFORT and his spouse. GATES worked for both DMP and DMI and served as MANAFORT's right-hand man.

10.   The Patty of Regions was a pro-Russia political party in Ukraine.

Beginning in approximately 2006, it retained MANAFORT, through DMP and then DMI, to advance its interests in Ukraine, including the election of its slate of candidates. In 2010, its candidate for President, Yanukovych, was elected President of Ukraine. In 2014, Yanukovych fled Ukraine for Russia in the wake of popular protests of widespread government corruption. Yanukovych, the Party of Regions, and the Government of Ukraine were MANAFORT, DMP, and DMI clients.

      11.   The European Centre for a Modern Ukraine (the Centre) was created in or about 2012 in Belgium as a mouthpiece for Yanukovych and the Party of Regions. The Centre was used by MANAFORT, GATES, and others in order to lobby and conduct a public relations campaign in the United States and Europe on behalf of the existing Ukraine regime. The Centre effectively ceased to operate upon the downfall of Yanukovych in 2014.

      12.   MANAFORT and GATES owned or controlled the following entities, which were used in the scheme (the MANAFORT/GATES entities):

Domestic Entities

Entity Name	Date Created	Incorporation Location
Bade LLC (RG)	January 2012	Delaware

Entity Name	Date Created	Incorporation Location
Daisy Manafort, LLC (PM)	August 2008	Virginia
	March 2011	Florida
Davis Manafort International LLC (PM)	March 2007	Delaware
DMP (PM)	March 2005	Virginia
	March 2011	Florida
Davis Manafort, Inc. (PM)	October 1999	Delaware
	November 1999	Virginia
	June 2011	Delaware

DMI (PM)	March 2012	Florida
Global Sites LLC (PM, RG)	July 2008	Delaware
Jemina LLC (RG)	July 2008	Delaware
Jesand Investment Corporation (PM)	April 2002	Virginia
Jesand Investments Corporation (PM)	March 2011	Florida
John Hannah, LLC (PM)	April 2006	Virginia
	March 2011	Florida
Jupiter Holdings Management, LLC (RG)	January 2011	Delaware
Lilred, LLC (PM)	December 2011	Florida
LOAV Ltd. (PM)	April 1992	Delaware
MC Brooklyn Holdings, LLC (PM)	November 2012	New York
MC Soho Holdings, LLC (PM)	January 2012	Florida
	April 2012	New York
Smythson LLC (also known as Symthson LLC) (PM, RG)	July 2008	Delaware

Cypriot Entities

Entity Name	Date Created	Incorporation Location
Actinet Trading Limited (PM, RG)	May 2009	Cyprus
Black Sea View Limited (PM, RG)	August 2007	Cyprus

Bletilla Ventures Limited (PM, RG)	October 2010	Cyprus
Cavenari Investments Limited (RG)	December 2007	Cyprus
Global Highway Limited (PM, RG)	August 2007	Cyprus
Leviathan Advisors Limited (PM, RG)	August 2007	Cyprus
LOAV Advisors Limited (PM, RG)	August 2007	Cyprus
Lucicle Consultants Limited (PM, RG)	December 2008	Cyprus
Marziola Holdings Limited (PM)	March 2012	Cyprus
Olivenia Trading Limited (PM, RG)	March 2012	Cyprus
Peranova Holdings Limited (Peranova) (PM, RG)	June 2007	Cyprus
Serangon Holdings Limited (PM, RG)	January 2008	Cyprus
Yiakora Ventures Limited (PM)	February 2008	Cyprus

Other Foreign Entities

Entity Name	Date Created	Incorporation Location
Global Endeavour Inc. (also known as Global Endeavor Inc.) (PM)	Unknown	Grenadines
Jeunet Ltd. (PM)	August 2011	Grenadines
Pompolo Limited (PM, RG)	April 2013	United Kingdom

13. The Internal Revenue Service (IRS) was a bureau in the United

States Department of the Treasury responsible for administering the tax laws of the United States and collecting taxes owed to the Treasury.

III. *The Scheme*

14. Between in or around 2008 and 2017, both dates being approximate and inclusive, in the District of Columbia and elsewhere, MANAFORT and GATES devised and intended to devise, and executed and attempted to execute, a scheme and artifice to defraud, and to obtain money and property by means of false and fraudulent pretenses, representations, and promises from the United States, banks, and other financial institutions. As part of the scheme, MANAFORT and GATES repeatedly provided false information to financial bookkeepers, tax accountants, and legal counsel, among others.

MANAFORT And GATES' Wiring Of Money From Offshore Accounts Into The United States

15. In order to use the money in the offshore nominee accounts of the MANAFORT/GATES entities without paying taxes on it, MANAFORT and GATES caused millions of dollars in wire transfers from these accounts to be made for goods, services, and real estate. They did not report these transfers as income to DMP, DMI, or MANAFORT.

16. From 2008 to 2014, MANAFORT caused the following wires, totaling over $12,000,000, to be sent to the vendors listed below for personal items. MANAFORT did not pay taxes on this income, which was used to make the purchases.

17. In 2012, MANAFORT caused the following wires to be sent to the entities listed below to purchase the real estate also listed below. MANAFORT did not report the money used to make these purchases on his 2012 tax return.

[For a list of the transactions referred to in paragraphs 16 and 17, please see the Wire Transaction Tables contained in later filings re this case, later on in this this Chapter. -Ed.]

MANAFORT And GATES' Hiding Of Ukraine Lobbying And Public Relations Work

18. It is illegal to act as an agent of a foreign principal engaged in certain United States influence activities without registering the affiliation. Specifically, a person who engages in lobbying or public relations work in the United States (hereafter collectively referred to as lobbying) for a foreign principal such as the Government of Ukraine or the Party of Regions is required to provide a detailed written registration statement to the United States Department of Justice. The filing, made under oath, must disclose the name of the foreign principal, the financial payments to the lobbyist, and the measures undertaken for the foreign principal,

among other information. A person required to make such a filing must further make in all lobbying material a "conspicuous statement" that the materials are distributed on behalf of the foreign principal, among other things. The filing thus permits public awareness and evaluation of the activities of a lobbyist who acts as an agent of a foreign power or foreign political party in the United States.

19. In furtherance of the scheme, from 2006 until 2014, both dates being approximate and inclusive, MANAFORT and GATES engaged in a multi-million dollar lobbying campaign in the United States at the direction of Yanukovych, the Party of Regions, and the Government of Ukraine. MANAFORT and GATES did so without registering and providing the disclosures required by law.

20. As part of the scheme, in February 2012, MANAFORT and GATES solicited two Washington, D.C., firms (Company A and Company B) to lobby in the United States on behalf of Yanukovych, the Party of Regions, and the Government of Ukraine. For instance, GATES wrote to Company A that it would be "representing the Government of Ukraine in [Washington,] DC."

21. MANAFORT repeatedly communicated in person and in writing with Yanukovych, and GATES passed on directions to Company A and Company B. For instance, MANAFORT wrote Yanukovych a memorandum dated April 8, 2012, in which he provided Yanukovych an update on the lobbying firms' activities "since the inception of the project a few weeks ago. It is my intention to provide you with a weekly update moving forward." Toward the end of that first year, in November 2012, GATES wrote to Company A and Company B that the firms needed to prepare an assessment of their past and prospective lobbying efforts so the "President" could be briefed by "Paul" "on what Ukraine has done well and what it can do better as we move into 2013."

22. At the direction of MANAFORT and GATES, Company A and Company B engaged in extensive lobbying. Among other things, they lobbied multiple Members of Congress and their staffs about Ukraine sanctions, the validity of Ukraine elections, and the propriety of Yanukovych's imprisoning his presidential rival, Yulia Tymoshenko (who had served as Ukraine President prior to Yanukovych). MANAFORT and GATES also lobbied in connection with the roll out of a report concerning the Tymoshenko trial commissioned by the Government of Ukraine. MANAFORT and GATES used one of their offshore accounts to funnel $4 million to pay secretly for the report.

23. To minimize public disclosure of their lobbying campaign, MANAFORT and GATES arranged for the Centre to be the nominal client of Company A and Company B, even though in fact the Centre was under the ultimate direction of the Government of Ukraine, Yanukovych, and the Party of Regions. For instance, MANAFORT and GATES selected Company A and Company B, and only thereafter did the Centre sign contracts with the lobbying firms without ever meeting either

company. Company A and Company B were paid for their services not by their nominal client, the Centre, but solely through offshore accounts associated with the MANAFORT/GATES entities, namely Bletilla Ventures Limited (in Cyprus) and Jeunet Ltd. and Global Endeavour Inc. (in Grenadines). In total, Company A and Company B were paid more than $2 million from these accounts between 2012 and 2014.

24. To conceal the scheme, MANAFORT and GATES developed a false and misleading cover story that would distance themselves and the Government of Ukraine, Yanukovych, and the Party of Regions from the Centre, Company A, and Company B. For instance, in the wake of extensive press reports on MANAFORT and his connections with Ukraine, on August 16, 2016, GATES communicated false talking points to Company B in writing, including:

a. Q: "Can you describe your initial contact with [Company B] and the lobbying goals he discussed with them?" A: "We provided an introduction between the [Centre] and [Company B/Company A] in 2012. The [Centre] was seeking to retain· representation in Washington, DC to support the mission of the NGO."

b. A: "Our [MANAFORT and GATES'] task was to assist the [Centre] find representation in Washington, but at no time did our firm or members provide any direct lobbying support." · A: "The structure of the arrangement between the [Centre] and [Company A and Company B] was worked out by the two parties,"

c. Q: "Can you say where the funding from for [sic] the [Centre] came from? (this ' amounted to well over a million dollars between 2012 and 2014)." A: "This is a question better asked of the [Centre] who contracted with the two firms."

d. Q: "Can you describe the lobbying work specifically undertaken by [Company B] on behalf of the Party of Regions/the [Centre]?" A: "This is a question better asked to Company B and/or the [Centre] as the agreement was between the parties. Our firm did not play a role in the structure, nor were we registered lobbyists."

e. Company B through a principal replied to GATES the same day that "there's a lot of email traffic that has you much more involved than this suggests[.] We will not disclose that but heaven knows what former employees of [Company B] or [Company A] might say."

25. In September 2016, after numerous recent press reports concerning MANAFORT, the Department of Justice informed MANAFORT, GATES, and DMI that it sought to determine whether they had acted as agents of a foreign principal under the Foreign Agents Registration Act (FARA), without registering. In November 2016 and February 2017, MANAFORT, GATES, and DMI caused false and misleading letters to be submitted to the Department of Justice, which mirrored the

false cover story set out above. The letters, both of which were approved by MANAFORT and GATES before they were submitted, represented, among other things, that:

   a.   DMI's "efforts on behalf of the Party of Regions" "did not include meetings or outreach within the U.S.";

   b.   MANAFORT and GATES did not "recall meeting with or conducting outreach to U.S. government officials or U.S. media outlets on behalf of the [Centre], nor do they recall being party to, arranging, or facilitating any such communications. Rather, it is the recollection and understanding of Messrs. Gates and Manafort that such communications would have been facilitated and conducted by the [Centre's] U.S. consultants, as directed by the [Centre]...";

   c.   MANAFORT and GATES had merely served as a means of introduction of Company A and Company B to the Centre and provided the Centre with a list of "potential U.S.-based consultants - including [Company A] and [Company B] - for, the [Centre's] reference and further consideration."

   d.   DMI "does not retain communications beyond thirty days" and as a result of this policy, a "search has returned no responsive documents." The November 2016 letter attached a one-page, undated document that purported to be a DMI "Email Retention Policy."

   26.   In fact, MANAFORT and GATES had: selected Company A and Company B; engaged in weekly scheduled calls and frequent emails with Company A and Company B to provide them directions as to specific lobbying steps that should be taken; sought and received detailed oral and written reports from these firms on the lobbying work they had performed; communicated with Yanukovych to brief him on their lobbying efforts; both congratulated and reprimanded Company A and Company B on their lobbying work; communicated directly with United States officials in connection with this work; and paid the lobbying firms over $2 million from offshore accounts they controlled, among other things. In addition, court-authorized searches of MANAFORT and GATES' DMI email accounts and MANAFORT's Virginia residence in July 2017 revealed numerous documents, including documents related to lobbying, which were more than thirty-days old at the time of the November 2016 letter to the Department of Justice.

MANAFORT And GATES' Hiding Of Foreign Bank Accounts And False Filings

   27.   United States citizens who have authority over certain foreign bank accounts -- whether or not the accounts are set up in the names of nominees who act for their principals -- have reporting obligations to the United States.

   28.   First, the Bank Secrecy Act and its implementing regulations

require United States citizens to report to the United States Treasury any financial interest in or signatory authority over, any bank account or other financial account held in foreign countries, for every calendar year in which the aggregate balance of all such foreign accounts exceeds $10,000 at any point during the year. This is commonly known as a foreign bank account report or "FBAR." The Bank Secrecy Act requires these reports because they have a high degree of usefulness in criminal, tax, or regulatory investigations or proceedings. The United States Treasury's Financial Crimes Enforcement Network (FinCEN) is the custodian for FBAR filings, and FinCEN provides access to its FBAR database to law enforcement entities, including the Federal Bureau of Investigation. The reports filed by individuals and businesses are used by law enforcement to identify, detect, and deter money laundering that furthers criminal enterprise activity, tax evasion, and other unlawful activities.

29. Second, United States citizens also are obligated to report information to the IRS regarding foreign bank accounts. For instance, in 2010 Form 1040, Schedule B had a "Yes" or "No" box to record an answer to the question: "At any time during [the calendar year], did you have an interest in or a signature or other authority over a financial account in a foreign country, such as a bank account, securities account, or other financial account?" If the answer was "Yes," then the form required the taxpayer to enter the name of the foreign country in which the financial account was located.

30. For each year in or about and between 2008 through at least 2014, MANAFORT had authority over foreign accounts that required an FBAR report. Specifically, MANAFORT was required to report to the United States Treasury each foreign bank account held by the foreign MANAFORT/GATES entities noted above in paragraph 12 that bear the initials PM. No FBAR reports were made by MANAFORT for these accounts.

31. For each year in or about and between 2008 through at least 2013, GATES had authority over foreign accounts that required an FBAR report. Specifically, GATES was required to report to the United States Treasury each foreign bank account held by the foreign MANAFORT/GATES entities noted above in paragraph 12 that bear the initials RG, as well as three other accounts in the United Kingdom. No FBAR reports were made by GATES for these accounts.

32. Furthermore, in each of MANAFORT's tax filings for 2008 through 2014, MANAFORT represented falsely that he did not have authority over any foreign bank accounts. MANAFORT and GATES had repeatedly and falsely represented in writing to MANAFORT's tax preparer that MANAFORT had no authority over foreign bank accounts, knowing that such false representations would result in false MANAFORT tax filings. For instance, on October 4, 2011, MANAFORT's tax preparer asked MANAFORT in writing: "At any time during 2010, did you [or your wife or_ children] have an interest in or a signature or other authority over a financial

account in a foreign country, such as a bank account, securities account or other financial account?" On the same day, MANAFORT falsely responded "NO." MANAFORT responded the same way as recently as October 3, 2016, when MANAFORT's tax preparer again emailed the question in connection with the preparation of MANAFORT's tax returns: "Foreign bank accounts etc.?" MANAFORT responded on or about the same day: "NONE."

MANAFORT And GATES' Fraud To Increase Access To Offshore Money

33. After MANAFORT used his offshore accounts to purchase real estate in the United States, he took out mortgages on the properties thereby allowing MANAFORT to have the benefits of liquid income without paying taxes on it. Further, MANAFORT defrauded the banks that loaned him the money so that he could withdraw more money at a cheaper rate than he otherwise would have been permitted.

34. In 2012, MANAFORT, through a corporate vehicle called "MC Soho Holdings, LLC" owned by him and his family, bought a condominium on Howard Street in the Soho neighborhood in Manhattan, New York. He paid approximately $2,850,000. All the money used to purchase the condominium came from MANAFORT entities in Cyprus. MANAFORT used the property from at least January 2015 through 2016 as an income-generating rental property, charging thousands of dollars a week on Airbnb, among other places. In his tax returns, MANAFORT took advantage of the beneficial tax consequences of owning this rental property,

35. In late 2015 through early 2016, MANAFORT applied for a mortgage on the condominium. Because the bank would permit a greater loan amount if the property were owner-occupied, MANAFORT falsely represented to the bank and its agents that it was a secondary home used as such by his daughter and son-in-law and was not a property held as a rental property. For instance, on January 26, 2016, MANAFORT wrote to his son-in-law to advise him that when the bank appraiser came to assess the condominium his son-in-law should "[r]emember, he believes that you and [MANAFORT's daughter] are living there." Based on a request from MANAFORT, GATES caused a document to be created which listed the Howard Street property as the second home of MANAFORT's daughter and son-in-law, when GATES knew this fact to be false. As a result of his false representations, in March 2016 the bank provided MANAFORT a loan for approximately $3,185,000.

36. Also in 2012, MANAFORT -- through a corporate vehicle called "MC Brooklyn Holdings, LLC" similarly owned by him and his family -- bought a brownstone on Union Street in the Carroll Gardens section of Brooklyn, New York. He paid approximately $3,000,000 in cash for the property. All of that money came from a MANAFORT entity in Cyprus. After purchase of the property, MANAFORT

began renovations to transform it from a multi-family dwelling into a single family home. In late 2015 through early 2016, MANAFORT sought to borrow cash against the property. The institution MANAFORT went to for the loan provided greater loan amounts for "construction loans" - that is, loans that required the loan amounts to be used to pay solely for construction of the property and thus increase the value of the property serving as the loan's collateral. The institution would thus loan money against the expected completed value of the property, which in the case of the Union Street property was estimated to be $8,000,000. In early 2016, MANAFORT was able to obtain a loan of approximately $5,000,000, after promising the bank that approximately $1,400,000 of the loan would be used solely for construction of the Union Street property. However, MANAFORT never intended to limit use of the proceeds to construction as required by the loan contracts. In December 2015, before the loan was made, MANAFORT wrote his tax preparer, among others, that the construction loan "will allow me to pay back the [another MANAFORT apartment] mortgage in full..." Further, when the construction loan closed, MANAFORT used hundreds of thousands of dollars from the construction loan to make a down payment on another property in California.

IV. Statutory Allegations
COUNT 1: Conspiracy Against the United States (18 U.S.C. § 371)

37.   Paragraphs 1 through 30 and 32 through 36 are incorporated here.

38.   From in or about and between 2006 and 2017, both dates being approximate and inclusive, in the District of Columbia and elsewhere, the defendants PAUL J. MANAFORT, JR., and RICHARD W. GATES III, together with others, knowingly and intentionally conspired to defraud the United States by impeding, impairing, obstructing, and defeating the lawful governmental functions of a government agency, namely the Department of Justice and the Department of the Treasury, and to commit offenses against the United States, to wit, the violations of law charged in Counts Three through Six and Ten through Twelve.

39.   In furtherance of the conspiracy and to effect its illegal object, MANAFORT and GATES committed the overt acts noted in Count Eleven and the overt acts, among others, in the District of Columbia and elsewhere as set forth in paragraphs 9, 16, 17, 20-25, 32, and 34-36, which are incorporated herein.

COUNT 2: Conspiracy To Launder Money (18 U.S.C. § 1956(h))

40.   Paragraphs 1 through 30 and 32 through 36 are incorporated here.

41.   In or around and between 2006 and 2016, both dates being approximate and inclusive, within the District of Columbia and elsewhere, the defendants PAUL J. MANAFORT, JR., and RICHARD W. GATES III, together with others, did knowingly and intentionally conspire to: (a) transport, transmit, and

transfer monetary instruments and funds from places outside the United States to and through places in the United States and from places in the United States to and through places outside the United States, with the intent to promote the carrying on of specified unlawful activity, to wit: a felony violation of the FARA, in violation of Title 22, United States Code, Sections 612 and 618 (the "Specified Unlawful Activity"), contrary to Title 18, United States Code, Section 1956(a)(2)(A); and (b) conduct financial transactions, affecting interstate and foreign commerce, knowing that the property involved in the financial transactions would represent the proceeds of some form of unlawful activity, and the transactions in fact would involve the proceeds of Specified Unlawful Activity, knowing that such financial transactions were designed in whole and in part (i) to engage in conduct constituting a violation of sections 7201 and 7206 of the Internal Revenue Code of 1986, and (ii) to conceal and disguise the nature, location, source, ownership, and control of the proceeds of the Specified Unlawful Activity, contrary to Title 18, United States Code, Section 1956(a)(l)(A)(ii) and 1956(a)(l)(B)(i). (18 u.s.c. § 1956(h))

COUNTS 3-6: Failure To Report Foreign Bank Accounts (31 U.S.C. §§ 5314 & 5322(b); 18 U.S.C. § 2)

42. Paragraphs 1 through 30 and 32 through 36 are incorporated here.

43. On the filing due dates listed below, in the District of Columbia and elsewhere, the defendant PAUL J. MANAFORT, JR., unlawfully, willfully, and knowingly did fail to file with the Department of the Treasury an FBAR disclosing that he has a financial interest in, and signature and other authority over, a bank, securities, and other financial account in a foreign country, which had an aggregate value of more than $10,000, while violating another law of the United States and as part of pattern of illegal activity involving more than $100,000 in a 12-month period, a total of 18 times, during the years: 2011, 2012, 2013, 2014.

COUNTS 7-9: Failure To Report Foreign Bank Accounts (31 U.S.C. §§ 5314 & 5322(b); 18 U.S.C. § 2)

44. Paragraphs 1 through 29 and 31 through 36 are incorporated here.

45. On the filing due dates listed below, in the District of Columbia and elsewhere, the defendant RICHARD W. GATES III unlawfully, willfully, and knowingly did fail to file with the Department of the Treasury an FBAR disclosing that he has a financial interest in, and signature and other authority over, a bank, securities, and other financial account in a foreign country, which had an aggregate value of more than $10,000, while violating another law of the United States and as part of pattern of illegal activity involving more than $100,000 in a 12-month period, a total of 24 times, during the years: 2011, 2012, 2013.

COUNT 10: Unregistered Agent Of A Foreign Principal (22 U.S.C. §§ 612 and 618(a)(1); 18 U.S.C. § 2)

46. Paragraphs 1 through 36 are incorporated here.

47. From in or about and between 2008 and 2014, both dates being approximate and inclusive, within the District of Columbia and elsewhere, the defendants PAUL J. MANAFORT, JR., and RICHARD W. GATES III knowingly and willfully, without registering with the Attorney General as required by law, acted as agents of a foreign principal, to wit, the Government of Ukraine, the Party of Regions, and Yanukovych.

COUNT 11: Making False and Misleading FARA Statements (22 U.S.C. §§ 612, 618(a)(2); 18 U.S.C. § 2)

48. Paragraphs 1 through 36 are incorporated here.

49. On or about November 23, 2016 and February 10, 2017, within the District of Columbia and elsewhere, the defendants PAUL J. MANAFORT, JR., and RICHARD W. GATES III knowingly and willfully caused to be made a false statement of a material fact, and omitted a material fact necessary to make the statements therein not misleading, in a document filed with and furnished to the Attorney General under the provisions of FARA, to wit the underlined statements: · "[DMI]'s efforts on behalf of the Party of Regions and Opposition Bloc did not include meetings or outreach within the U.S."

    a. "[N]either [DMI] nor Messrs. Manafort or Gates had any agreement with the [Centre] to provide services."

    b. "[DMI] did provide the [Centre], at the request of members of the Party of Regions, with a list of potential U.S.-based consultants-including [Company A and Company B]-for the [Centre]'s reference and further consideration. [The Centre] then contracted directly with [Company A and Company B] to provide services within the United States for which these entities registered under the Lobbying Disclosure Act."

    c. "To Gates' recollection, these efforts included providing policy briefings to the [Centre] and its consultants on key initiatives and political developments in Ukraine, including participation in and/or coordination of related conference calls and meetings. Although Gates recalls interacting with [the Centre]'s consultants regarding efforts in the Ukraine and Europe, neither Gates nor Mr. Manafort recall meeting with or conducting outreach to U.S. government officials or U.S. media outlets on behalf of the [the Centre], nor do they recall being party to, arranging. or facilitating any such communications. Rather, it is the recollection and understanding of Messrs. Gates and Manafort that such communications would have been facilitated and conducted by the [Centre]'s U.S. consultants, as directed by the

[Centre], pursuant to the agreement reached between those parties (to which fDMI] was not a party)."

    d.   "[Al search has been conducted for correspondence containing additional information related to the matters described in [the government's] Letters. However. as a result of [DMl's] Email Retention Policy, which does not retain communications beyond thirty days, the search has returned no responsive communications."

COUNT 12: Making False Statements (18 U.S.C. §§ 2, l00l(a))

50.   Paragraphs 1 through 36 and paragraph 49 are incorporated here.

51.   On or about November 23, 2016 and February 10, 2017, within the District of Columbia and elsewhere, in a matter within the jurisdiction of the executive branch of the Government of the United States, the defendants PAUL J. MANAFORT, JR., and RICHARD W. GATES III knowingly and willfully did cause another: to falsify, conceal, and cover up by a scheme and device a material fact; to make a materially false, fictitious, and fraudulent' statement and representation; and to make and use a false writing and document knowing the same to contain a materially false, fictitious, and fraud~lent statement, to wit, the statements in the November 23, 2016 and February 10, 2017 submissions to the Department of Justice quoted in paragraph 49.

FORFEITURE ALLEGATION

52.   Pursuant to Fed. R. Crim. P. 32.2, notice is hereby given to the defendants that the United States will seek forfeiture as part of any sentence in accordance with Title 18, United States Code, Sections 981(a)(l)(C) and 982(a)(l) and (a)(2), and Title 28, United States Code, Section 2461(c), in the event of the defendants' convictions under Count Two of this Indictment. Upon conviction of the offense charged in Count Two, the defendants PAUL J. MANAFORT, JR., and RICHARD W. GATES III shall forfeit to the United States any property, real or personal, involved in such offense, and any property traceable to such property. Upon conviction of the offenses charged in Counts Ten and Eleven, the defendants PAUL J. MANAFORT, JR., and RICHARD W. GATES III shall forfeit to the United States any property, real or personal, which constitutes or is derived from proceeds traceable to the offense(s) of conviction. Notice is further given that, upon conviction, the United States intends to seek a judgment against each defendant for a sum of money representing the property described in this paragraph, as applicable to each defendant (to be offset by the forfeiture of any specific property).

53.   The grand jury finds probable cause to believe that the property subject to forfeiture by PAUL J. MANAFORT, JR., includes, but is not limited to, the following listed assets:

1) The real property and premises commonly known as 377 Union Street, Brooklyn, New York 11231 (Block 429, Lot 65), including all appurtenances, improvements, and attachments thereon, and any property traceable thereto;

2) The real property and premises commonly known as 29 Howard Street, #4D, New York, New York 10013 (Block 209, Lot 1104), including all appurtenances, improvements, and attachments thereon, and any property traceable thereto;

3) The real property and premises commonly known as 174 Jobs Lane, Water Mill, New York 11976, including all appurtenances, improvements, and attachments thereon, and any property traceable thereto;

4) Northwestern Mutual Universal Life Insurance Policy and any property traceable thereto; and

5) The real property and premises commonly known as 1046 N. Edgewood Street, Ailington, Virginia, 22201, including all appurtenances, improvements, and attachments thereon, and any property traceable thereto.

Substitute Assets

54. If any of the property described above as being subject to forfeiture, as a result of any act or omission of any defendant -- a cannot be located upon the exercise of due diligence; b. has been transferred or sold to, or deposited with, a third party; c. has been placed beyond the jurisdiction of the court; d. has been substantially diminished in value; or e. has been commingled with other property that cannot be subdivided without difficulty; it is the intent of the United States of America, pursuant to Title 18, United States Code, Section 982(b) and Title 28, United States Code, Section 2461(c), incorporating Title 21, United States Code, Section 853, to seek forfeiture of any other property of said defendant.

(18 U.S.C. §§ 981(a)(1)(C) and 982; 28 U.S.C. § 2461(c))

Signed: Robert S. Mueller, III

Special Counsel

Part 2

UNITED STATES v. RICHARD W. GATES III

FILED: February 23, 2018 in the U.S. District Court for the District of Columbia

Editor's Note: This Statement of the Offense for Rick Gates' guilty plea details in greater relief the elaborate and highly illegal schemes that Gates and Manafort used to funnel money from governments, political parties and other (often bad) actors overseas, to bank accounts in tax havens with low or no financial reporting requirements and then on to their bank accounts in the U.S. This allowed Gates and Manafort to both maintain an opulent lifestyle for themselves and their families while hiding the illegal sources of their income and shielding a lion's share of their assets from the prying eyes of the IRS.

Statement of the Offense

Pursuant to the Federal Rules of Criminal Procedure 11, the United States and the defendant RICHARD W. GATES III (GATES) stipulate and agree that the following facts are true and accurate. These facts do not constitute all of the facts known to the parties concerning the charged offense and covered conduct. This statement is being submitted to demonstrate that sufficient facts exist to establish that the defendant committed the offense to which he is pleading guilty.

Count 1: Conspiracy to Defraud the United States (18 U.S.C. § 371)

1. At all relevant times herein, GATES worked as an employee at companies run by Paul J. Manafort, Jr., and other principals, namely Davis Manafort Partners, Inc. (DMP) and DMP International, LLC. (DMI). Manafort engaged in a variety of criminal schemes, and GATES as part of his work for Manafort, DMP, and DMI knowingly and intentionally conspired with Manafort to assist him in the criminal schemes that make up Count One of the Indictment, as more fully set forth below.

    A.   Tax and FBAR Scheme (26 U.S.C. §§ 7206(1) & 7206(2); 31 U.S.C. §§ 5314 & 5322(b))

2. From 2008 through 2014, Manafort, with the assistance of GATES, caused millions of dollars of wire transfers to be made from offshore nominee accounts, without Manafort paying taxes on that income. The payments were made for goods, services, and real estate. Manafort, again with the assistance of GATES, also hid income by denominating various overseas payments as "loans," thereby evading payment of any taxes on that income by Manafort.

3. GATES, acting on the authority of Manafort, routinely dealt with Manafort's tax accountants in the preparation of Manafort's tax returns. GATES was

authorized by Manafort to answer questions from Manafort's accountants, to provide documents and other information, and to review Manafort's draft and finalized income tax returns. In doing so, GATES, with Manafort's knowledge and agreement, repeatedly misled Manafort's accountants, including by not disclosing Manafort's overseas accounts and the income. Further, GATES, acting at Manafort's instruction, continued to classify overseas payments made to Manafort as "loans" to avoid incurring additional taxes on the income.

4. Manafort, with GATES' assistance, owned and controlled a range of foreign bank accounts in Cyprus and the Grenadines. GATES helped maintain these accounts and arranged substantial transfers from the accounts to both Manafort and himself. GATES was aware that any of these accounts held well in excess of $10,000 in the aggregate at some point during each year in which they existed. GATES, acting at Manafort's instruction, did not report the accounts' existence to Manafort's tax accountants in an effort to hide them, and to allow Manafort to avoid disclosing their existence on an FBAR filing.

5. GATES was aware at the time that it was illegal to hide income from the Internal Revenue Service (IRS) by failing to account for reportable income on Manafort's income tax returns. GATES was also aware that it was illegal to fail to report information to the IRS regarding the existence of foreign bank accounts, as required by Schedule B of the IRS Form 1040. GATES also understood at the time that a U.S. person who had a financial interest in, or signature or other authority over, a bank account or other financial account in a foreign country, which exceeded $10,000 in any one year (at any time during that year), was required to report the account to the Department of the Treasury. GATES also understood, after 2010, that the failure to make such a report constituted a crime.

B. **FARA Scheme (22 U.S.C. §§ 612 & 618(a)(l))**

6. GATES understood that it was illegal to engage in certain activities in the United States as an agent of a foreign principal without registering with the United States Government. Specifically, a person who engages in lobbying or public relations work in the United States (hereafter collectively referred to as lobbying) for a foreign principal such as the Government of Ukraine or the Party of Regions is required to register. Manafort, together with GATES' assistance, engaged in a scheme to avoid this registration requirement for DMT, Manafort, and others.

7. It was part of this scheme that in or about 2012 Manafort and others obtained the approval of Ukraine President Yanukovych to implement a global lobbying strategy to promote Ukraine's interests, including entry into the European Union. This was dubbed the anti-crisis project or AC project. Thereafter, DMI, through Manafort, and with the assistance of GATES, worked with various entities and people to lobby in the United States, among other locations. As part of this scheme, the European Centre for a Modern Ukraine (the Centre) was set up by the

Government of Ukraine lo coordinate lobbying principally in Europe, as well as to act as the ostensible client for two lobbying firms in the United States. The Centre reported to Ukraine Party of Regions member, and Ukraine First Vice Prime Minister, Andriy Klyuyev. The Centre largely oversaw European lobbying and Manafort and GATES generally oversaw the work of lobbyists in the United States.

8. As one part of the AC Project, in February 2012, GATES solicited two Washington, D.C., firms (Company A and Company B) to lobby in the United States on behalf of the Party of Regions. For instance on February 21, 2012, GATES wrote to Company A that il would be "representing the Government of Ukraine in [Washington,] DC."

9. The general division of labor in managing Companies A and B's lobbying activities was that Manafort would communicate with Yanukovych and his staff, and GATES dealt with coordinating the work of the two firms. For instance, in November 2012, GATES wrote to the firms that they needed to prepare an assessment of their past and prospective lobbying efforts so the "President" could be briefed by "Paul" "on what Ukraine has done well and what it can do better as we move into 2013." The two firms engaged in extensive United States lobbying. Among other things, they lobbied multiple Members of Congress and their staffs about Ukraine sanctions, the validity of Ukraine elections, and the propriety of Yanukovych's imprisoning his presidential rival, Yulia Tymoshenko.

10. GATES, at Manafort's instruction, worked with Company A to arrange for Manafort to lobby personally in the United States. Specifically, they arranged a meeting in March 2013 in Washington, D.C. attended by Manafort, a senior Company A lobbyist, and a Member of Congress who was on a subcommittee that had Ukraine within its purview. After the meeting, Manafort, with GATES' assistance, prepared a March 2013 report to Yanukovych's office that the meeting "went well," and reported a series of positive developments from the meeting.

11. To distance their public United States lobbying work from the Government of Ukraine, GATES and others arranged for the Centre to represent falsely that it was not "directly or indirectly supervised, directed, [or] controlled" in whole or in major part by the Government of Ukraine or the Party of Regions. GATES knew at the time that the Centre was under the direction of Party of Regions. GATES provided false and misleading representations to a law firm for Company A, which was assessing whether a filing was required under FARA. GATES understood that the false and misleading representations would permit Companies A and B not to register their activities pursuant to FARA.

12. In September 2016, the Department of Justice informed Manafort, GATES, and DMI that it sought to determine whether they had acted as agents of a foreign principal under FARA without registering. In November 2016 and February 2017, GATES and Manafort caused false and misleading letters to be submitted to the

Department of Justice. The letters represented, among other things, that:

    a.   DMI's "efforts on behalf of the Party of Regions" "did not include meetings or outreach within the U.S.";

    b.   GATES did not "recall meeting with or conducting outreach to U.S. government officials or U.S. media outlets on behalf of the [Centre], nor do they recall being party to, arranging, or facilitating any such communications. Rather, it is the recollection and understanding of Messrs. Gates and Manafort that such communications would have been facilitated and conducted by the [Centre's] U.S. consultants, as directed by the [Centre].";

    c.   GATES had merely served as a means of introduction of Companies A and B to the Centre and provided the Centre with a list of "potential U.S.-based consultants - including [Company A] and [Company B] - for the [Centre's] reference and further consideration."

    d.   DMI "does not retain communications beyond thirty days" and as a result of this policy, a "search has returned no responsive documents." The November 2016 letter attached a one-page, undated document that purported to be a DMI "Email Retention Policy."

13.   In fact, GATES knew that the above was false or misleading. He and Manafort had selected Companies A and B without the Centre. Further, GATES engaged in weekly scheduled calls and frequent emails with them to provide them directions as to specific lobbying steps that should be taken; sought and received detailed oral and written reports from these firms on the lobbying work they had performed; wrote communications for Manafort, at his request, to brief Yanukovych on their lobbying efforts; and arranged for payment to the lobbying firms of over $2 million from offshore accounts, among other things. In addition, GATES had provided his then FARA counsel a DMI document retention policy to create the misleading appearance that DMI and its employees did not have responsive documents to provide to the Department of Justice, when he knew that they in fact did.

14.   As another part of the lobbying scheme, in or about and between 2012 and 2013 the Party of Regions, through Manafort, GATES and others, secretly retained a group of former senior European politicians to take positions favorable to Ukraine, including lobbying in the United States. Although the former politicians would appear to be providing their independent assessments of actions by the Government of Ukraine, in fact they were paid lobbyists for Ukraine. In or about 2012 through 2013, GATES, at Manafort's instruction, used at least four offshore accounts to wire more than 2 million euros to pay the group of former politicians. GATES understood that none of the former politicians registered under FARA.

15.   In 2013, foreign politicians who were part of this group lobbied

United States Members of Congress, the Executive Branch, and their staffs in coordination with Manafort, GATES, and Companies A and B.

COUNT 2: *Criminal Information/Making False Statements (18 U.S.C. § 1001)*

16. On February I, 2018, GATES attended a proffer session with his counsel at the Special Counsel's Office, which included Special Agents from the Federal Bureau of Investigation. During questioning concerning a March 19, 2013 meeting involving Manafort, a senior Company A lobbyist, and a Member of Congress who was on a subcommittee that had Ukraine within its purview, GATES stated falsely that he was told by Manafort and the senior Company A lobbyist that there were no discussions of Ukraine at the meeting. At the time of his proffer statement, GATES knew that: (a) Manafort and the senior Company A lobbyist had not made the above statements to him; (b) Manafort and the senior Company A lobbyists had told him that the meeting went well; (c) GATES had participated with Manafort in preparing a report that memorialized for Ukraine leadership the pertinent Ukraine discussions that Manafort represented had taken place at the meeting; and (d) Manafort told GATES in 2016 that Manafort told his FARA lawyer that there had been no discussion of Ukraine at the Meeting.

Plea Agreement

17. On February 23, 2018, GATES pled guilty in federal court to one count of making false statements to the FBI and the Special Counsel (Part C, above) and one count of conspiracy against the United States (Parts A & B, above).

18. GATES' sentencing has been delayed until at least March 15, 2019 at the request of the Special Counsel, so that GATES can continue offering the Government his cooperation and assist in both Mueller's inquiry as well as other federal investigations currently underway. This has been supported by GATES and his lawyer as, in their view, the more helpful he can be the less time he hopes he'll have to serve in federal prison.

19. According to federal sentencing guidelines, when GATES' sentencing does finally arrive (likely around the same time the Special Counsel investigation wraps up), he could face up to 6 years in a federal correctional institution for his part in this.

Signed: Robert S. Mueller, lII
Special Counsel

Prepared By: Andrew Weissmann, Jeannie S. Rhee, Greg D. Andres & Kyle R. Freeny
Senior/Assistant Special Counsels

Part 3
UNITED STATES v. PAUL J. MANAFORT, JR.

FILED: September 14, 2018 in the U.S. District Court for the District of Columbia

Editor's Note: This Statement of the Offenses and Other Acts for Paul Manafort's first attempt at a successful guilty plea (more on this later) further details Manafort and Gates' nefarious operations overseas, while also beginning to hint at the pandora's box of legal pitfalls still ahead for Paul Manafort at this stage in the game. Also, at present, Manafort's failure to live up to the deals he's made with prosecutors (such as this one) is making it look increasingly likely that - barring a presidential pardon - Manafort will end up being incarcerated for the rest of his natural life when all is said and done.

Statement of the Offenses and Other Acts

Pursuant to the Federal Rules of Criminal Procedure 11, the United States and the defendant PAUL J. MANAFORT, JR. ("MANAFORT") stipulate and agree that the following facts are true and accurate. These facts do not constitute all of the facts known to the parties concerning the charged offense and covered conduct. This statement is being submitted by the parties to demonstrate that sufficient facts exist to establish that the defendant committed the offenses to which he is pleading guilty.

COUNT 1: *Conspiracy Against the United States (18 U.S.C. § 371)*

1.   At all relevant times herein, MANAFORT was an owner of Davis Manafort Partners, Inc. (DMP) or DMP International, LLC (DMI) or both. MANAFORT engaged in a variety of criminal schemes, and knowingly, intentionally, and willfully conspired with Richard W. Gates, Konstantin Kilimnik, and others to carry out the criminal schemes that make up Counts One and Two of the Information, as more fully set forth below.

      A.   **Foreign Agent Registration Act Conspiracy (22 U.S.C. §§ 612 and 618(a)(l))**

MANAFORT's Lobbying in the United States on Behalf of the Government of Ukraine

2.   MANAFORT knew it was illegal to lobby government officials and engage in public relations activities (hereinafter collectively referred to as lobbying) in the United States on behalf of a foreign government or political party, without registering with the United States Government under the Foreign Agents Registration Act. MANAFORT knew he was lobbying in the United States for the Government of Ukraine, President Viktor F. Yanukovych, the Party of Regions, and

the Opposition Bloc (the latter two being political parties in Ukraine), and thus he was supposed to submit a written registration statement to the United States Department of Justice. MANAFORT knew that the filing was required to disclose the name of the foreign country, all the financial payments to the lobbyist, and the specific steps undertaken for the foreign country in the United States, among other information.

3.   MANAFORT knew that Ukraine had a strong interest in the United States' taking economic and policy positions favorable to Ukraine, including not imposing sanctions on Ukraine. MANAFORT also knew that the trial and treatment of President Yanukovych's political rival, former Prime Minister Yulia Tymoshenko, was strongly condemned by leading United States executive and legislative branch officials, and was a major hurdle to improving United States and Ukraine relations.

4.   From 2006 until 2015, MANAFORT led a multi-million dollar lobbying campaign in the United States at the direction of the Government of Ukraine, President Yanukovych, the Party of Regions, and the Opposition Bloc. MANAFORT intentionally did so without registering and providing the disclosures required by law.

5.   As part of the lobbying scheme, MANAFORT hired numerous firms and people to assist in his lobbying campaign in the United States. He hired Companies A, B, C, D, and E, and Law Firm A, among others, to participate in what he described to President Yanukovych in writing as a global "Engage Ukraine" lobbying campaign that he devised and led. These companies and law firm were paid the equivalent of over $11 million for their Ukraine work.

6.   MANAFORT viewed secrecy for himself and for the actions of his lobbyists as integral to the effectiveness of the lobbying offensive he orchestrated for Ukraine. Filing under the Foreign Agents Registration Act would have thwarted the secrecy MANAFORT sought in order to conduct an effective campaign for Ukraine to influence both American leaders and the American public.

7.   MANAFORT took steps to avoid any of these firms and people disclosing their lobbying efforts under the Foreign Agents Registration Act. As one example, even though MANAFORT engaged Company E in 2007 to lobby in the United States for the Government of Ukraine, MANAFORT tried to dissuade Company E from filing under the Foreign Agents Registration Act. Only after MANAFORT ceased to use Company E in the fall of 2007 did Company E disclose its work for Ukraine, in a belated filing under the Act in 2008.

8.   MANAFORT took other measures to keep the Ukraine lobbying as secret as possible. For example, MANAFORT, in written communications on or about May 16, 2013, directed his lobbyists (including Persons D1 and D2, who worked for Company D) to write and disseminate within the United States news stories that alleged that Tymoshenko had paid for the murder of a Ukrainian official. MANAFORT

stated that it should be "push[ed]" "[w]ith no fingerprints." "It is very important we have no connection." MANAFORT stated that "[m]y goal is to plant some stink on Tymo." Person D1 objected to the plan, but ultimately Persons DI and D2 complied with MANAFORT's direction. The Foreign Agents Registration Act required MANAFORT to disclose such lobbying, as MANAFORT knew. He did not.

The Hapsburg Group & Company D

9. As part of the lobbying scheme, starting in 2011, MANAFORT secretly retained Company D and a group of four former European heads of state and senior officials (including a former Austrian Chancellor, Italian Prime Minister, and Polish President) to lobby in the United States and Europe on behalf of Ukraine. The former politicians, called the Hapsburg Group by MANAFORT, appeared to be providing solely their independent assessments of Government of Ukraine policies, when in fact they were paid by Ukraine. MANAFORT explained in an "EYES ONLY" memorandum in or about June 2012 that his purpose was to "assemble a small group of high-level European infuencial [sic] champions and politically credible friends who can act informally and without any visible relationship with the Government of Ukraine."

10. Through MANAFORT, the Government of Ukraine retained an additional group of lobbyists (Company D and Persons D1 and D2). In addition to lobbying itself, Company D secretly served as intermediaries between the Hapsburg Group and MANAFORT and the Government of Ukraine. In or about 2012 through 2013, MANAFORT directed more than the equivalent of 700,000 euros to be wired from at least three of his offshore accounts to the benefit of Company D to pay secretly for its services.

11. All four Hapsburg Group members, at the direction, and with the direct assistance, of MANAFORT, advocated positions favorable to Ukraine in meetings with United States lawmakers, interviews with United States journalists, and ghost written op-eds in American publications. In or about 2012 through 2014, MANAFORT directed more than 2 million euros to be wired from at least four of his offshore accounts to pay secretly the Hapsburg Group. To avoid European taxation, the contract with the Hapsburg Group falsely stated that none of its work would take place in Europe.

12. One of the Hapsburg Group members, a former Polish President, was also a representative of the European Parliament with oversight responsibility for Ukraine. MANAFORT solicited that official to provide MANAFORT inside information about the European Parliament's views and actions toward Ukraine and to take actions favorable to Ukraine. MANAFORT also used this Hapsburg Group member's current European Parliament position to Ukraine's advantage in his lobbying efforts in the United States. In the fall of 2012, the United States Senate was

considering and ultimately passed a resolution critical of President Yanukovych's treatment of former Prime Minister Tymoshenko. MANAFORT engaged in an all-out campaign to try to kill or delay the passage of this resolution. Among the steps he took was having the Hapsburg Group members reach out to United States Senators, as well as directing Companies A and B to have private conversations with Senators to lobby them to place a "hold" on the resolution. MANAFORT told his lobbyists to stress to the Senators that the former Polish President who was advocating against the resolution was currently a designated representative of the President of the European Parliament, to give extra clout to his supposedly independent judgment against the Senate resolution. MANAFORT never revealed to the Senators or to the American public that any of these lobbyists or Hapsburg Group members were paid by Ukraine.

13.   In another example, on May 16, 2013, another member of the Hapsburg Group lobbied in the United States for Ukraine. The Hapsburg Group member accompanied his country's prime minister to the Oval Office and met with the President and Vice President of the United States, as well as senior United States officials in the executive and legislative branches. In written communications sent to MANAFORT, Person D1 reported that the Hapsburg Group member delivered the message of not letting "Russians Steal Ukraine from the West." The Foreign Agents Registration Act required MANAFORT to disclose such lobbying, as MANAFORT knew. He did not.

Law Firm Report and Tymoshenko

14.   As another part of the lobbying scheme, in 2012, on behalf of President Yanukovych and the Government of Ukraine's Ministry of Justice, MANAFORT solicited a United States law firm to write a report evaluating the trial of Yanukovych's political opponent Yulia Tymoshenko. MANAFORT caused Ukraine to hire the law firm so that its report could be used in the United States and elsewhere to defend the Tymoshenko criminal trial and argue that President Yanukovych and Ukraine had not engaged in selective prosecution.

15.   MANAFORT retained a public relations firm (Company C) to prepare a media roll-out plan for the law firm report. MANAFORT used one of his offshore accounts to pay Company C the equivalent of more than $1 million for its services.

16.   MANAFORT worked closely with Company C to develop a detailed written lobbying plan in connection with what MANAFORT termed the "selling" of the report. This campaign included getting the law firm's report "seeded" to the press in the United States-that is, to leak the report ahead of its official release to a prominent United States newspaper and then use that initial article to influence reporting globally. As part of the roll-out plan, on the report's issuance on December

13, 2012, MANAFORT arranged to have the law firm disseminate hard copies of the report to numerous government officials, including senior United States executive and legislative branch officials.

17.   MANAFORT reported on the law firm's work on the report and Company C's lobbying plan to President Yanukovych and other representatives of the Government of Ukraine. For example, in a July 27, 2012 memorandum to President Yanukovych's Chief of Staff, MANAFORT reported on "the global rollout strategy for the [law firm's] legal report, and provide[d] a detailed plan of action" which included step-by-step lobbying outreach in the United States.

18.   MANAFORT directed lobbyists to tout the report as showing that President Yanukovych had not selectively prosecuted Tymoshenko. But in November 2012 MANAFORT had been told privately in writing by the law firm that the evidence of Tymoshenko's criminal intent "is virtually non-existent" and that it was unclear even among legal experts that Tymoshenko lacked power to engage in the conduct central to the Ukraine criminal case. These facts, known by MANAFORT, were not disclosed to the public.

19.   MANAFORT knew that the report also did not disclose that the law firm, in addition to being retained to write the report, was retained to represent Ukraine itself, including in connection with the Tymoshenko case and to provide training to the trial team prosecuting Tymoshenko.

20.   MANAFORT also knew that the Government of Ukraine did not want to disclose how much the report cost. More than $4.6 million was paid to the law firm for its work. MANAFORT used one of his offshore accounts to funnel $4 million to pay the law firm, a fact that MANAFORT did not disclose to the public. Instead, the Government of Ukraine reported falsely that the report cost just $12,000.

21.   MANAFORT and others knew that the actual cost of the report and the scope of the law firm's work would undermine the report's being perceived as an independent assessment and thus being an effective lobbying tool for MANAFORT to use to support the incarceration of President Yanukovych's political opponent.

22.   In addition to the law firm report, MANAFORT took other steps on behalf of the Government of Ukraine to tarnish Tymoshenko in the United States. In addition to disseminating stories about her soliciting murder, noted above, in October 2012, MANAFORT orchestrated a scheme to have, as he wrote in a contemporaneous communication, "[O]bama jews" put pressure on the Administration to disavow Tymoshenko and support Yanukovych. MANAFORT sought to undermine United States support for Tymoshenko by spreading stories in the United States that a senior Cabinet official (who had been a prominent critic of Yanukovych's treatment of Tymoshenko) was supporting anti-Semitism because the official supported Tymoshenko, who in turn had formed a political alliance with a

Ukraine party that espoused anti-Semitic views. MANAFORT coordinated privately with a senior Israeli government official to issue a written statement publicizing this story. MANAFORT then, with secret advance knowledge of that Israeli statement, worked to disseminate this story in the United States, writing to Person D1 "I have someone pushing it on the NY Post. Bada bing bada boom." MANAFORT sought to have the Administration understand that "the Jewish community will take this out on Obama on election day if he does nothing." MANAFORT then told his United States lobbyist to inform the Administration that Ukraine had worked to prevent the Administration's presidential opponent from including damaging language in the Israeli statement, so as not to harm the Administration, and thus further ingratiate Yanukovych with the Administration.

Company A and Company B

23. As a third part of the lobbying scheme, in February 2012, MANAFORT solicited two Washington , D.C. lobbying firms (Company A and Company B) to lobby in the United States on behalf of President Yanukovych, the Party of Regions and the Government of Ukraine. For instance, in early 2012 at the inception of the relationship, Company B wrote in an email to its team about a "potential representation for the Ukraine," having been contacted "at the suggestion of Paul Manafort who has been working on the current PM elections."

24. MANAFORT arranged to pay Companies A and B over $2 million from his offshore accounts for their United States lobbying work for Ukraine.

25. MANAFORT provided direction to Companies A and B in their lobbying efforts, including providing support for numerous United States visits by numerous senior Ukrainian officials. Companies A and B, at MANAFORT's direction, engaged in extensive United States lobbying. Among other things, they lobbied dozens of Members of Congress, their staff, and White House and State Department officials about Ukraine sanctions, the validity of Ukraine elections, and the propriety of President Yanukovych's imprisoning Tymoshenko, his presidential rival.

26. In addition, with the assistance of Company A, MANAFORT also personally lobbied in the United States. He drafted and edited numerous ghost-written op-eds for publication in United States newspapers. He also personally met in March 2013 in Washington, D.C., with a Member of Congress who was on a subcommittee that had Ukraine within its purview. After the meeting, MANAFORT prepared a report for President Yanukovych that the meeting "went well" and reported a series of positive developments for Ukraine from the meeting.

27. Indeed, MANAFORT repeatedly communicated in person and in writing with President Yanukovych and his staff about the lobbying activities of Companies A and B and he tasked the companies to prepare assessments of their work so he, in turn, could brief President Yanukovych. For instance, MANAFORT

wrote President Yanukovych a memorandum dated April 8, 2012, in which he provided an update on the lobbying firms' activities "since the inception of the project a few weeks ago. It is my intention to provide you with a weekly update moving forward." In November 2012, Gates wrote to Companies A and B that the firms needed to prepare an assessment of their past and prospective lobbying efforts so the "President" could be briefed by "Paul" "on what Ukraine has done well and what it can do better as we move into 2013." The resulting memorandum from Companies A and B, with input from Gates, noted among other things that the "client" had not been as successful as hoped given that it had an Embassy in Washington.

28. To distance their United States lobbying work from the Government of Ukraine, and to avoid having to register as agents of Ukraine under the Foreign Agents Registration Act, MANAFORT with others arranged for Companies A and B to be engaged by a newly-formed Brussels entity called the European Centre for the Modern Ukraine (the Centre), instead of directly by the Government of Ukraine.

29. MANAFORT described the Centre as "the Brussels NGO that we have formed" to coordinate lobbying for Ukraine. The Centre was founded by a Ukraine Party of Regions member and Ukraine First Vice-Prime Minister. The head of its Board was another member of the Party of Regions, who became the Ukraine Foreign Minister.

30. In spite of these ties to Ukraine, MANAFORT and others arranged for the Centre to represent falsely that it was not "directly or indirectly supervised, directed, [or] controlled" in whole or in major part by the Government of Ukraine or the Party of Regions. MANAFORT knew that the false and misleading representations would lead Companies A and B not to register their activities pursuant to the Foreign Agents Registration Act.

31. Despite the Centre being the ostensible client of Companies A and B, MANAFORT knew that the Centre did not direct or oversee their work. The firms received direction from MANAFORT and his subordinate Gates, on behalf of the Government of Ukraine.

32. As MANAFORT knows from giving directions to Companies A and B, and from the discovery material provided herein, various employees of Companies A and B understood that they were receiving direction from MANAFORT and President Yanukovych, not the Centre, which was not even operational when Companies A and B began lobbying for Ukraine. MANAFORT, Gates, and employees of both Companies A and B referred to the client in ways that made clear they knew it was Ukraine, for instance noting that the "client" had an Embassy in Washington D.C. The head of Company B told his team to think the President of Ukraine "is the client." As a Company A employee noted to another company employee: the lobbying

for the Centre was "in name only. [Y]ou've gotta see through the nonsense of that[.]" "It's like Alice in Wonderland." An employee of Company B described the Centre as a fig leaf, and the Centre's written certification that it was not related to the Party of Regions as "a fig leaf on a fig leaf," referring to the Centre in an email as the "European hot dog stand for a Modern Ukraine."

Conspiring to Obstruct Justice (False and Misleading Submissions to the Department of Justice)

33. In September 2016, after numerous press reports concerning MANAFORT had appeared in August, the Department of Justice National Security Division informed MANAFORT, Gates, and DMI in writing that it sought to determine whether they had acted as agents of a foreign principal under the Foreign Agents Registration Act, without registering. In November 2016 and February 2017, MANAFORT and Gates conspired to knowingly and intentionally cause false and misleading letters to be submitted to the Department of Justice, through his unwitting legal counsel. The letters, both of which were approved by MANAFORT before they were submitted by his counsel, represented falsely, among other things, that:

    a.   DMl's "efforts on behalf of the Party of Regions" "did not include meetings or outreach within the U.S.";

    b.   MANAFORT did not "recall meeting with or conducting outreach to U.S. government officials or U.S. media outlets on behalf of the [Centre], nor do they recall being party to, arranging, or facilitating any such communications. Rather, it is the recollection and understanding of Messrs. Gates and Manafort that such communications would have been facilitated and conducted by the [Centre's] U.S. consultants, as directed by the [Centre] ";

    c.   MANAFORT had merely served as a means of introduction of Company A and Company B to the Centre and provided the Centre with a list of "potential U.S.-based consultants-including [Company A] and [Company B]-for the [Centre's] reference and further consideration."

    d.   DMI "does not retain communications beyond thirty days" and as a result of this policy, a "search has returned no responsive documents." The November 2016 letter attached a one-page, undated document that purported to be a DMI "Email Retention Policy."

34. In fact, MANAFORT had: selected Companies A and B; engaged in weekly scheduled calls and frequent emails with Companies A and B to provide them directions as to specific lobbying steps that should be taken; sought and received detailed oral and written reports from these firms on the lobbying work they had performed; communicated with Yanukovych to brief him on their lobbying efforts;

both congratulated and reprimanded Companies A and B on their lobbying work; communicated directly with United States officials in connection with this work; and paid the lobbying firms over $2.5 million from offshore accounts he controlled, among other things.

35. Although MANAFORT had represented to the Department of Justice in November 2016 and February 2017 that he had no relevant documents, in fact MANAFORT had numerous incriminating documents in his possession, as he knew at the time. The Federal Bureau of Investigation conducted a court-authorized search of MANAFORT'S home in Virginia in the summer of 2017. The documents attached hereto as Government Exhibits 503, 504, 517, 532, 594, 604, 606, 616, 691, 692, 697, 706 and 708, among numerous others, were all documents that MANAFORT had in his possession (and were found in the search) and all pre-dated the November 2016 letter.

B.   Money Laundering Conspiracy

36. In or around and between 2006 and 2016, MANAFORT, together with others, did knowingly and intentionally conspire (a) to conduct financial transactions, affecting interstate and foreign commerce, which involved the proceeds of specified unlawful activity, to wit, felony violations of FARA in violation of Title 22, United States Code, Sections 612 and 618, knowing that the property involved in the financial transactions represented proceeds of some form of unlawful activity, with intent to engage in conduct constituting a violation of sections 7201 and 7206 of the Internal Revenue Code of 1986; and (b) to transport, transmit, and transfer monetary instruments and funds from places outside the United States to and through places in the United States and from places in the United States to and through places outside the United States, with the intent to promote the carrying on of specified unlawful activity, to wit: a felony violation of FARA, in violation of Title 22, United States Code, Sections 612 and 618, contrary to Title 18, United States Code, Section 1956(a)(l)(A)(ii) and (a)(2)(A).

37. MANAFORT caused the following transfers to be made, knowing that they were being made to entities to carry on activities that were required to be timely reported under the Foreign Agents Registration Act, but were not:

Payee	Date	Payer	Originating Bank Account	Country of... Origin	Destination	Amount (USD)
	8/2/2012	Bletilla Ventures Ltd.	Bank of Cyprus Account - 0480	Cyprus	us	$270,000.00
	10/10/2012	Bletilla Ventures Ltd.	Bank of Cyprus Account - 0480	Cyprus	us	$90,000.00
	11/16/2012	Bletilla Ventures Ltd.	Bank of Cyprus Account - 0480	Cyprus	us	$120,000.00
	11/20/2012	Bletilla Ventures Ltd.	Bank of Cyprus Account -0480	Cyprus	us	$182,968.07
	12/21/2012	Bletilla Ventures Ltd.	Bank of Cyprus Account -0480	Cyprus	us	$25,000.0C
	3/15/2013	Bletilla Ventures Ltd.	Hellenic Bank Account - 2501	Cyprus	us	$90,000.0C
	9/18/2013	Global Endeavour Inc.	Loyal Bank Limited Account -1840	SVG*	us	$135,937.37

P ayee	Date	Payer	Originating Bank Account	Country of... Origin	Desti nation	Amount (USD)
	10/31/ 2013	Jeunet Ltd.	Loyal Bank Limited Account -4978	SV G*	us	$167,689. 40
	3/28/2 014	Jeunet Ltd.	Loyal Bank Limited Account -4978	SV G*	us	$135,639. 65
	4/3/20 14	Jeunet Ltd.	Loyal Bank Limited Account -4978	SV G*	us	$82,979. 93
Total Company A Transfers						$1,300,21 4.42
	5/30/2 012	Bletill a Ventures Ltd.	Bank of Cyprus Account - 0480	Cy prus	us	$130,000. 00
	8/2/20 12	Bletill a Ventures Ltd.	Bank of Cyprus Account - 0480	Cy prus	us	$195,000. 00
	10/10/ 2012	Bletill a Ventures Ltd.	Bank of Cyprus Account - 0480	Cy prus	us	$130,000. 00
	11/16/2 012	Bletill a Ventures Ltd.	Bank of Cyprus Account - 0480	Cy prus	us	$50,000. 00
	12/21/ 2012	Bletill a	Bank of Cyprus	Cy prus	us	$54,649. 51

		Ventures Ltd.	Account - 0480			
3/15/2 013	Bletill a Ventures Ltd.	Hellenic Bank Account - 2501	Cy prus	us	$150,000. 00
9/3/20 13	Jeunet Ltd.	Loyal Bank Limited Account -4978	SV G*	us	$175,857. 51
10/31/ 2013	Jeunet Ltd.	Loyal Bank Limited Account -4978	SV G*	us	$195,857. 51
3/12/2 014	Jeunet Ltd.	Loyal Bank Limited Account -4978	SV G*	us	$26,891.7 8
3/21/2 014	Jeunet Ltd.	Loyal Bank Limited Account -4978	SV G*	us	$138,026. 00
4/15/2 014	Jeunet Ltd.	Loyal Bank Limited Account -4978	SV G*	us	$4,728.81
4/25/2 014	Jeunet Ltd.	Loyal Bank Limited Account -4978	SV G*	us	$4,739.23
Total Company B Transfers					$1,255,75 0.35

P ayee	Date	Payer	Originat ing Bank Account	Country of... Origin	Desti nation	Amount (.USD)
	4/19/ 2012	Black Sea View Limited	Bank of Cyprus Account- 7412	Cy prus	us	$2,000,00 0.00
	5/30/ 2012	Black Sea View Limited	Bank of Cyprus Account- 7412	Cy prus	us	$1,000,00 0.00
	7/13/2 012	Black Sea View Limited	Bank of Cyprus Account - 7412	Cy prus	us	$1,000,00 0.00
Total Law Firm A Transfers						$4,000,00 0.00
TOTAL TRANSFERS						$6.555.96 4. 77

* SVG refers to St. Vincent and the Grenadines.

C.   **Tax & Foreign Bank Account Conspiracy**
(26 U.S.C. § 7206(1) & 31 U.S.C. §§ 5314/5322(a))

38.   From 2008 through 2014, MANAFORT caused millions of dollars of wire transfers to be made from offshore nominee accounts, without paying taxes on that income. The payments were made for goods, services, and real estate. MANAFORT also hid income by denominating various overseas payments as "loans," thereby evading payment of any taxes on that income by MANAFORT.

39.   MANAFORT directly and through Gates repeatedly misled his bookkeeper and tax accountants, including by not disclosing Manafort's overseas accounts and income. Further, MANAFORT and Gates, acting at Manafort's instruction, classified overseas payments made to MANAFORT falsely as "loans" to avoid incurring additional taxes on the income.

40.   MANAFORT owned and controlled a range of foreign bank accounts in Cyprus, the Grenadines, and the United Kingdom. MANAFORT directly and through Gates maintained these accounts, including by managing them and by

making substantial transfers from the accounts to both himself and vendors for personal items for him and his family. MANAFORT was aware that many of these accounts held well in excess of $10,000 in the aggregate at some point during each year in which they existed. MANAFORT did not report the accounts' existence to his bookkeeper and his tax preparers in an effort to hide them, and to allow him to avoid disclosing their existence on an FBAR filing.

41.   MANAFORT was aware at the time that it was illegal to hide income from the Internal Revenue Service (IRS) by failing to account for reportable income on his income tax returns. MANAFORT was also aware that it was illegal to fail to report information to the IRS regarding the existence of foreign bank accounts, as required by Schedule B of the IRS Form 1040. MANAFORT also understood at the time that a U.S. person who had a financial interest in, or signature or other authority over, a bank account or other financial account in a foreign country, which exceeded $10,000 in any one year (at any time during that year), was required to report the account to the Department of the Treasury. MANAFORT also understood, after 2010, that the failure to make such a report constituted a crime.

42.   Knowing the existence of his reportable foreign accounts and hidden income, MANAFORT knowingly, intentionally, and willfully filed and conspired to file false tax returns from 2006-2015 in that he said he did not have reportable foreign bank accounts when he knew that he did, he did not report income that he knew he in fact had earned, and he did not file Foreign Bank Account Reports. MANAFORT failed to report over $15 million in income during the period 2010-2014.

FORFEITURE NOTICE

43.   The following assets constitute or were derived from proceeds of MANAFORT's conspiracy to violate the Foreign Agents Registration Act and/or they constitute property involved in MANAFORT's conspiracy to launder money in violation of 18 U.S.C. § 1956 or are traceable thereto and/or they represent substitute assets for such property which has been made unavailable for forfeiture by the acts or omissions of MANAFORT:

1) The real property and premises commonly known as 377 Union Street, Brooklyn, New York 11231 (Block 429, Lot 65), including all appurtenances, improvements, and attachments thereon, and any property traceable thereto;

2) The real property and premises commonly known as 29 Howard Street, #4D, New York, New York 10013 (Block 209, Lot 1104), including all appurtenances, improvements, and attachments thereon, and any property traceable thereto;

3) The real property and premises commonly known as 174 Jobs Lane, Water Mill, New York 11976, including all appurtenances, improvements, and attachments thereon, and any property traceable thereto;

4) All funds held in account number XXXXXX0969 at The Federal Savings Bank, and any property traceable thereto;

5) All funds seized from account number XXXXXX1388 at Capital One N.A. and any property traceable thereto;

6) All funds seized from account number XXXXXX9952 at The Federal Savings Bank and any property traceable thereto;

7) Northwestern Mutual Universal Life Insurance Policy and any property traceable thereto;

8) The real property and premises commonly known as 123 Baxter Street, #5D, New York, New York 10016 in lieu of 1046 N. Edgewood Street; and

9) The real property and premises commonly known as 721 Fifth Avenue, #43G, New York, New York 10022 in lieu of all funds from account number at Charles Schwab & Co. Inc., and any property traceable thereto.

COUNT 2: Witness Tampering Conspiracy (18 TI.S.C. § 371)

44. From in or about and between February 23, 2018, and April 2018, both dates being approximate and inclusive, within the District of Columbia and elsewhere, the defendant PAUL J. MANAFORT, JR., together with others, including Konstantin Kilimnik, knowingly and intentionally conspired to corruptly persuade another person, to wit: Persons D1 and D2, with intent to influence, delay and prevent the testimony of any person in an official proceeding, in violation of 18 U.S.C. § 15 1 2(b)(1). The facts set forth with respect to Count One are incorporated herein.

45. On February 22, 2018, MANAFORT was charged in the District of Columbia in a Superseding Indictment that for the first time included allegations about the Hapsburg Group and MANAFORT's use of that group to lobby illegally in the United States in violation of the Foreign Agent Registration Act. MANAFORT knew that the Act prescribed only United States lobbying. Immediately after February 22, 2018, MANAFORT began reaching out directly and indirectly to Persons D1 and D2 to induce them to say falsely that they did not work in the United States as part of the lobbying campaign, even though MANAFORT then and there well knew that they did lobby in the United States.

46. MANAFORT committed the following overt acts directly and through his conspirators.

OTHER ACTS

A.   Bank Fraud & Bank Fraud Conspiracy (18 U.S.C. §§ 1344 and 1349) Citizens Bank / $3.4 million loan (Charged as Count 24 in the Eastern District of Virginia Superseding Indictment)

47.   Between December 2015 and March 2016, MANAFORT conspired to intentionally defraud Citizens Bank in connection with his application for a mortgage for approximately $3.4 million. The mortgage related to a condominium on Howard Street in the Soho neighborhood of Manhattan, New York. During the course of the conspiracy, MANAFORT made and caused to be made, a series of false and fraudulent representations to the bank in order to secure the loan, including the following:

a.   MANAFORT falsely represented the amount of debt he had by failing to disclose on his loan application the existence of a mortgage on his Union Street property (from Genesis Capital);

b.   MANAFORT caused an insurance broker to provide Citizens Bank false information, namely, an outdated insurance report that did not list the Union Street loan (from Genesis Capital);

c.   MANAFORT falsely stated that a $1.5 million Peranova loan had been forgiven in 2015; and

d.   MANAFORT falsely represented to the lender and its agents that the Howard Street property was a secondary home used as such by his daughter and son-in-law and was not held as a rental property. These statements were material to Citizens Bank.

48.   Citizens Bank was a financial institution chartered by the United States.

B.   Bank Fraud & Bank Fraud Conspiracy (18 U.S.C. §§ 1344 and 1349) Banc of California / $1 million loan (Charged as·Count 26 in the Eastern District of Virginia Superseding Indictment)

49.   In approximately February 2016, MANAFORT conspired to intentionally defraud Banc of California in connection with his application for a business loan. During the course of the conspiracy, MANAFORT made and caused to be made a series of false and fraudulent representations to the bank, including the following: (a) the submission of a false statement of assets and liabilities that failed to disclose a loan on the Union Street property (from Genesis Capital) and misrepresented, among other things, the amount of the mortgage on the Howard Street property; and (b) the submission of a doctored 2015 DMI profit and loss statement (P&L) that overstated DMI's 2015 income by more than $4 million. These statements were material to Banc of California.

50.   Banc of California was a financial institution chartered by the

United States.

C.   Bank Fraud & Bank Fraud Conspiracy (18 U.S.C. §§ 1344 and 1349) Citizens Bank / $5.5 million loan (Charged as·Count 28 in the Eastern District of Virginia Superseding Indictment)

51.   Between December 2015 and March 2016, MANAFORT conspired to intentionally defraud Citizens Bank in connection with his application for a mortgage for approximately $5.5 million on a property at Union Street in Brooklyn, New York. During the course of the conspiracy, MANAFORT made or caused to be made a series of false and fraudulent material representations to the bank in order to secure the loan, including the following: (a) the submission of a false statement of assets and liabilities that hid a prior loan on the Union Street property (from Genesis Capital), among other liabilities; and (b) the submission of a falsified 2016 DMI P&L that overstated DMl's income by more than $2 million.

D.   Bank Fraud & Bank Fraud Conspiracy (18 U.S.C. §§ 1344 and 1349) The Federal Savings Bank / $9.5 million loan (Charged as·Count 28 in the Eastern District of Virginia Superseding Indictment)

52.   Between April 2016 and January 2017, MANAFORT conspired to intentionally defraud, and did defraud, The Federal Savings Bank in connection with his applications for the following two loans: (a) a loan for approximately $9.5 million related to various properties, including a house in Bridgehampton, New York, and (b) a loan for approximately $6.5 million related to his Union Street property. During the course of the fraudulent scheme, MANAFORT made and caused to be made a series of false and fraudulent material representations to the bank in order to secure both loans, including the following: (a) MANAFORT provided the bank with doctored P&Ls for DMI for both 2015 and 2016, overstating its income by millions of dollars; and (b) MANAFORT falsely represented to The Federal Savings Bank that he had lent his credit card to a friend who had incurred more than $200,000 in charges relating to the purchase of Yankee tickets.

53.   Both loans were extended by The Federal Savings Bank.

54.   The Federal Savings Bank was a financial institution chartered by the United States.

Plea Agreement

55.   MANAFORT had his bail revoked on June 15, 2018, after the special counsel's office accused him of witness tampering while out awaiting trial between February and April, 2018. This could seriously damage the tentative agreements he's struck with federal prosecutors in his two recent, high-profile criminal cases (more on this in later chapters).

56. MANAFORT is scheduled to be sentenced in both of his still pending court cases on March 8 and March 13, 2019. The special counsel has made it clear that he would certainly not mind if MANAFORT spent the rest of his life in prison, so even if his plea deals stays in place, MANAFORT still faces an uphill battle trying to catch a break at either of his sentencing hearings.

57. Additionally, Mueller may not be the end of MANAFORT's legal troubles as there are still multiple open investigations around the country looking at many years worth of MANAFORT's characteristically shady banking, business and political practices. Including one out of the New York State Attorney General's office that is rumored to have legs and which, if brought, would open MANAFORT up to serious legal jeopardy, the outcome of which cannot be reversed by a presidential pardon if it doesn't work out in his favor.

Signed: Robert S. Mueller, III
Special Counsel

Prepared By: Andrew Weissmann, Jeannie S. Rhee, Greg D. Andres & Kyle R. Freeny
Senior/Assistant Special Counsels

CHAPTER 3: MICHAEL FLYNN, DEC. 1, 2017

UNITED STATES v. MICHAEL T. FLYNN

FILED: December 1, 2017 in the U.S. District Court for the District of Columbia

Editor's Note: Michael Flynn was formerly the head of the Defense Intelligence Agency and a senior foreign policy advisor to the Trump campaign, before being named the Trump administration's first National Security Advisor. He lasted less than a month, resigning on February 13, 2017, for conduct related to the charges below.

Timeline of Events

December 10, 2015: FLYNN is paid $45,000 to attend a 10th anniversary gala for RT (the world-reaching, Russian-government-backed, english-language broadcast network) in Moscow and sit next to Vladimir Putin for the evening. FLYNN is later quoted as saying, "I didn't even really talk to him."

On or around August 6, 2015: FLYNN meets with Trump to advise him on foreign policy and assist in debate prep ahead of the Republican presidential primary debate in Cleveland, OH.

February 2016: FLYNN joins the Trump campaign in an official role as a senior foreign policy and national security advisor, adding gravitas to a roster of aides with largely little experience in foreign policy.

July 2016: Prior to the start of the Republican convention, FLYNN is reported to be on short list of candidates being looked at to be Trump's running mate.

November 10, 2016: President Obama in a closed-door meeting with Trump after his election victory, warns Trump that FLYNN's ties to and support for Turkey and other foreign governments through his personal lobbying firm, Flynn Intel Group, made him an unsuitable to choice to serve as the president's National Security Advisor. The next day, The Daily Caller, publishes the first of many news reports beginning to detail FLYNN's secretive dealings with Erdogan's government in Turkey.

November 18, 2016: President-elect Trump officially names FLYNN as his pick to be National Security Advisor in the new administration.

December 2016: FLYNN has conversations with Russian ambassador Sergey

Kislyak about a possible easement of U.S. sanctions. Vice-President Mike Pence will later claim that FLYNN deceived him as to the nature of these talks at the time.

January 2017: FLYNN is interviewed by the FBI about his personal and professional ties to Russia as part of the ongoing FBI investigation into possible election interference. FLYNN later admits to making misrepresentations and lying throughout the interview about his relationships with and support for both the Erdogan government in Turkey and Putin's government in Russia.

January 26, 2017: Sally Yates, the acting attorney general at the time, warns the Trump White House about FLYNN's conversations with Russian operatives.

February 14, 2017: FLYNN resigns from his post as National Security Advisor.

March 2017: FLYNN registers as a foreign agent under the Foreign Agents Registration Act.

December 1, 2017: FLYNN pleads guilty to lying to the FBI and begins cooperating with federal investigators, including Special Counsel Mueller.

December 4, 2018: Mueller recommends no prison time for Flynn due to his cooperation with the special counsel investigation and other criminal inquiries.

Statement of the Offense

Pursuant to Federal Rule of Criminal Procedure 11, the United States of America and the defendant, MICHAEL T. FLYNN, stipulate and agree that the following facts are true and accurate. These facts do not constitute all of the facts known to the parties concerning the charged offense; they are being submitted to demonstrate that sufficient facts exist that the defendant committed the offense to which he is pleading guilty.

1.   The defendant, MICHAEL T. FLYNN, who served as a surrogate and national security advisor for the presidential campaign of Donald J. Trump ("Campaign"), as a senior member of President-Elect Trump's Transition Team ("Presidential Transition Team"), and as the National Security Advisor to President Trump, made materially false statements and omissions during an interview with the Federal Bureau of Investigation ("FBI") on January 24, 2017, in Washington, D.C. At the time of the interview, the FBI had an open investigation into the Government of Russia's ("Russia") efforts to interfere in the 2016 presidential election, including the nature of any links between individuals associated with the Campaign and Russia, and whether there was any coordination between the Campaign and Russia's efforts.

2.   FLYNN's false statements and omissions impeded and otherwise had a material impact on the FBI's ongoing investigation into the existence of any links or coordination between individuals associated with the Campaign and Russia's efforts to interfere with the 2016 presidential election.

False Statements: Regarding FLYNN's Request to the Russian Ambassador that Russia Refrain from Escalating the Situation in Response to U.S. Sanctions against Russia

3.   On or about January 24, 2017, FLYNN agreed to be interviewed by agents from the FBI ("January 24 voluntary interview"). During the interview, FLYNN falsely stated that he did not ask Russia's Ambassador to the United States ("Russian Ambassador") to refrain from escalating the situation in response to sanctions that the United States had imposed against Russia. FLYNN also falsely stated that he did not remember a follow-up conversation in which the Russian Ambassador stated that Russia had chosen to moderate its response to those sanctions as a result of FLYNN's request. In truth and in fact, however, FLYNN then and there knew that the following had occurred:

a.   On or about December 28, 2016, then-President Barack Obama signed Executive Order 13757, which was to take effect the following day. The executive order announced sanctions against Russia in response to that government's actions intended to interfere with the 2016 presidential election ("U.S. Sanctions").

b.   On or about December 28, 2016, the Russian Ambassador contacted FLYNN.

c.   On or about December 29, 2016, FLYNN called a senior official of the Presidential Transition Team ("PTT official"), who was with other senior members of the Presidential Transition Team at the Mar-a-Lago resort in Palm Beach, Florida, to discuss what, if anything, to communicate to the Russian Ambassador about the U.S. Sanctions. On that call, FLYNN and the PTT official discussed the U.S. Sanctions, including the potential impact of those sanctions on the incoming administration's foreign policy goals. The PTT official and FLYNN also discussed that the members of the Presidential Transition Team at Mar-a-Lago did not want Russia to escalate the situation

d.   Immediately after his phone call with the PIT official, FLYNN called the Russian Ambassador and requested that Russia not escalate the situation and only respond to the U.S. Sanctions in a reciprocal manner.

e.   Shortly after his phone call with the Russian Ambassador, FLYNN spoke with the PTT official to report on the substance of his call with the Russian Ambassador, including their discussion of the U.S. Sanctions.

f.   On or about December 30, 2016, Russian President Vladimir Putin released a statement indicating that Russia would not take retaliatory measures in response to the U.S. Sanctions at that time.

g.   On or about December 31, 2016, the Russian Ambassador called FLYNN and informed him that Russia had chosen not to retaliate in response to FLYNN's request.

h.   After his phone call with the Russian Ambassador, FLYNN spoke with senior members of the Presidential Transition Team about FLYNN's conversations with the Russian Ambassador regarding the U.S. Sanctions and Russia's decision not to escalate the situation.

False Statements: Regarding FLYNN's Request for Foreign Officials to Vote Against or Delay the vote on a UN Security Council Resolution on Israeli Settlements

4.   During the January 24 voluntary interview, FLYNN made additional false statements about calls he made to Russia and several other countries regarding a resolution submitted by Egypt to the United Nations Security Council on December 21, 2016. Specifically FLYNN falsely stated that he only asked the countries' positions on the vote, and that he did not request that any of the countries take any particular action on the resolution. FLYNN also falsely stated that the Russian Ambassador never described to him Russia's response to FLYNN's request regarding the resolution. In truth and in fact, however, FLYNN then and there knew that the following had occurred:

a.   On or about December 21, 2016, Egypt submitted a resolution to the United Nations Security Council on the issue of Israeli settlements ("resolution"). The United Nations Security Council was scheduled to vote on the resolution the following day.

b.   On or about December 22, 2016, a very senior member of the Presidential Transition Team directed FLYNN to contact officials from foreign governments, including Russia, to learn where each government stood on the resolution and to influence those governments to delay the vote or defeat the resolution.

c.   On or about December 22, 2016, FLYNN contacted the Russian Ambassador about the pending vote. FLYNN informed the Russian Ambassador about the incoming administration's opposition to the resolution, and requested that Russia vote against or delay the resolution.

d. On or about December 23, 2016, FLYNN again spoke with the Russian Ambassador, who informed FLYNN that if it came to a vote Russia would not vote against the resolution.

False Statements: Regarding FLYNN's Contacts with Foreign Governments

5. On March 7, 2017, FLYNN filed multiple documents with the Department of Justice pursuant to the Foreign Agents Registration Act ("FARA") pertaining to a project performed by him and his company, the Flynn Intel Group, Inc. ("FIG"), for the principal benefit of the Republic of Turkey ("Turkey project"). In the FARA filings, FLYNN made materially false statements and omissions, including by falsely stating that (a) FIG did not know whether or the extent to which the Republic of Turkey was involved in the Turkey project, (b) the Turkey project was focused on improving U.S. business organizations' confidence regarding doing business in Turkey, and (c) an op-ed by FLYNN published in *The Hill* on November 8, 2016, was written at his own initiative; and by omitting that officials from the Republic of Turkey provided supervision and direction over the Turkey project.

Plea Agreement
COUNT 1: Making False Statements to the FBI (Title 18, United States Code, Section 1001(a)(2))

6. On or about January 24, 2017, defendant MICHAEL T. FLYNN did willfully and knowingly make materially false, fictitious, and fraudulent statements and representations in a matter within the jurisdiction of the executive branch of the Government of the United States, to wit, the defendant falsely stated and represented to agents of the Federal Bureau of Investigation, in Washington, D.C., that: \

7. On or about December 29, 2016, FLYNN did not ask the Government of Russia's Ambassador to the United States ("Russian Ambassador") to refrain from escalating the situation in response to sanctions that the United States had imposed against Russia that same day; and FLYNN did not recall the Russian Ambassador subsequently telling him that Russia had chosen to moderate its response to those sanctions as a result of his request; and

8. On or about December 22, 2016, FLYNN did not ask the Russian Ambassador to delay the vote on or defeat a pending United Nations Security Council resolution; and that the Russian Ambassador subsequently never described to FLYNN Russia's response to his request.

SENTENCE: Delayed by the judge assigned to the case as of December 18, 2018.

FLYNN will be sentenced once his cooperation with the government's larger case has ended, though Mueller has said that he will not recommend that Flynn serve time.

Signed: Robert S. Mueller, III

Special Counsel

Prepared By: Brandon L. Van Grack & Zainab Ahmed
Assistant Special Counsels

CHAPTER 4: RICHARD PINEDO, FEB. 12, 2018

UNITED STATES v. RICHARD PINEDO

FILED: February 12, 2018 in the U.S. District Court for the District of Columbia

Editor's note: Richard Pinedo ran an online fake-account business, and was unlucky enough to have sold his product to a group of Russian agents who became the subject of Mueller's probe.

Statement of the Offense

Pursuant to Federal Rule of Criminal Procedure I I, the United States of America and the defendant, RICHARD PINEDO, stipulate and agree that the following facts are true and accurate. These facts do not constitute all of the facts known to the parties concerning the charged offense; they are being submitted to demonstrate that sufficient facts exist that the defendant committed the offense to which he is pleading guilty.

1. From approximately 2014 through December 2017, the defendant, RICHARD PINEDO, operated an online service called "Auction Essistance." Through Auction Essistance, Pinedo offered a variety of services designed to circumvent the security features of large online digital payment companies, including a large digital payments company hereinafter referred to as Company I.

2. PINEDO sold bank account numbers through interstate and foreign commerce, specifically over the internet. PINEDO obtained bank account numbers either by registering accounts in his own name or by purchasing accounts in the names of other people through the internet. Many of the bank accounts purchased by PINEDO over the internet were created using stolen identities of U.S. persons. Although PINEDO was not directly involved in the registration of these accounts using stolen identities, he willfully and intentionally avoided learning about the use of stolen identities.

3. Company 1 required users to submit bank account numbers as a means of verifying a user's identity. To circumvent this requirement, certain users (hereinafter "Users") registered for Company 1's online services with bank account numbers in the names of other people. PINEDO sold Users bank account

numbers over the internet to aid and abet, and in connection with, this scheme to defraud Company 1 by means of internet communications in interstate and foreign commerce.

4.   After acquiring bank account numbers from PINEDO, Users linked the bank account numbers to their accounts with Company 1 as if they were the real owners of the bank accounts. Company 1 sought to verify the bank account numbers by making the minimal trial deposits into the accounts and asking Users to identity the amount of those trial deposits. PINEDO told Users the amounts of those trial deposits, thereby further aiding the Users in their scheme to circumvent verification processes by Company 1.

5.   PINEDO frequently purchased bank account numbers from an individual he knew to be outside the United States. Similarly, based on IP addresses and other information, PINEDO knew that many of the persons to whom he sold bank account numbers were outside the United States.

6.   In total, PINEDO knowingly transferred, possessed, and used, without lawful authority, hundreds of bank account numbers to aid and abet, and in connection with, the use of the wires in interstate and foreign commerce to defeat security measures employed by Company 1. PINEDO personally collected tens of thousands of dollars, and more than $1,000 during a one- year period, through the sale of these bank account numbers.

Plea Information
COUNT 1: Identity Fraud (18 U.S.C. § 1028)

7.   The Special Counsel informs the Court: From approximately 2014 through November 2017, defendant RICHARD PINEDO did knowingly transfer, possess, and use, in and affecting interstate and foreign commerce, and without lawful authority, means of identification of other persons with the intent to commit, and to aid or abet, and in connection with, unlawful activity that constitutes a violation of Federal law, to wit, wire fraud, in violation of Title 18, United States Code, Section 1343. As a result of the offense, PINEDO obtained $1,000 or more during a one-year period. **(Title 18, United States Code, Sections 1028(a)(7), (b)(l)(D) & (c)(3)(A).)**

SENTENCE: Six months in federal prison, six months house arrest and two years of court supervised release.

Signed: Robert S. Mueller, III
Special Counsel

Prepared By: Jeannie S. Rhee, Ryan K. Dickey & L. Rush Atkinson
Senior/Assistant Special Counsel

CHAPTER 5: THE INTERNET RESEARCH AGENCY, FEB. 16, 2018

UNITED STATES v. INTERNET RESEARCH AGENCY LLC (A/K/A MEDIASINTEZ LLC A/K/A GLAVSET LLC A/K/A MIXINFO LLC A/K/A AZIMUT LLC A/K/A NOVINFO LLC), CONCORD MANAGEMENT AND CONSULTING LLC, CONCORD CATERING, YEVGENIY VIKTOROVICH PRIGOZHIN, MIKHAIL IVANOVICH BYSTROV, MIKHAIL LEONIDOVICH BURCHIK (A/K/A MIKHAIL ABRAMOV), ALEKSANDRA YURYEVNA KRYLOVA, ANNA VLADISLAVOVNA BOGACHEVA, SERGEY PAVLOVICH POLOZOV, MARIA ANATOLYEVNA BOVDA (A/K/A MARIA ANATOLYEVNA BELYAEVA), ROBERT SERGEYEVICH BOVDA, DZHEYKHUN NASIMI OGLY ASLANOV (A/K/A JAYHOON ASLANOV A/K/A JAY ASLANOV), VADIM VLADIMIROVICH PODKOPAEV, GLEB IGOREVICH VASILCHENKO, IRINA VIKTOROVNA KAVERZINA, and VLADIMIR VENKOV.

FILED: February 16, 2018 in the U.S. District Court for the District of Columbia

Editor's note: The Internet Research Agency is a Russian organization whose bots and trolls engage in online political conversations in countries foreign to it, posing as concerned local voters.

Indictment

Introduction

1. The United States of America, through its departments and agencies, regulates the activities of foreign individuals and entities in and affecting the United States in order to prevent, disclose, and counteract improper foreign influence on U.S. elections and on the U.S. political system. U.S. law bans foreign nationals from making certain expenditures or financial disbursements for the purpose of influencing federal elections. U.S. law also bars agents of any foreign entity from engaging in political activities within the United States without first registering with the Attorney General. And U.S. law requires certain foreign nationals seeking entry to the United States to obtain a visa by providing truthful and accurate information to the government. Various federal agencies, including the Federal Election

Commission, the U.S. Department of Justice, and the U.S. Department of State, are charged with enforcing these laws.

2. Defendant INTERNET RESEARCH AGENCY LLC ("ORGANIZATION") is a Russian organization engaged in operations to interfere with elections and political processes. Defendants MIKHAIL IVANOVICH BYSTROV, MIKHAIL LEONIDOVICH BURCHIK, ALEKSANDRA YURYEVNA KRYLOVA, ANNA VLADISLAVOVNA BOGACHEVA, SERGEY PAVLOVICH POLOZOV, MARIA ANATOLYEVNA BOVDA, ROBERT SERGEYEVICH BOVDA, DZHEYKHUN NASIMI OGLY ASLANOV, VADIM VLADIMIROVICH PODKOPAEV, GLEB IGOREVICH VASILCHENKO, IRINA VIKTOROVNA KAVERZINA, and VLADIMIR VENKOV worked in various capacities to carry out Defendant ORGANIZATION's interference operations targeting the United States. From in or around 2014 to the present, Defendants knowingly and intentionally conspired with each other (and with persons known and unknown to the Grand Jury) to defraud the United States by impairing, obstructing, and defeating the lawful functions of the government through fraud and deceit for the purpose of interfering with the U.S. political and electoral processes, including the presidential election of 2016.

3. Beginning as early as 2014, Defendant ORGANIZATION began operations to interfere with the U.S. political system, including the 2016 U.S. presidential election. Defendant ORGANIZATION received funding for its operations from Defendant YEVGENIY VIKTOROVICH PRIGOZHIN and companies he controlled, including Defendants CONCORD MANAGEMENT AND CONSULTING LLC and CONCORD CATERING (collectively "CONCORD"). Defendants CONCORD and PRIGOZHIN spent significant funds to further the ORGANIZATION's operations and to pay the remaining Defendants, along with other uncharged ORGANIZATION employees, salaries and bonuses for their work at the ORGANIZATION.

4. Defendants, posing as U.S. persons and creating false U.S. personas, operated social media pages and groups designed to attract U.S. audiences. These groups and pages, which addressed divisive U.S. political and social issues, falsely claimed to be controlled by U.S. activists when, in fact, they were controlled by Defendants. Defendants also used the stolen identities of real U.S. persons to post on ORGANIZATION-controlled social media accounts. Over time, these social media accounts became Defendants' means to reach significant numbers of Americans for purposes of interfering with the U.S. political system, including the presidential election of 2016.

5. Certain Defendants traveled to the United States under false pretenses for the purpose of collecting intelligence to inform Defendants' operations. Defendants also procured and used computer infrastructure, based

partly in the United States, to hide the Russian origin of their activities and to avoid detection by U.S. regulators and law enforcement.

6.   Defendant ORGANIZATION had a strategic goal to sow discord in the U.S. political system, including the 2016 U.S. presidential election. Defendants posted derogatory information about a number of candidates, and by early to mid-2016, Defendants' operations included supporting the presidential campaign of then-candidate Donald J. Trump ("Trump Campaign") and disparaging Hillary Clinton. Defendants made various expenditures to carry out those activities, including buying political advertisements on social media in the names of U.S. persons and entities. Defendants also staged political rallies inside the United States, and while posing as U.S. grassroots entities and U.S. persons, and without revealing their Russian identities and ORGANIZATION affiliation, solicited and compensated real U.S. persons to promote or disparage candidates. Some Defendants, posing as U.S. persons and without revealing their Russian association, communicated with unwitting individuals associated with the Trump Campaign and with other political activists to seek to coordinate political activities.

7.   In order to carry out their activities to interfere in U.S. political and electoral processes without detection of their Russian affiliation, Defendants conspired to obstruct the lawful functions of the United States government through fraud and deceit, including by making expenditures in connection with the 2016 U.S. presidential election without proper regulatory disclosure; failing to register as foreign agents carrying out political activities within the United States; and obtaining visas through false and fraudulent statements.

COUNT 1: Conspiracy to Defraud the United States (18 U.S.C. § 371)

8.   Paragraphs 1 through 7 of this Indictment are re-alleged and incorporated by reference as if fully set forth herein.

9.   From in or around 2014 to the present, in the District of Columbia and elsewhere, defendants, together with others known and unknown to the Grand Jury, knowingly and intentionally conspired to defraud the United States by impairing, obstructing, and defeating the lawful functions of the Federal Election Commission, the U.S. Department of Justice, and the U.S. Department of State in administering federal requirements for disclosure of foreign involvement in certain domestic activities.

I.   *Defendants*

10.   Defendant INTERNET RESEARCH AGENCY LLC (Агентство Интернет Исследований) is a Russian organization engaged in political and electoral interference operations. In or around July 2013, the ORGANIZATION registered with the Russian government as a Russian corporate entity. Beginning in

or around June 2014, the ORGANIZATION obscured its conduct by operating through a number of Russian entities, including Internet Research LLC, MediaSintez LLC, GlavSet LLC, MixInfo LLC, Azimut LLC, and NovInfo LLC. Starting in or around 2014, the ORGANIZATION occupied an office at 55 Savushkina Street in St. Petersburg, Russia. That location became one of the ORGANIZATION's operational hubs from which Defendants and other co-conspirators carried out their activities to interfere in the U.S. political system, including the 2016 U.S. presidential election.

a.　　The ORGANIZATION employed hundreds of individuals for its online operations, ranging from creators of fictitious personas to technical and administrative support. The ORGANIZATION's annual budget totaled the equivalent of millions of U.S. dollars.

b.　　The ORGANIZATION was headed by a management group and organized into departments, including: a graphics department; a data analysis department; a search-engine optimization ("SEO") department; an information-technology ("IT).

c.　　The ORGANIZATION sought, in part, to conduct what it called "information warfare against the United States of America" through fictitious U.S. personas on social media platforms and other Internet-based media. By in or around April 2014, the ORGANIZATION formed a department that went by various names but was at times referred to as the "translator project." This project focused on the U.S. population and conducted operations on social media platforms such as YouTube, Facebook, Instagram, and Twitter. By approximately July 2016, more than eighty ORGANIZATION employees were assigned to the translator project.

d.　　By in or around April 2014, the ORGANIZATION formed a department that went by various names but was at times referred to as the "translator project." This project focused on the U.S. population and conducted operations on social media platforms such as YouTube, Facebook, Instagram, and Twitter. By approximately July 2016, more than eighty ORGANIZATION employees were assigned to the translator project.

e.　　By in or around May 2014, the ORGANIZATION's strategy included interfering with the 2016 U.S. presidential election, with the stated goal of "spread[ing] distrust towards the candidates and the political system in general."

11.　　Defendants CONCORD MANAGEMENT AND CONSULTING LLC (Конкорд Менеджмент и Консалтинг) and CONCORD CATERING are related Russian entities with various Russian government contracts. CONCORD was the ORGANIZATION's primary source of funding for its interference operations. CONCORD controlled funding, recommended personnel, and oversaw

ORGANIZATION activities through reporting and interaction with ORGANIZATION management.

  a. CONCORD funded the ORGANIZATION as part of a larger CONCORD-funded interference operation that it referred to as "Project Lakhta." Project Lakhta had multiple components, some involving domestic audiences within the Russian Federation and others targeting foreign audiences in various countries, including the United States.

  b. By in or around September 2016, the ORGANIZATION's monthly budget for Project Lakhta submitted to CONCORD exceeded 73 million Russian rubles (over 1,250,000 U.S. dollars), including approximately one million rubles in bonus payments.

  c. To conceal its involvement, CONCORD labeled the monies paid to the ORGANIZATION for Project Lakhta as payments related to software support and development. To further conceal the source of funds, CONCORD distributed monies to the ORGANIZATION through approximately fourteen bank accounts held in the names of CONCORD affiliates, including Glavnaya Liniya LLC, Merkuriy LLC, Obshchepit LLC, Potentsial LLC, RSP LLC, ASP LLC, MTTs LLC, Kompleksservis LLC, SPb Kulinariya LLC, Almira LLC, Pishchevik LLC, Galant LLC, Rayteks LLC, and Standart LLC.

  12. Defendant YEVGENIY VIKTOROVICH PRIGOZHIN (Пригожин Евгений Викторович) is a Russian national who controlled CONCORD.

  a. PRIGOZHIN approved and supported the ORGANIZATION's operations, and Defendants and their co-conspirators were aware of PRIGOZHIN's role.

  b. For example, on or about May 29, 2016, Defendants and their co-conspirators, through an ORGANIZATION-controlled social media account, arranged for a real U.S. person to stand in front of the White House in the District of Columbia under false pretenses to hold a sign that read "Happy 55th Birthday Dear Boss." Defendants and their co-conspirators informed the real U.S. person that the sign was for someone who "is a leader here and our boss ... our funder." PRIGOZHIN's Russian passport identifies his date of birth as June 1, 1961.

  13. Defendant MIKHAIL IVANOVICH BYSTROV (Быстров Михаил Иванович) joined the ORGANIZATION by at least in or around February 2014.

  a. By approximately April 2014, BYSTROV was the general director, the ORGANIZATION's highest-ranking position. BYSTROV subsequently served as the head of various other entities used by the ORGANIZATION to mask its activities, including, for example, Glavset LLC, where he was listed as that entity's general director.

  b. In or around 2015 and 2016, BYSTROV frequently

communicated with PRIGOZHIN about Project Lakhta's overall operations, including through regularly scheduled in-person meetings.

14. Defendant MIKHAIL LEONIDOVICH BURCHIK (Бурчик Михаил Леонидович) A/K/A MIKHAIL ABRAMOV joined the ORGANIZATION by at least in or around October 2013. By approximately March 2014, BURCHIK was the executive director, the ORGANIZATION's second-highest ranking position. Throughout the ORGANIZATION's operations to interfere in the U.S political system, including the 2016 U.S. presidential election, BURCHIK was a manager involved in operational planning, infrastructure, and personnel. In or around 2016, BURCHIK also had in-person meetings with PRIGOZHIN.

15. Defendant ALEKSANDRA YURYEVNA KRYLOVA (Крылова Александра Юрьевна) worked for the ORGANIZATION from at least in or around September 2013 to at least in or around November 2014. By approximately April 2014, KRYLOVA served as director and was the ORGANIZATION's third-highest ranking employee. In 2014, KRYLOVA traveled to the United States under false pretenses for the purpose of collecting intelligence to inform the ORGANIZATION's operations.

16. Defendant SERGEY PAVLOVICH POLOZOV (Полозов Сергей Павлович) worked for the ORGANIZATION from at least in or around April 2014 to at least in or around October 2016. POLOZOV served as the manager of the IT department and oversaw the procurement of U.S. servers and other computer infrastructure that masked the ORGANIZATION's Russian location when conducting operations within the United States.

17. Defendant ANNA VLADISLAVOVNA BOGACHEVA (Богачева Анна Владиславовна) worked for the ORGANIZATION from at least in or around April 2014 to at least in or around July 2014. BOGACHEVA served on the translator project and oversaw the project's data analysis group. BOGACHEVA also traveled to the United States under false pretenses for the purpose of collecting intelligence to inform the ORGANIZATION's operations.

18. Defendant MARIA ANATOLYEVNA BOVDA (Бовда Мария Анатольевна) A/K/A MARIA ANATOLYEVNA BELYAEVA ("M. BOVDA") worked for the ORGANIZATION from at least in or around November 2013 to at least in or around October 2014. M. BOVDA served as the head of the translator project, among other positions.

19. Defendant ROBERT SERGEYEVICH BOVDA (Бовда Роберт Сергеевич) ("R. BOVDA") worked for the ORGANIZATION from at least in or around November 2013 to at least in or around October 2014. R. BOVDA served as the deputy head of the translator project, among other positions. R. BOVDA attempted to travel to the United States under false pretenses for the purpose of collecting intelligence to inform the ORGANIZATION's operations but could not obtain the necessary visa.

20.   Defendant DZHEYKHUN NASIMI OGLY ASLANOV (Асланов Джейхун Насими Оглы) A/K/A JAYHOON ASLANOV A/K/A JAY ASLANOV joined the ORGANIZATION by at least in or around September 2014. ASLANOV served as head of the translator project and oversaw many of the operations targeting the 2016 U.S. presidential election. ASLANOV was also listed as the general director of Azimut LLC, an entity used to move funds from CONCORD to the ORGANIZATION.

21.   Defendant VADIM VLADIMIROVICH PODKOPAEV (Подкопаев Вадим Владимирович) joined the ORGANIZATION by at least in or around June 2014. PODKOPAEV served as an analyst on the translator project and was responsible for conducting U.S.-focused research and drafting social media content for the ORGANIZATION.

22.   Defendant GLEB IGOREVICH VASILCHENKO (Васильченко Глеб Игоревич) worked for the ORGANIZATION from at least in or around August 2014 to at least in or around September 2016. VASILCHENKO was responsible for posting, monitoring, and updating the social media content of many ORGANIZATION-controlled accounts while posing as U.S. persons or U.S. grassroots organizations. VASILCHENKO later served as the head of two sub-groups focused on operations to interfere in the U.S. political system, including the 2016 U.S. presidential election.

23.   Defendant IRINA VIKTOROVNA KAVERZINA (Каверзина Ирина Викторовна) joined the ORGANIZATION by at least in or around October 2014. KAVERZINA served on the translator project and operated multiple U.S. personas that she used to post, monitor, and update social media content for the ORGANIZATION.

24.   Defendant VLADIMIR VENKOV (Венков Владимир) joined the ORGANIZATION by at least in or around March 2015. VENKOV served on the translator project and operated multiple U.S. personas, which he used to post, monitor, and update social media content for the ORGANIZATION.

II.   *Federal Regulatory Agencies*

25.   The Federal Election Commission is a federal agency that administers the Federal Election Campaign Act ("FECA"). Among other things, FECA prohibits foreign nationals from making any contributions, expenditures, independent expenditures, or disbursements for electioneering communications. FECA also requires that individuals or entities who make certain independent expenditures in federal elections report those expenditures to the Federal Election Commission. The reporting requirements permit the Federal Election Commission to fulfill its statutory duties of providing the American public with accurate data about the financial activities of individuals and entities supporting federal candidates, and enforcing FECA's limits and prohibitions, including the ban on foreign expenditures.

26.   The U.S. Department of Justice administers the Foreign Agent

Registration Act ("FARA"). FARA establishes a registration, reporting, and disclosure regime for agents of foreign principals (which includes foreign non-government individuals and entities) so that the U.S. government and the people of the United States are informed of the source of information and the identity of persons attempting to influence U.S. public opinion, policy, and law. FARA requires, among other things, that persons subject to its requirements submit periodic registration statements containing truthful information about their activities and the income earned from them. Disclosure of the required information allows the federal government and the American people to evaluate the statements and activities of such persons in light of their function as foreign agents.

27.   The U.S. Department of State is the federal agency responsible for the issuance of non- immigrant visas to foreign individuals who need a visa to enter the United States. Foreign individuals who are required to obtain a visa must, among other things, provide truthful information in response to questions on the visa application form, including information about their employment and the purpose of their visit to the United States.

III.   Object of the Conspiracy

28.   The conspiracy had as its object impairing, obstructing, and defeating the lawful governmental functions of the United States by dishonest means in order to enable the Defendants to interfere with U.S. political and electoral processes, including the 2016 U.S. presidential election.

IV.   Manner and Means of the Conspiracy
Intelligence Gathering to Inform U.S. Operations

29.   Starting at least in or around 2014, Defendants and their co-conspirators began to track and study groups on U.S. social media sites dedicated to U.S. politics and social issues. In order to gauge the performance of various groups on social media sites, the ORGANIZATION tracked certain metrics like the group's size, the frequency of content placed by the group, and the level of audience engagement with that content, such as the average number of comments or responses to a post.

30.   Defendants and their co-conspirators also traveled, and attempted to travel, to the United States under false pretenses in order to collect intelligence for their interference operations.

a. KRYLOVA and BOGACHEVA, together with other Defendants and co- conspirators, planned travel itineraries, purchased equipment (such as cameras, SIM cards, and drop phones), and discussed security measures (including "evacuation scenarios") for Defendants who traveled to the United States.

b. To enter the United States, KRYLOVA, BOGACHEVA, R. BOVDA, and another co-conspirator applied to the U.S. Department of State for visas to travel. Duringtheir application process, KRYLOVA, BOGACHEVA, R. BOVDA, and their co- conspirator falsely claimed they were traveling for personal reasons and did not fully disclose their place of employment to hide the fact that they worked for the ORGANIZATION.

c. Only KRYLOVA and BOGACHEVA received visas, and from approximately June 4, 2014 through June 26, 2014, KRYLOVA and BOGACHEVA traveled in and around the United States, including stops in Nevada, California, New Mexico, Colorado, Illinois, Michigan, Louisiana, Texas, and New York to gather intelligence. After the trip, KRYLOVA and BURCHIK exchanged an intelligence report regarding the trip.

d. Another co-conspirator who worked for the ORGANIZATION traveled to Atlanta, Georgia from approximately November 26, 2014 through November 30, 2014. Following the trip, the co-conspirator provided POLOZOV a summary of his trip's itinerary and expenses.

31.   In order to collect additional intelligence, Defendants and their co-conspirators posed as U.S. persons and contacted U.S. political and social activists. For example, starting in or around June 2016, Defendants and their co-conspirators, posing online as U.S. persons, communicated with a real U.S. person affiliated with a Texas-based grassroots organization. During the exchange, Defendants and their co-conspirators learned from the real U.S. person that they should focus their activities on "purple states like Colorado, Virginia & Florida." After that exchange, Defendants and their co-conspirators commonly referred to targeting "purple states" in directing their efforts.

Use of U.S. Social Media

32.   Defendants and their co-conspirators, through fraud and deceit, created hundreds of social media accounts and used them to develop certain fictitious U.S. personas into "leader[s] of public opinion" in the United States.

33.   ORGANIZATION employees, referred to as "specialists," were tasked to create social media accounts that appeared to be operated by U.S. persons. The specialists were divided into day-shift and night-shift hours and instructed to make posts in accordance with the appropriate U.S. time zone. The ORGANIZATION also circulated lists of U.S. holidays so that specialists could develop and post appropriate account activity. Specialists were instructed to write about topics germane to the United States such as U.S. foreign policy and U.S. economic issues. Specialists were directed to create "political intensity through supporting radical groups, users dissatisfied with [the] social and economic situation and oppositional social movements."

34.   Defendants and their co-conspirators also created thematic group pages on social media sites, particularly on the social media platforms Facebook and Instagram. ORGANIZATION- controlled pages addressed a range of issues, including: immigration (with group names including "Secured Borders"); the Black Lives Matter movement (with group names including "Blacktivist"); religion (with group names including "United Muslims of America" and "Army of Jesus"); and certain geographic regions within the United States (with group names including "South United" and "Heart of Texas"). By 2016, the size of many ORGANIZATION-controlled groups had grown to hundreds of thousands of online followers.

35.   Starting at least in or around 2015, Defendants and their co-conspirators began to purchase advertisements on online social media sites to promote ORGANIZATION-controlled social media groups, spending thousands of U.S. dollars every month. These expenditures were included in the budgets the ORGANIZATION submitted to CONCORD.

36.   Defendants and their co-conspirators also created and controlled numerous Twitter accounts designed to appear as if U.S. persons or groups controlled them. For example, the ORGANIZATION created and controlled the Twitter account "Tennessee GOP," which used the handle @TEN_GOP. The @TEN_GOP account falsely claimed to be controlled by a U.S. state political party. Over time, the @TEN_GOP account attracted more than 100,000 online followers.

37.   To measure the impact of their online social media operations, Defendants and their co- conspirators tracked the performance of content they posted over social media. They tracked the size of the online U.S. audiences reached through posts, different types of engagement with the posts (such as likes, comments, and reposts), changes in audience size, and other metrics. Defendants and their co-conspirators received and maintained metrics reports on certain group pages and individualized posts.

38.   Defendants and their co-conspirators also regularly evaluated the content posted by specialists (sometimes referred to as "content analysis") to ensure they appeared authentic—as if operated by U.S. persons. Specialists received feedback and directions to improve the quality of their posts. Defendants and their co-conspirators issued or received guidance on: ratios of text, graphics, and video to use in posts; the number of accounts to operate; and the role of each account (for example, differentiating a main account from which to post information and auxiliary accounts to promote a main account through links and reposts).

Use of U.S. Computer Infrastructure

39.   To hide their Russian identities and ORGANIZATION affiliation, Defendants and their co- conspirators—particularly POLOZOV and the ORGANIZATION's IT department—purchased space on computer servers located

inside the United States in order to set up virtual private networks ("VPNs"). Defendants and their co-conspirators connected from Russia to the U.S.-based infrastructure by way of these VPNs and conducted activity inside the United States— including accessing online social media accounts, opening new accounts, and communicating with real U.S. persons—while masking the Russian origin and control of the activity.

40. Defendants and their co-conspirators also registered and controlled hundreds of web-based email accounts hosted by U.S. email providers under false names so as to appear to be U.S. persons and groups. From these accounts, Defendants and their co-conspirators registered or linked to online social media accounts in order to monitor them; posed as U.S. persons when requesting assistance from real U.S. persons; contacted media outlets in order to promote activities inside the United States; and conducted other operations, such as those set forth below.

Use of Stolen U.S. Identities

41. In or around 2016, Defendants and their co-conspirators also used, possessed, and transferred, without lawful authority, the social security numbers and dates of birth of real U.S. persons without those persons' knowledge or consent. Using these means of identification, Defendants and their co-conspirators opened accounts at PayPal, a digital payment service provider; created false means of identification, including fake driver's licenses; and posted on ORGANIZATION-controlled social media accounts using the identities of these U.S. victims. Defendants and their co-conspirators also obtained, and attempted to obtain, false identification documents to use as proof of identity in connection with maintaining accounts and purchasing advertisements on social media sites.

Actions Targeting the 2016 U.S. Presidential Election

42. By approximately May 2014, Defendants and their co-conspirators discussed efforts to interfere in the 2016 U.S. presidential election. Defendants and their co-conspirators began to monitor U.S. social media accounts and other sources of information about the 2016 U.S. presidential election.

43. By 2016, Defendants and their co-conspirators used their fictitious online personas to interfere with the 2016 U.S. presidential election. They engaged in operations primarily intended to communicate derogatory information about Hillary Clinton, to denigrate other candidates such as Ted Cruz and Marco Rubio, and to support Bernie Sanders and then-candidate Donald Trump.

a. On or about February 10, 2016, Defendants and their co-conspirators internally circulated an outline of themes for future content to be posted to ORGANIZATION-controlled social media accounts. Specialists were instructed to post content that focused on "politics in the USA" and to "use any opportunity to criticize Hillary and the rest (except Sanders and Trump—we support them)."

b. On or about September 14, 2016, in an internal review of an ORGANIZATION- created and controlled Facebook group called "Secured Borders," the account specialist was criticized for having a "low number of posts dedicated to criticizing Hillary Clinton" and was told "it is imperative to intensify criticizing Hillary Clinton" in future posts.

44. Certain ORGANIZATION-produced materials about the 2016 U.S. presidential election used election-related hashtags, including: "#Trump2016," "#TrumpTrain," "#MAGA," "#IWontProtectHillary," and "#Hillary4Prison." Defendants and their co-conspirators also established additional online social media accounts dedicated to the 2016 U.S. presidential election, including the Twitter account "March for Trump" and Facebook accounts "Clinton FRAUDation" and "Trumpsters United."

45. Defendants and their co-conspirators also used false U.S. personas to communicate with unwitting members, volunteers, and supporters of the Trump Campaign involved in local community outreach, as well as grassroots groups that supported then-candidate Trump. These individuals and entities at times distributed the ORGANIZATION's materials through their own accounts via retweets, reposts, and similar means. Defendants and their co-conspirators then monitored the propagation of content through such participants.

46. In or around the latter half of 2016, Defendants and their co-conspirators, through their ORGANIZATION-controlled personas, began to encourage U.S. minority groups not to vote in the 2016 U.S. presidential election or to vote for a third-party U.S. presidential candidate.

a. On or about October 16, 2016, Defendants and their co-conspirators used the ORGANIZATION-controlled Instagram account "Woke Blacks" to post the following message: "[A] particular hype and hatred for Trump is misleading the people and forcing Blacks to vote Killary. We cannot resort to the lesser of two devils. Then we'd surely be better off without voting AT ALL."

b. On or about November 3, 2016, Defendants and their co-conspirators purchased an advertisement to promote a post on the ORGANIZATION-controlled Instagram account "Blacktivist" that read in part: "Choose peace and vote for Jill Stein. Trust me, it's not a wasted vote."

c. By in or around early November 2016, Defendants and their co-conspirators used the ORGANIZATION-controlled "United Muslims of America" social media accounts to post anti-vote messages such as:

"American Muslims [are] boycotting elections today, most of the American Muslim voters refuse to vote for Hillary Clinton because she wants to continue the war on Muslims in the middle east and voted yes for invading Iraq."

47. Starting in or around the summer of 2016, Defendants and their co-conspirators also began to promote allegations of voter fraud by the Democratic Party through their fictitious U.S. personas and groups on social media. Defendants and their co-conspirators purchased advertisements on Facebook to further promote the allegations.

a. On or about August 4, 2016, Defendants and their co-conspirators began purchasing advertisements that promoted a post on the ORGANIZATION-controlled Facebook account "Stop A.I." The post alleged that "Hillary Clinton has already committed voter fraud during the Democrat Iowa Caucus."

b. On or about August 11, 2016, Defendants and their co-conspirators posted that allegations of voter fraud were being investigated in North Carolina on the ORGANIZATION-controlled Twitter account @TEN_GOP.

c. On or about November 2, 2016, Defendants and their co-conspirators used the same account to post allegations of "#VoterFraud by counting tens of thousands of ineligible mail in Hillary votes being reported in Broward County, Florida."

Political Advertisements

48. From at least April 2016 through November 2016, Defendants and their co-conspirators, while concealing their Russian identities and ORGANIZATION affiliation through false personas, began to produce, purchase, and post advertisements on U.S. social media and other online sites expressly advocating for the election of then-candidate Trump or expressly opposing Clinton. Defendants and their co-conspirators did not report their expenditures to the Federal Election Commission, or register as foreign agents with the U.S. Department of Justice.

49. From at least April 2016 through November 2016, Defendants and their co-conspirators, while concealing their Russian identities and ORGANIZATION affiliation through false personas, began to produce, purchase, and post advertisements on U.S. social media and other online sites expressly advocating for the election of then-candidate Trump or expressly opposing Clinton. Defendants and their co-conspirators did not report their expenditures to the Federal Election Commission, or register as foreign agents with the U.S. Department of Justice.

50. The political advertisements included the following:

Approximate Date	Excerpt of Advertisement
April 6, 2016	"You know, a great number of black people support us saying that #HillaryClintonIsNotMyPresident"
April 7, 2016	"I say no to Hillary Clinton / I say no to manipulation"
April 19, 2016	"JOIN our #HillaryClintonForPrison2016"
May 10, 2016	"Donald wants to defeat terrorism . . . Hillary wants to sponsor it"
May 19, 2016	"Vote Republican, vote Trump, and support the Second Amendment!"
May 24, 2016	"Hillary Clinton Doesn't Deserve the Black Vote"
June 7, 2016	"Trump is our only hope for a better future!"
June 30, 2016	"#NeverHillary #HillaryForPrison #Hillary4Prison #HillaryForPrison2016 #Trump2016 #Trump #Trump4President"
July 20, 2016	"Ohio Wants Hillary 4 Prison"
August 4, 2016	"Hillary Clinton has already committed voter fraud during the Democrat Iowa Caucus."
August 10, 2016	"We cannot trust Hillary to take care of our veterans!"
October 14, 2016	"Among all the candidates Donald Trump is the one and only who can defend the police from terrorists."
October 19, 2016	"Hillary is a Satan, and her crimes and lies had proved just how evil she is."

Staging U.S. Political Rallies in the United States

51.   Starting in approximately June 2016, Defendants and their co-

conspirators organized and coordinated political rallies in the United States. To conceal the fact that they were based in Russia, Defendants and their co-conspirators promoted these rallies while pretending to be U.S. grassroots activists who were located in the United States but unable to meet or participate in person. Defendants and their co-conspirators did not register as foreign agents with the U.S. Department of Justice.

52. In order to build attendance for the rallies, Defendants and their co-conspirators promoted the events through public posts on their false U.S. persona social media accounts. In addition, Defendants and their co-conspirators contacted administrators of large social media groups focused on U.S. politics and requested that they advertise the rallies.

53. In or around late June 2016, Defendants and their co-conspirators used the Facebook group "United Muslims of America" to promote a rally called "Support Hillary. Save American Muslims" held on July 9, 2016 in the District of Columbia. Defendants and their co-conspirators recruited a real U.S. person to hold a sign depicting Clinton and a quote attributed to her stating "I think Sharia Law will be a powerful new direction of freedom." Within three weeks, on or about July 26, 2016, Defendants and their co-conspirators posted on the same Facebook page that Muslim voters were "between Hillary Clinton and a hard place."

54. In or around June and July 2016, Defendants and their co-conspirators used the Facebook group "Being Patriotic," the Twitter account @March_for_Trump, and other ORGANIZATION accounts to organize two political rallies in New York. The first rally was called "March for Trump" and held on June 25, 2016. The second rally was called "Down with Hillary" and held on July 23, 2016.

    a. In or around June through July 2016, Defendants and their co-conspirators purchased advertisements on Facebook to promote the "March for Trump" and "Down with Hillary" rallies.

    b. Defendants and their co-conspirators used false U.S. personas to send individualized messages to real U.S. persons to request that they participate in and help organize the rally. To assist their efforts, Defendants and their co-conspirators, through false U.S. personas, offered money to certain U.S. persons to cover rally expenses.

    c. On or about June 5, 2016, Defendants and their co-conspirators, while posing as a U.S. grassroots activist, used the account @March_for_Trump to contact a volunteer for the Trump Campaign in New York. The volunteer agreed to provide signs for the "March for Trump" rally.

55. In or around late July 2016, Defendants and their co-conspirators used the Facebook group "Being Patriotic," the Twitter account @March_for_Trump, and other false U.S. personas to organize a series of

coordinated rallies in Florida. The rallies were collectively referred to as "Florida Goes Trump" and held on August 20, 2016.

  a. In or around August 2016, Defendants and their co-conspirators used false U.S. personas to communicate with Trump Campaign staff involved in local community outreach about the "Florida Goes Trump" rallies.

  b. Defendants and their co-conspirators purchased advertisements on Facebook and Instagram to promote the "Florida Goes Trump" rallies.

  c. Defendants and their co-conspirators also used false U.S. personas to contact multiple grassroots groups supporting then-candidate Trump in an unofficial capacity. Many of these groups agreed to participate in the "Florida Goes Trump" rallies and serve as local coordinators.

  d. Defendants and their co-conspirators also used false U.S. personas to ask real U.S. persons to participate in the "Florida Goes Trump" rallies. Defendants and their co-conspirators asked certain of these individuals to perform tasks at the rallies. For example, Defendants and their co-conspirators asked one U.S. person to build a cage on a flatbed truck and another U.S. person to wear a costume portraying Clinton in a prison uniform. Defendants and their co-conspirators paid these individuals to complete the requests.

  56. After the rallies in Florida, Defendants and their co-conspirators used false U.S. personas to organize and coordinate U.S. political rallies supporting then-candidate Trump in New York and Pennsylvania. Defendants and their co-conspirators used the same techniques to build and promote these rallies as they had in Florida, including: buying Facebook advertisements; paying U.S. persons to participate in, or perform certain tasks at, the rallies; and communicating with real U.S. persons and grassroots organizations supporting then-candidate Trump.

  57. After the election of Donald Trump in or around November 2016, Defendants and their co- conspirators used false U.S. personas to organize and coordinate U.S. political rallies in support of then president-elect Trump, while simultaneously using other false U.S. personas to organize and coordinate U.S. political rallies protesting the results of the 2016 U.S. presidential election. For example, in or around November 2016, Defendants and their co-conspirators organized a rally in New York through one ORGANIZATION-controlled group designed to "show your support for President-Elect Donald Trump" held on or about November 12, 2016. At the same time, Defendants and their co-conspirators, through another ORGANIZATION-controlled group, organized a rally in New York called "Trump is NOT my President" held on or about November 12, 2016. Similarly, Defendants and their co-conspirators organized a rally entitled "Charlotte Against

Trump" in Charlotte, North Carolina, held on or about November 19, 2016.

Destruction of Evidence

58.   In order to avoid detection and impede investigation by U.S. authorities of Defendants' operations, Defendants and their co-conspirators deleted and destroyed data, including emails, social media accounts, and other evidence of their activities

a.   Beginning in or around June 2014, and continuing into June 2015, public reporting began to identify operations conducted by the ORGANIZATION in the United States. In response, Defendants and their co-conspirators deleted email accounts used to conduct their operations.

b.   Beginning in or around September 2017, U.S. social media companies, starting with Facebook, publicly reported that they had identified Russian expenditures on their platforms to fund political and social advertisements. Facebook's initial disclosure of the Russian purchases occurred on or about September 6, 2017, and included a statement that Facebook had "shared [its] findings with US authorities investigating these issues."

c.   Media reporting on or about the same day as Facebook's disclosure referred to Facebook working with investigators for the Special Counsel's Office of the U.S. Department of Justice, which had been charged with investigating the Russian government's efforts to interfere in the 2016 presidential election.

d.   Defendants and their co-conspirators thereafter destroyed evidence for the purpose of impeding the investigation. On or about September 13, 2017, KAVERZINA wrote in an email to a family member: "We had a slight crisis here at work: the FBI busted our activity (not a joke). So, I got preoccupied with covering tracks together with the colleagues." KAVERZINA further wrote, "I created all these pictures and posts, and the Americans believed that it was written by their people."

Overt Acts

59.   In furtherance of the Conspiracy and to effect its illegal object, Defendants and their co- conspirators committed the following overt acts in connection with the staging of U.S. political rallies, as well as those as set forth in paragraphs 1 through 7, 9 through 27, and 29 through 58, which are re-alleged and incorporated by reference as though fully set forth herein.

60.   On or about June 1, 2016, Defendants and their co-conspirators created and purchased Facebook advertisements for their "March for Trump" rally.

61.   On or about June 4, 2016, Defendants and their co-conspirators

used allforusa@yahoo.com, the email address of a false U.S. persona, to send out press releases for the "March for Trump" rally to New York media outlets.

62. On or about June 23, 2016, Defendants and their co-conspirators used the Facebook account registered under a false U.S. persona "Matt Skiber" to contact a real U.S. person to serve as a recruiter for the "March for Trump" rally, offering to "give you money to print posters and get a megaphone."

63. On or about June 24, 2016, Defendants and their co-conspirators purchased advertisements on Facebook to promote the "Support Hillary. Save American Muslims" rally.

64. On or about July 5, 2016, Defendants and their co-conspirators ordered posters for the "Support Hillary. Save American Muslims" rally, including the poster with the quote attributed to Clinton that read "I think Sharia Law will be a powerful new direction of freedom."

65. On or about July 8, 2016, Defendants and their co-conspirators communicated with a real U.S. person about the posters they had ordered for the "Support Hillary. Save American Muslims" rally.

66. On or about July 12, 2016, Defendants and their co-conspirators created and purchased Facebook advertisements for the "Down With Hillary" rally in New York.

67. On or about July 23, 2016, Defendants and their co-conspirators used the email address of a false U.S. persona, joshmilton024@gmail.com, to send out press releases to over thirty media outlets promoting the "Down With Hillary" rally at Trump Tower in New York City.

68. On or about July 28, 2016, Defendants and their co-conspirators posted a series of tweets through the false U.S. persona account @March_for_Trump stating that "[w]e're currently planning a series of rallies across the state of Florida" and seeking volunteers to assist.

69. On or about August 2, 2016, Defendants and their co-conspirators used the false U.S. persona "Matt Skiber" Facebook account to send a private message to a real Facebook account, "Florida for Trump," set up to assist then-candidate Trump in the state of Florida. In the first message, Defendants and their co-conspirators wrote, "Hi there! I'm a member of Being Patriotic online community. Listen, we've got an idea. Florida is still a purple state and we need to paint it red. If we lose Florida, we lose America. We can't let it happen, right? What about organizing a YUGE pro-Trump flash mob in every Florida town? We are currently reaching out to local activists and we've got the folks who are okay to be in charge of organizing their events almost everywhere in FL. However, we still need your support. What do you think about that? Are you in?"

70. On or about August 2, 2016, and August 3, 2016, Defendants and their co-conspirators, through the use of a stolen identity of a real U.S. person, T.W.,

sent emails to certain grassroots groups located in Florida that stated in part, "My name is [T.W.] and I represent a conservative patriot community named as "Being Patriotic." … So we're gonna organize a flash mob across Florida to support Mr. Trump. We clearly understand that the elections winner will be predestined by purple states. And we must win Florida   We got a lot of volunteers in ~25 locations and it's just the beginning. We're currently choosing venues for each location and recruiting more activists. This is why we ask you to spread this info and participate in the flash mob.

71.   On or about August 4, 2016, Defendants and their co-conspirators created and purchased Facebook advertisements for the "Florida Goes Trump" rally. The advertisements reached over 59,000 Facebook users in Florida, and over 8,300 Facebook users responded to the advertisements by clicking on it, which routed users to the ORGANIZATION's "Being Patriotic" page.

72.   Beginning on or about August 5, 2016, Defendants and their co-conspirators used the false U.S. persona @March_for_Trump Twitter account to recruit and later pay a real U.S. person to wear a costume portraying Clinton in a prison uniform at a rally in West Palm Beach.

73.   Beginning on or about August 11, 2016, Defendants and their co-conspirators used the false U.S. persona "Matt Skiber" Facebook account to recruit a real U.S. person to acquire signs and a costume depicting Clinton in a prison uniform.

74.   On or about August 15, 2016, Defendants and their co-conspirators received an email at one of their false U.S. persona accounts from a real U.S. person, a Florida-based political activist identified as the "Chair for the Trump Campaign" in a particular Florida county. The activist identified two additional sites in Florida for possible rallies. Defendants and their co-conspirators subsequently used their false U.S. persona accounts to communicate with the activist about logistics and an additional rally in Florida.

75.   On or about August 16, 2016, Defendants and their co-conspirators used a false U.S. persona Instagram account connected to the ORGANIZATION-created group "Tea Party News" to purchase advertisements for the "Florida Goes Trump" rally.

76.   On or about August 18, 2016, the real "Florida for Trump" Facebook account responded to the false U.S. persona "Matt Skiber" account with instructions to contact a member of the Trump Campaign ("Campaign Official 1") involved in the campaign's Florida operations and provided Campaign Official 1's email address at the campaign domain donaldtrump.com. On approximately the same day, Defendants and their co-conspirators used the email address of a false U.S. persona, joshmilton024@gmail.com, to send an email to Campaign Official 1 at that donaldtrump.com email account, which read in part, "Hello [Campaign Official

1], [w]e are organizing a state-wide event in Florida on August, 20 to support Mr. Trump. Let us introduce ourselves first. "Being Patriotic" is a grassroots conservative online movement trying to unite people offline [W]e gained a huge lot of followers and decided to somehow help Mr. Trump get elected. You know, simple yelling on the Internet is not enough.There should be real action. We organized rallies in New York before. Now we're focusing on purple states such as Florida. The email also identified thirteen "confirmed locations" in Florida for the rallies and requested the campaign provide "assistance in each location."

77.   On or about August 18, 2016, Defendants and their co-conspirators sent money via interstate wire to another real U.S. person recruited by the ORGANIZATION, using one of their false U.S. personas, to build a cage large enough to hold an actress depicting Clinton in a prison uniform.

78.   On or about August 19, 2016, a supporter of the Trump Campaign sent a message to the ORGANIZATION-controlled "March for Trump" Twitter account about a member of the Trump Campaign ("Campaign Official 2") who was involved in the campaign's Florida operations and provided Campaign Official 2's email address at the domain donaldtrump.com. On or about the same day, Defendants and their co-conspirators used the false U.S. persona joshmilton024@gmail.com account to send an email to Campaign Official 2 at that donaldtrump.com email account.

79.   On or about August 19, 2016, the real "Florida for Trump" Facebook account sent another message to the false U.S. persona "Matt Skiber" account to contact a member of the Trump Campaign ("Campaign Official 3") involved in the campaign's Florida operations. On or about August 20, 2016, Defendants and their co-conspirators used the "Matt Skiber" Facebook account to contact Campaign Official 3.

80.   On or about August 19, 2016, Defendants and their co-conspirators used the false U.S. persona "Matt Skiber" account to write to the real U.S. person affiliated with a Texas-based grassroots organization who previously had advised the false persona to focus on "purple states like Colorado, Virginia & Florida." Defendants and their co-conspirators told that U.S. person, "We were thinking about your recommendation to focus on purple states and this is what we're organizing in FL." Defendants and their co-conspirators then sent a link to the Facebook event page for the Florida rallies and asked that person to send the information to Tea Party members in Florida. The real U.S. person stated that he/she would share among his/her own social media contacts, who would pass on the information.

81.   On or about August 24, 2016, Defendants and their co-conspirators updated an internal ORGANIZATION list of over 100 real U.S. persons contacted through ORGANIZATION- controlled false U.S. persona accounts and tracked to monitor recruitment efforts and requests. The list included contact information for

the U.S. persons, a summary of their political views, and activities they had been asked to perform by Defendants and their co-conspirators.

82. On or about August 31, 2016, Defendants and their co-conspirators, using a U.S. persona, spoke by telephone with a real U.S. person affiliated with a grassroots group in Florida. That individual requested assistance in organizing a rally in Miami, Florida. On or about September 9, 2016, Defendants and their co-conspirators sent the group an interstate wire to pay for materials needed for the Florida rally on or about September 11, 2016.

83. On or about August 31, 2016, Defendants and their co-conspirators created and purchased Facebook advertisements for a rally they organized and scheduled in New York for September 11, 2016.

84. On or about September 9, 2016, Defendants and their co-conspirators, through a false U.S. persona, contacted the real U.S. person who had impersonated Clinton at the West Palm Beach rally. Defendants and their co-conspirators sent that U.S. person money via interstate wire as an inducement to travel from Florida to New York and to dress in costume at another rally they organized.

85. On or about September 22, 2016, Defendants and their co-conspirators created and purchased Facebook advertisements for a series of rallies they organized in Pennsylvania called "Miners for Trump" and scheduled for October 2, 2016.

(All in violation of Title 18, United States Code, Section 371)

COUNT 2: Conspiracy to Commit Wire Fraud and Bank Fraud (18 U.S.C. § 1349)

86. Paragraphs 1 through 7, 9 through 27, and 29 through 85 of this Indictment are re-alleged and incorporated by reference as if fully set forth herein.

87. From in or around 2016 through present, in the District of Columbia and elsewhere, Defendants INTERNET RESEARCH AGENCY LLC, DZHEYKHUN NASIMI OGLY ASLANOV, and GLEB IGOREVICH VASILCHENKO, together with others known and unknown to the Grand Jury, knowingly and intentionally conspired to commit certain offenses against the United States, to wit:

a. To knowingly, having devised and intending to devise a scheme and artifice to defraud, and to obtain money and property by means of false and fraudulent pretenses, representations, and promises, transmit and cause to be transmitted, by means of wire communications in interstate and foreign commerce, writings, signs, signals, pictures, and sounds, for the purposes of executing such scheme and artifice, in violation of Title 18, United States Code, Section 1343; and

b. To knowingly execute and attempt to execute a scheme and artifice to defraud a federally insured financial institution, and to obtain monies, funds, credits, assets, securities and other property from said financial institution by means of false and fraudulent pretenses, representations, and promises, all in violation of Title 18, United States Code, Section 1344.

I. *Object of the Conspiracy*

88. The conspiracy had as its object the opening of accounts under false names at U.S. financial institutions and a digital payments company in order to receive and send money into and out of the United States to support the ORGANIZATION's operations in the United States and for self-enrichment.

II. *Manner and Means of the Conspiracy*

89. Beginning in at least 2016, Defendants and their co-conspirators used, without lawful authority, the social security numbers, home addresses, and birth dates of real U.S. persons without their knowledge or consent. Using these means of stolen identification, Defendants and their co- conspirators opened accounts at a federally insured U.S. financial institution ("Bank 1"), including the following accounts:

Approximate Date	Account Name	Means of Identification
June 16, 2016	T.B.	Social Security Number Date of Birth
July 21, 2016	A.R.	Social Security Number Date of Birth
July 27, 2016	T.C.	Social Security Number Date of Birth
August 2, 2016	T.W.	Social Security Number Date of Birth

90. Defendants and their co-conspirators also used, without lawful authority, the social security numbers, home addresses, and birth dates of real U.S. persons to open accounts at PayPal, a digital payments company, including the following accounts:

Approximate Date	Initials of Identity Theft Victim	Means of Identification
June 16, 2016	T.B.	Social Security Number Date of Birth
July 21, 2016	A.R.	Social Security Number Date of Birth
August 2, 2016	T.W.	Social Security Number Date of Birth
November 11, 2016	J.W.	Home Address
January 18, 2017	V.S.	Social Security Number

91. Defendants and their co-conspirators also established other accounts at PayPal in the names of false and fictitious U.S. personas. Some personas used to register PayPal accounts were the same as the false U.S. personas used in

connection with the ORGANIZATION's social media accounts. Defendants and their co-conspirators purchased credit card and bank account numbers from online sellers for the unlawful purpose of evading security measures at PayPal, which used account numbers to verify a user's identity. Many of the bank account numbers purchased by Defendants and their co-conspirators were created using the stolen identities of real U.S. persons. After purchasing the accounts, Defendants and their co-conspirators submitted these bank account numbers to PayPal.

92. On or about the dates identified below, Defendants and their co-conspirators obtained and used the following fraudulent bank account numbers for the purpose of evading PayPal's security measures:

Approximate Date	Card/Bank Account Number	Financial Institution	Email Used to Acquire Account Number
June 13, 2016	xxxxxxxxx8902	Bank 2	wemakeweather@gmail.com
June 16, 2016	xxxxxx8731	Bank 1	allforusa@yahoo.com
July 21, 2016	xxxxxx2215	Bank 3	antwan_8@yahoo.com
August 2, 2016	xxxxxx5707	Bank 1	xtimwaltersx@gmail.com
October 18, 2016	xxxxxxxxx5792	Bank 4	unitedvetsofamerica@gmail.com
October 18, 2016	xxxxxxxxx4743	Bank 4	patriototus@gmail.com
November 11, 2016	xxxxxxxxx2427	Bank 4	beautifullelly@gmail.com
November 11, 2016	xxxxxxxxx7587	Bank 5	staceyredneck@gmail.com
November 11, 2016	xxxxxxxx7590	Bank 5	ihatecrime1@gmail.com
November 11, 2016	xxxxxxxx1780	Bank 6	staceyredneck@gmail.com

November 11, 2016	xxxxxxxx176 2	Bank 6	ihatecrime1@gmail.com
December 13, 2016	xxxxxxxx616 8	Bank 6	thetaylorbrooks@aol.com
March 30, 2017	xxxxxxxxx63 16	Bank 3	wokeaztec@outlook.com
March 30, 2017	xxxxx9512	Bank 3	wokeaztec@outlook.com

93.   Additionally, and in order to maintain their accounts at PayPal and elsewhere, including online cryptocurrency exchanges, Defendants and their co-conspirators purchased and obtained false identification documents, including fake U.S. driver's licenses. Some false identification documents obtained by Defendants and their co-conspirators used the stolen identities of real U.S. persons, including U.S. persons T.W. and J.W.

94.   After opening the accounts at Bank 1 and PayPal, Defendants and their co-conspirators used them to receive and send money for a variety of purposes, including to pay for certain ORGANIZATION expenses. Some PayPal accounts were used to purchase advertisements on Facebook promoting ORGANIZATION-controlled social media accounts. The accounts were also used to pay other ORGANIZATION-related expenses such as buttons, flags, and banners for rallies.

95.   Defendants and their co-conspirators also used the accounts to receive money from real U.S. persons in exchange for posting promotions and advertisements on the ORGANIZATION- controlled social media pages. Defendants and their co-conspirators typically charged certain U.S. merchants and U.S. social media sites between 25 and 50 U.S. dollars per post for promotional content on their popular false U.S. persona accounts, including Being Patriotic, Defend the 2nd, and Blacktivist.

All in violation of Title 18, United States Code, Section 1349.

COUNTS 3-8: Aggravated Identity Theft (18 U.S.C. § 1028A(a)(1) & (2))

96.   Paragraphs 1 through 7, 9 through 27, and 29 through 85, and 89 through 95 of this Indictment are re-alleged and incorporated by reference as if fully set forth herein.

97.   On or about the dates specified below, in the District of Columbia and elsewhere, Defendants INTERNET RESEARCH AGENCY LLC, DZHEYKHUN NASIMI OGLY ASLANOV, GLEB IGOREVICH VASILCHENKO, IRINA VIKTOROVNA KAVERZINA, and VLADIMIR VENKOV did knowingly transfer, possess, and use,

without lawful authority, a means of identification of another person during and in relation to a felony violation enumerated in 18 U.S.C. § 1028A(c), to wit, wire fraud and bank fraud, knowing that the means of identification belonged to another real person:

Count	Approximate Date	Initials of Identity Theft Victim	Means of Identification
3	June 16, 2016	T.B.	Social Security Number Date of Birth
4	July 21, 2016	A.R.	Social Security Number Date of Birth
5	July 27, 2016	T.C.	Social Security Number Date of Birth
6	August 2, 2016	T.W.	Social Security Number Date of Birth
7	January 18, 2017	V.S.	Social Security Number
8	May 19, 2017	J.W.	Home Address Date of Birth

All in violation of Title 18, United States Code, Sections 1028A(a)(1) and (2).
FORFEITURE ALLEGATION

98.   Pursuant to Federal Rule of Criminal Procedure 32.2, notice is hereby given to Defendants that the United States will seek forfeiture as part of any sentence in accordance with Title 18, United States Code, Sections 981(a)(1)(C) and 982(a)(2), and Title 28, United States Code, Section 2461(c), in the event of Defendants' convictions under Count Two of this Indictment. Upon conviction of the offense charged in Count Two, Defendants INTERNET RESEARCH AGENCY LLC, DZHEYKHUN NASIMI OGLY ASLANOV, and GLEB IGOREVICH VASILCHENKO shall forfeit to the United States any property, real or personal, which constitutes or is derived from proceeds traceable to the offense of conviction. Upon conviction of the offenses charged in Counts Three through Eight, Defendants INTERNET RESEARCH AGENCY LLC, DZHEYKHUN NASIMI OGLY ASLANOV, GLEB IGOREVICH VASILCHENKO, IRINA VIKTOROVNA KAVERZINA, and VLADIMIR VENKOV shall forfeit to the United States any property, real or personal, which constitutes or is derived from proceeds traceable to the offense(s) of conviction. Notice is further

given that, upon conviction, the United States intends to seek a judgment against each Defendant for a sum of money representing the property described in this paragraph, as applicable to each Defendant (to be offset by the forfeiture of any specific property).

Substitute Assets

99. If any of the property described above as being subject to forfeiture, as a result of any act or omission of any defendant:

    a.   cannot be located upon the exercise of due diligence;

    b.   has been transferred or sold to, or deposited with, a third party;

    c,   has been placed beyond the jurisdiction of the court;

    d.   has been substantially diminished in value; or

    e.   has been commingled with other property that cannot be subdivided without difficulty;

100. It is the intent of the United States of America, pursuant to Title 18, United States Code, Section 982(b) and Title 28, United States Code, Section 2461(c), incorporating Title 21, United States Code, Section 853, to seek forfeiture of any other property of said Defendant. *(18 U.S.C. §§ 981(a)(1)(C) and 982; 28 U.S.C. § 2461(c))*

Signed: Robert S. Mueller, III
Special Counsel

CHAPTER 6: ALEX VAN DER ZWAAN, FEB. 20, 2018

UNITED STATES v. ALEX VAN DER ZWAAN

FILED: February 20, 2018 in the U.S. District Court for the District of Columbia

Editor's note: Alex van der Zwaan was a lawyer sentenced to prison for lying to Mueller's investigators, the first person to enter prison as a result of the probe.

Statement of the Offense

Pursuant to Federal Rule of Criminal Procedure 11, the United States of America and the defendant, ALEX VAN DER ZWAAN, stipulate and agree that the following facts are true and accurate. These facts do not constitute all of the facts known to the parties concerning the charged offense; they are being submitted to demonstrate that sufficient facts exist that the defendant committed the offense to which he is pleading guilty.

1. The At all relevant times herein, the Special Counsel's Office had an open investigation into Paul J. Manafort, Jr. and Richard W. Gates III in connection with, among other things, their work in the United States on behalf of foreign principals as to which they had not registered under the Foreign·Agents Registration Act (FARA). The investigation encompassed United States lobbying and public relations work on behalf of the Ukraine Ministry of Justice in 2012, including the dissemination to the United States media and others of a report written by an international law firm (Law Firm A) concerning the trial of Yulia Tymoshenko (the Report). On October 27, 2017, arising in part from this investigation, a Grand Jury indicted Manafort and Gates, among other things, for acting as unregistered agents of a foreign principal in violation of FARA, 22 U.S.C. §§ 615 and 618(a)(l). The indictment was unsealed on October 30, 2017.

2. The defendant, ALEX VAN DER ZWAAN, was an English lawyer associated with Law Firm A. He had worked on the Report.

3. On November 3, 2017, in Washington, D.C., VAN DER ZWAAN was interviewed by the Special Counsel's Office, including Department of Justice

prosecutors and Special Agents of the Federal Bureau of investigation. He was represented by counsel. He was warned that intentionally false statements to the Office could subject him to criminal charges. He indicated that he understood.

4.   VAN DER ZWAAN thereafter made materially false statements during the interview

5.   During the November 3, 2017, interview, VAN DER ZWAAN knowingly and intentionally falsely stated the following:

a.   His last communication with Gates was in mid-August 2016, which consisted of an innocuous text message;

b.   His last communication with a longtime business associate of Manafort and Gates in Ukraine (Person A) was in 2014, when he talked with Person A about Person A's family; and

c.   he did not know why Law Firm A had not produced to the Special Counsel's Office a September 2016 e-mail between him and Person A.

6.   In truth and in fact, VAN DER ZWAAN well knew and believed the following facts, when he made each of the above statements:

a.   In or about September 2016, VAN DER ZWAAN spoke with both Gates and Person A regarding the Report. In early September 2016, Gates called VAN DER ZWAAN and told him to contact Person A. After the call, Gates sent VAN DER ZWAAN documents including a preliminary criminal complaint in Ukraine via an electronic application called Viber. VAN DER ZWAAN then called Person A and discussed in Russian that formal criminal charges might be brought against a former Ukrainian Minister of Justice, Law Finn A, and Manafort. VAN DER ZWAAN recorded the call. VAN DER ZWAAN then called the senior partner on the Report at Law Firm A and partially recorded that call. Finally, VAN DER ZWAAN called Gates and recorded the call. VAN DER ZWAAN also took notes of the calls.

b.   Prior to the November 3, 2017, interview, VAN DER ZWAAN did not produce to Law Firm A and deleted and otherwise did not produce emails he possessed that he understood had been requested by either the Special Counsel's Office or Law Firm A, or both, including an email in Russian dated September 12, 2016 in which Person A asked VAN DER ZWAAN to contact Person A and to use an encrypted application.

7.   During the November 3, 2017, interview, VAN DER ZWAAN stated that he played a passive role in the roll out of the Report, limited to defending the Report to ensure Law Firm A's work was properly portrayed. However, in or about late July-early August 2012, VAN DER ZWAAN gave, without authorization, an advance draft of the Report to the public relations firm retained by the Ukraine Ministry of Justice to manage the global press and lobbying strategy for the Report,

and in September 2012 provided Gates talking points for use in the public relations campaign as to how to describe the Report in ways favorable to the client. For instance, VAN DER ZWAAN advised that the text of the Report could be used to Ukraine's advantage if one looked beyond the Report's description of "procedural" infractions in Tymoshenko's trial and focused instead on the fact that her defense was weak.

Plea Information
COUNT 1: Making False Statements (18 U.S.C. § 1001)

The Special Counsel informs the Court: On November 3, 2017, the defendant, ALEX VAN DER ZWAAN, did willfully and knowingly make materially false, fictitious, and fraudulent statements and representations in a matter within the jurisdiction of the executive branch of the Government of the United States, to wit, the defendant falsely stated and represented to the Special Counsel's Office, including Special Agents of the Federal Bureau of Investigation, in Washington, D.C., in the course of answering questions concerning his work as an attorney employed by a law firm engaged in 2012 by the Ukraine Ministry of Justice to prepare a report on the trial of Yulia Tymoshenko:

1)   his last communication with Richard W. Gates III was in mid-August 2016 (which consisted of an innocuous text message) and his last communication with Person A was in 2014 (when VAN DER ZWAAN and Person A discussed Person A's family); and

2)   he did not know why an email between him and Person A in September 2016 was not produced to the Special Counsel's Office,

when in fact, as he then and there well knew and believed:

1)   in or about September 2016, he spoke with both Gates and Person A regarding the Report, and surreptitiously recorded the calls; and

2)   he deleted and otherwise did not produce emails sought by the Special Counsel's Office and Law Firm A, including the email between Person A and him in September 2016.

(Title 18, United States Code, Section 1001(a)(2))

SENTENCE: 30 days in federal prison, a $20,000 fine and two months of court supervised release.

Signed: Robert S. Mueller, III
Special Counsel

Prepared By: Andrew Weissman, Greg Donald Andres, Kyle Freeny, Brian M. Richardson
Senior/Associate Special Counsel

CHAPTER 7: PAUL MANAFORT ET AL, FEB. 22, 2018

UNITED STATES v. PAUL J. MANAFORT, JR. (Counts 1–5, 11–14 & 24–32) & RICHARD W. GATES III (Counts 6–10 & 15–32)

FILED: February 22, 2018 in the U.S. District Court for the Eastern District of Virginia

Editor's Note: This is the second indictment (of two) charging Paul Manafort and Rick Gates with a laundry list of serious crimes and it's where things really started to go from bad to much worse for Paul Manafort. This can be seen in how quickly Manafort's longtime confidant and protegee, Rick Gates, jumped ship. Gates cut a deal to cooperate with federal investigators and plead guilty to two counts the day after this indictment was filed.

Charges Contained in the Superseding Indictment of February 22, 2018

COUNTS 1–5: 26 U.S.C. § 7206(1); 18 U.S.C. §§ 2 and 3551 et seq. <u>Subscribing to False United States Individual Income Tax Returns</u>

COUNTS 6–10: 26 U.S.C. § 7206(2); 18 U.S.C. § 3551 et seq. <u>Assisting in the Preparation of False United States Individual Income</u>

COUNTS 11–14: 31 U.S.C. §§ 5314 and 5322(a); 18 U.S.C. §§ 2 and 3551 et seq. <u>Failure To File Reports Of Foreign Bank And Financial Accounts</u>

COUNTS 15–19: 26 U.S.C. § 7206(1); 18 U.S.C. §§ 2 and 3551 et seq. <u>Subscribing to False United States Individual Income Tax Returns</u>

COUNT 20: 26 U.S.C. § 7206(1); 18 U.S.C. §§ 2 and 3551 et seq. <u>Subscribing to a False Amended United States Individual Income Tax Return</u>

COUNTS 21–23: 31 U.S.C. §§ 5314 and 5322(a); 18 U.S.C. §§ 2 and 3551 et seq. <u>Failure To File Reports Of Foreign Bank And Financial Accounts</u>

COUNT 24: 18 U.S.C. §§ 1349 and 3551 et seq. <u>Bank Fraud Conspiracy</u>

COUNT 25: 18 U.S.C. §§ 1344, 2, and 3551 et seq. <u>Bank Fraud</u>

COUNT 26: 18 U.S.C. §§ 1349 and 3551 et seq. <u>Bank Fraud Conspiracy</u>

COUNTS 27: 18 U.S.C. §§ 1344, 2, and 3551 et seq. <u>Bank Fraud</u>

COUNT 28–29: 18 U.S.C. §§ 1349 and 3551 et seq. <u>Bank Fraud Conspiracy</u>

COUNT 30: 18 U.S.C. §§ 1344, 2, and 3551 et seq. <u>Bank Fraud</u>
COUNT 31: 18 U.S.C. §§ 1349 and 3551 et seq. <u>Bank Fraud Conspiracy</u>
COUNT 32: 18 U.S.C. §§ 1344, 2, and 3551 et seq. <u>Bank Fraud</u>

FORFEITURE NOTICE

Superseding Indictment

I. Introduction

At all times relevant to this Superseding Indictment:

1.   Defendants PAUL J. MANAFORT, JR. (MANAFORT) and RICHARD W. GATES III (GATES) served for years as political consultants and lobbyists. Between at least 2006 and 2015, MANAFORT and GATES acted as unregistered agents of a foreign government and foreign political parties. Specifically, they represented the Government of Ukraine, the President of Ukraine (Viktor Yanukovych, who was President from 2010 to 2014), the Party of Regions (a Ukrainian political party led by Yanukovych), and the Opposition Bloc (a successor to the Party of Regions after Yanukovych fled to Russia).

2.   MANAFORT and GATES generated tens of millions of dollars in income as a result of their Ukraine work. From approximately 2006 through the present, MANAFORT and GATES engaged in a scheme to hide income from United States authorities, while enjoying the use of the money. During the first part of the scheme between approximately 2006 and 2015, MANAFORT, with GATES' assistance, failed to pay taxes on this income by disguising it as alleged "loans" from nominee offshore corporate entities and by making millions of dollars in unreported payments from foreign accounts to bank accounts they controlled and United States vendors. MANAFORT also used the offshore accounts to purchase United States real estate, and MANAFORT and GATES used the undisclosed income to make improvements to and refinance their United States properties.

3.   In the second part of the scheme, between approximately 2015 and at least January 2017, when the Ukraine income dwindled after Yanukovych fled to Russia, MANAFORT, with the assistance of GATES, extracted money from MANAFORT's United States real estate by, among other things, using those properties as collateral to obtain loans from multiple financial institutions. MANAFORT and GATES fraudulently secured more than twenty million dollars in loans by falsely inflating MANAFORT's and his company's income and by failing to disclose existing debt in order to qualify for the loans.

4.   In furtherance of the scheme, MANAFORT and GATES funneled millions of dollars in payments into numerous foreign nominee companies and bank accounts, opened by them and their accomplices in nominee names and in various foreign countries, including Cyprus, Saint Vincent & the Grenadines (Grenadines),

and the Seychelles. MANAFORT and GATES hid the existence and ownership of the foreign companies and bank accounts, falsely and repeatedly reporting to their tax preparers and to the United States that they had no foreign bank accounts.

5. In furtherance of the scheme, MANAFORT used his hidden overseas wealth to enjoy a lavish lifestyle in the United States, without paying taxes on that income. MANAFORT, without reporting the income to his tax preparer or the United States, spent millions of dollars on luxury goods and services for himself and his extended family through payments wired from offshore nominee accounts to United States vendors. MANAFORT also used these offshore accounts to purchase multi-million dollar properties in the United States and to improve substantially another property owned by his family.

6. In furtherance of the scheme, GATES used millions of dollars from these offshore accounts to pay for his personal expenses, including his mortgage, children's tuition, and interior decorating and refinancing of his Virginia residence.

7. In total, more than \$75,000,000 flowed through the offshore accounts. MANAFORT, with the assistance of GATES, laundered more than \$30,000,000, income that he concealed from the United States Department of the Treasury (Treasury), the Department of Justice, and others. GATES obtained more than \$3,000,000 from the offshore accounts, income that he too concealed from the Treasury, the Department of Justice, and others.

II. *Relevant Individuals & Entities*

8. MANAFORT was a United States citizen. He resided in homes in Virginia, Florida, and Long Island, New York.

9. GATES was a United States citizen. He resided in Virginia.

10. In 2005, MANAFORT and another partner created Davis Manafort Partners, Inc. (DMP) to engage principally in political consulting. DMP had staff in the United States, Ukraine, and Russia. In 2011, MANAFORT created DMP International, LLC (DMI) to engage in work for foreign clients, in particular political consulting, lobbying, and public relations for the Government of Ukraine, the Party of Regions, and members of the Party of Regions. DMI was a partnership solely owned by MANAFORT and his spouse. GATES worked for both DMP and DMI and served as MANAFORT's right-hand man.

11. The Party of Regions was a pro-Russia political party in Ukraine. Beginning in approximately 2006, it retained MANAFORT, through DMP and then DMI, to advance its interests in Ukraine, the United States, and elsewhere, including the election of its slate of candidates. In 2010, its candidate for President, Yanukovych, was elected President of Ukraine. In 2014, Yanukovych fled Ukraine for Russia in the wake of popular protests of widespread government corruption. Yanukovych, the Party of Regions, and the Government of Ukraine were MANAFORT,

DMP, and DMI clients.

    12.   MANAFORT and GATES owned or controlled the following entities, which were used in the scheme (the MANAFORT–GATES entities):

Domestic Entities

Entity Name	Date Created	Incorporation Location
Bade LLC (RG)	January 2012	Delaware

Entity Name	Date Created	Incorporation Location
Daisy Manafort, LLC (PM)	August 2008	Virginia
	March 2011	Florida
Davis Manafort International LLC (PM)	March 2007	Delaware
DMP (PM)	March 2005	Virginia
	March 2011	Florida
Davis Manafort, Inc. (PM)	October 1999	Delaware
	November 1999	Virginia
DMI (PM)	June 2011	Delaware
	March 2012	Florida
Global Sites LLC (PM, RG)	July 2008	Delaware
Jemina LLC (RG)	July 2008	Delaware
Jesand Investment Corporation (PM)	April 2002	Virginia
Jesand Investments Corporation (PM)	March 2011	Florida
	April 2006	Virginia

John Hannah, LLC (PM)	March 2011	Florida
Jupiter Holdings Management, LLC (RG)	January 2011	Delaware
Lilred, LLC (PM)	December 2011	Florida
LOAV Ltd. (PM)	April 1992	Delaware
MC Brooklyn Holdings, LLC (PM)	November 2012	New York
MC Soho Holdings, LLC (PM)	January 2012	Florida
	April 2012	New York
Smythson LLC (also known as Symthson LLC) (PM, RG)	July 2008	Delaware

Cypriot Entities

Entity Name	Date Created	Incorporation Location
Actinet Trading Limited (PM, RG)	May 2009	Cyprus
Black Sea View Limited (PM, RG)	August 2007	Cyprus
Bletilla Ventures Limited (PM, RG)	October 2010	Cyprus
Cavenari Investments Limited (RG)	December 2007	Cyprus
Global Highway Limited (PM, RG)	August 2007	Cyprus
Leviathan Advisors Limited (PM, RG)	August 2007	Cyprus
LOAV Advisors Limited (PM, RG)	August 2007	Cyprus
Lucicle Consultants Limited (PM, RG)	December 2008	Cyprus

Marziola Holdings Limited (PM)	March 2012	Cyprus
Olivenia Trading Limited (PM, RG)	March 2012	Cyprus
Peranova Holdings Limited (Peranova) (PM, RG)	June 2007	Cyprus
Serangon Holdings Limited (PM, RG)	January 2008	Cyprus
Yiakora Ventures Limited (PM)	February 2008	Cyprus

Other Foreign Entities

Entity Name	Date Created	Incorporation Location
Global Endeavour Inc. (also known as Global Endeavor Inc.) (PM)	Unknown	Grenadines
Jeunet Ltd. (PM)	August 2011	Grenadines
Pompolo Limited (PM, RG)	April 2013	United Kingdom

13.   The Internal Revenue Service (IRS) was a bureau in the Treasury responsible for administering the tax laws of the United States and collecting taxes owed to the Treasury.

III.   *The Tax Scheme*

MANAFORT And GATES' Wiring Money From Offshore Accounts Into The United States

14.   In order to use the money in the offshore nominee accounts of the MANAFORT–GATES entities without paying taxes on it, MANAFORT and GATES caused millions of dollars in wire transfers from these accounts to be made for goods, services, and real estate. They did not report these transfers as income.

15.   From 2008 to 2014, MANAFORT caused the following wires, totaling over $12,000,000, to be sent to the vendors listed below for personal items. MANAFORT did not pay taxes on this income, which was used to make the

purchases.

Payee	Transaction Date	Originating Account Holder	Country of Origination	Amount of Transaction
Vendor A (Home Improvement Company in the Hamptons, New York)	6/10/2008	LOAV Advisors Limited	Cyprus	$107,000
	6/25/2008	LOAV Advisors Limited	Cyprus	$23,500
	7/7/2008	LOAV Advisors Limited	Cyprus	$20,000
	8/5/2008	Yiakora Ventures Limited	Cyprus	$59,000
	9/2/2008	Yiakora Ventures Limited	Cyprus	$272,000
	10/6/2008	Yiakora Ventures Limited	Cyprus	$109,000
	10/24/2008	Yiakora Ventures Limited	Cyprus	$107,800
	11/20/2008	Yiakora Ventures Limited	Cyprus	$77,400
	12/22/2008	Yiakora Ventures Limited	Cyprus	$100,000
	1/14/2009	Yiakora Ventures Limited	Cyprus	$9,250
	1/29/2009	Yiakora Ventures Limited	Cyprus	$97,670
	2/25/2009	Yiakora Ventures Limited	Cyprus	$108,100
	4/16/2009	Yiakora Ventures Limited	Cyprus	$94,394
	5/7/2009	Yiakora Ventures Limited	Cyprus	$54,000
	5/12/2009	Yiakora Ventures Limited	Cyprus	$9,550
	6/1/2009	Yiakora Ventures Limited	Cyprus	$86,650
	6/18/2009	Yiakora Ventures	Cyprus	$34,400

Payee	Transaction Date	Originating Account Holder	Country of Origination	Amount of Transaction
	09	Limited		
	7/31/2009	Yiakora Ventures Limited	Cyprus	$106,000
	8/28/2009	Yiakora Ventures Limited	Cyprus	$37,000
	9/23/2009	Yiakora Ventures Limited	Cyprus	$203,500
	10/26/2009	Yiakora Ventures Limited	Cyprus	$38,800
	11/18/2009	Global Highway Limited	Cyprus	$130,906
	3/8/2010	Global Highway Limited	Cyprus	$124,000
	5/11/2010	Global Highway Limited	Cyprus	$25,000
	7/8/2010	Global Highway Limited	Cyprus	$28,000
	7/23/2010	Leviathan Advisors Limited	Cyprus	$26,500
	8/12/2010	Leviathan Advisors Limited	Cyprus	$138,900
	9/2/2010	Yiakora Ventures Limited	Cyprus	$31,500
	10/6/2010	Global Highway Limited	Cyprus	$67,600
	10/14/2010	Yiakora Ventures Limited	Cyprus	$107,600
	10/18/2010	Leviathan Advisors Limited	Cyprus	$31,500
	12/16/2010	Global Highway Limited	Cyprus	$46,160
	2/7/2011	Global Highway Limited	Cyprus	$36,500

	3/22/20 11	Leviathan Advisors Limited	Cyprus	$26,800
	4/4/201 1	Leviathan Advisors Limited	Cyprus	$195,00 0
	5/3/2011	Global Highway Limited	Cyprus	$95,000
	5/16/20 11	Leviathan Advisors Limited	Cyprus	$6,500
	5/31/201 1	Leviathan Advisors Limited	Cyprus	$70,000
	6/27/20 11	Leviathan Advisors Limited	Cyprus	$39,900
	7/27/20 11	Leviathan Advisors Limited	Cyprus	$95,000
	10/24/2 011	Global Highway Limited	Cyprus	$22,000
	10/25/2 011	Global Highway Limited	Cyprus	$9,300
	11/15/20 11	Global Highway Limited	Cyprus	$74,000
	11/23/20 11	Global Highway Limited	Cyprus	$22,300
	11/29/2 011	Global Highway Limited	Cyprus	$6,100
	12/12/20 11	Leviathan Advisors Limited	Cyprus	$17,800
	1/17/201 2	Global Highway Limited	Cyprus	$29,800
	1/20/20 12	Global Highway Limited	Cyprus	$42,600
	2/9/201 2	Global Highway Limited	Cyprus	$22,300
	2/23/20 12	Global Highway Limited	Cyprus	$75,000
	2/28/20 12	Global Highway Limited	Cyprus	$22,300
	3/28/20 12	Peranova	Cyprus	$37,500

	4/18/20 12	Lucicle Consultants Limited	Cyprus	$50,000
	5/15/201 2	Lucicle Consultants Limited	Cyprus	$79,000
	6/5/201 2	Lucicle Consultants Limited	Cyprus	$45,000
	6/19/20 12	Lucicle Consultants Limited	Cyprus	$11,860

Payee	Transaction Date	Originating Account Holder	Country of Origination	Amount of Transaction
	7/9/201 2	Lucicle Consultants Limited	Cyprus	$10,800
	7/18/201 2	Lucicle Consultants Limited	Cyprus	$88,000
	8/7/201 2	Lucicle Consultants Limited	Cyprus	$48,800
	9/27/20 12	Lucicle Consultants Limited	Cyprus	$100,000
	11/20/2 012	Lucicle Consultants Limited	Cyprus	$298,000
	12/20/2 012	Lucicle Consultants Limited	Cyprus	$55,000
	1/29/20 13	Lucicle Consultants Limited	Cyprus	$149,000
	3/12/201 3	Lucicle Consultants Limited	Cyprus	$375,000
	8/29/20 13	Global Endeavour Inc.	Grenadines	$200,000
	11/13/20 13	Global Endeavour Inc.	Grenadines	$75,000
	11/26/2 013	Global Endeavour Inc.	Grenadines	$80,000
	12/6/20 13	Global Endeavour Inc.	Grenadines	$130,000

	12/12/2013	Global Endeavour Inc.	Grenadines	$90,000
	4/22/2014	Global Endeavour Inc.	Grenadines	$56,293
	8/18/2014	Global Endeavour Inc.	Grenadines	$34,660
Vendor A Total				$5,434,793
Vendor B (Home Automation, Lighting and Home Entertainment Company in Florida)	3/22/2011	Leviathan Advisors Limited	Cyprus	$12,000
	3/28/2011	Leviathan Advisors Limited	Cyprus	$25,000
	4/27/2011	Leviathan Advisors Limited	Cyprus	$12,000
	5/16/2011	Leviathan Advisors Limited	Cyprus	$25,000
	11/15/2011	Global Highway Limited	Cyprus	$17,006
	11/23/2011	Global Highway Limited	Cyprus	$11,000
	2/28/2012	Global Highway Limited	Cyprus	$6,200
	10/31/2012	Lucicle Consultants Limited	Cyprus	$290,000
	12/17/2012	Lucicle Consultants Limited	Cyprus	$160,600
	1/15/2013	Lucicle Consultants Limited	Cyprus	$194,000
	1/24/2013	Lucicle Consultants Limited	Cyprus	$6,300
	2/12/2013	Lucicle Consultants Limited	Cyprus	$51,600
	2/26/2013	Lucicle Consultants Limited	Cyprus	$260,000
	7/15/2013	Pompolo Limited	United Kingdom	$175,575
	11/5/2013	Global Endeavour Inc.	Grenadines	$73,000

Vendor B Total				$1,319,281
Vendor C (Antique Rug Store in Alexandria, Virginia)	10/7/2008	Yiakora Ventures Limited	Cyprus	$15,750
	3/17/2009	Yiakora Ventures Limited	Cyprus	$46,200
	4/16/2009	Yiakora Ventures Limited	Cyprus	$7,400
	4/27/2009	Yiakora Ventures Limited	Cyprus	$65,000
	5/7/2009	Yiakora Ventures Limited	Cyprus	$210,000

Payee	Transaction Date	Originating Account Holder	Country of Origination	Amount of Transaction
	7/15/2009	Yiakora Ventures Limited	Cyprus	$200,000
	3/31/2010	Yiakora Ventures Limited	Cyprus	$140,000
	6/16/2010	Global Highway Limited	Cyprus	$250,000
Vendor C Total				$934,350
Vendor D (Related to Vendor C)	2/28/2012	Global Highway Limited	Cyprus	$100,000
Vendor D Total				$100,000
Vendor E (Men's Clothing Store in New York)	11/7/2008	Yiakora Ventures Limited	Cyprus	$32,000
	2/5/2009	Yiakora Ventures Limited	Cyprus	$22,750
	4/27/2009	Yiakora Ventures Limited	Cyprus	$13,500
	10/26/2	Yiakora Ventures	Cyprus	$32,500

	009	Limited		
	3/30/2010	Yiakora Ventures Limited	Cyprus	$15,000
	5/11/2010	Global Highway Limited	Cyprus	$39,000
	6/28/2010	Leviathan Advisors Limited	Cyprus	$5,000
	8/12/2010	Leviathan Advisors Limited	Cyprus	$32,500
	11/17/2010	Global Highway Limited	Cyprus	$11,500
	2/7/2011	Global Highway Limited	Cyprus	$24,000
	3/22/2011	Leviathan Advisors Limited	Cyprus	$43,600
	3/28/2011	Leviathan Advisors Limited	Cyprus	$12,000
	4/27/2011	Leviathan Advisors Limited	Cyprus	$3,000
	6/30/2011	Global Highway Limited	Cyprus	$24,500
	9/26/2011	Leviathan Advisors Limited	Cyprus	$12,000
	11/2/2011	Global Highway Limited	Cyprus	$26,700
	12/12/2011	Leviathan Advisors Limited	Cyprus	$46,000
	2/9/2012	Global Highway Limited	Cyprus	$2,800
	2/28/2012	Global Highway Limited	Cyprus	$16,000
	3/14/2012	Lucicle Consultants Limited	Cyprus	$8,000
	4/18/2012	Lucicle Consultants Limited	Cyprus	$48,550
	5/15/2012	Lucicle Consultants Limited	Cyprus	$7,000
	6/19/2010	Lucicle Consultants	Cyprus	$21,600

12	Limited			
8/7/2012	Lucicle Consultants Limited	Cyprus	$15,500
11/20/2012	Lucicle Consultants Limited	Cyprus	$10,900
12/20/2012	Lucicle Consultants Limited	Cyprus	$7,500
1/15/2013	Lucicle Consultants Limited	Cyprus	$37,000
2/12/2013	Lucicle Consultants Limited	Cyprus	$7,000
2/26/2013	Lucicle Consultants Limited	Cyprus	$39,000
9/3/2013	Global Endeavour Inc.	Grenadines	$81,500

Payee	Transaction Date	Originating Account Holder	Country of Origination	Amount of Transaction
	10/15/2013	Global Endeavour Inc.	Grenadines	$53,000
	11/26/2013	Global Endeavour Inc.	Grenadines	$13,200
	4/24/2014	Global Endeavour Inc.	Grenadines	$26,680
	9/11/2014	Global Endeavour Inc.	Grenadines	$58,435
Vendor E Total				$849,215
Vendor F (Landscaper in the Hamptons, New York)	4/27/2009	Yiakora Ventures Limited	Cyprus	$34,000
	5/12/2009	Yiakora Ventures Limited	Cyprus	$45,700
	6/1/2009	Yiakora Ventures Limited	Cyprus	$21,500
	6/18/2009	Yiakora Ventures Limited	Cyprus	$29,000
	9/21/2009	Yiakora Ventures Limited	Cyprus	$21,800
	5/11/2010	Global Highway Limited	Cyprus	$44,000
	6/28/2010	Leviathan Advisors Limited	Cyprus	$50,000
	7/23/2010	Leviathan Advisors Limited	Cyprus	$19,000
	9/2/2010	Yiakora Ventures Limited	Cyprus	$21,000
	10/6/2010	Global Highway Limited	Cyprus	$57,700
	10/18/2010	Leviathan Advisors Limited	Cyprus	$26,000
	12/16/2	Global Highway	Cyprus	$20,000

	010	Limited		
	3/22/2011	Leviathan Advisors Limited	Cyprus	$50,000
	5/3/2011	Global Highway Limited	Cyprus	$40,000
	6/1/2011	Leviathan Advisors Limited	Cyprus	$44,000
	7/27/2011	Leviathan Advisors Limited	Cyprus	$27,000
	8/16/2011	Leviathan Advisors Limited	Cyprus	$13,450
	9/19/2011	Leviathan Advisors Limited	Cyprus	$12,000
	10/24/2011	Global Highway Limited	Cyprus	$42,000
	11/2/2011	Global Highway Limited	Cyprus	$37,350
Vendor F Total				$655,500
Vendor G (Antique Dealer in New York)	9/2/2010	Yiakora Ventures Limited	Cyprus	$165,000
	10/18/2010	Leviathan Advisors Limited	Cyprus	$165,000
	2/28/2012	Global Highway Limited	Cyprus	$190,600
	3/14/2012	Lucicle Consultants Limited	Cyprus	$75,000
	2/26/2013	Lucicle Consultants Limited	Cyprus	$28,310
Vendor G Total				$623,910
Vendor H (Clothing Store in Beverly Hills, California)	6/25/2008	LOAV Advisors Limited	Cyprus	$52,000
	12/16/2008	Yiakora Ventures Limited	Cyprus	$49,000
	12/22/2008	Yiakora Ventures Limited	Cyprus	$10,260
	8/12/20	Yiakora Ventures	Cyprus	$76,400

	09	Limited		
	5/11/2010	Global Highway Limited	Cyprus	$85,000
	11/17/2010	Global Highway Limited	Cyprus	$128,280

Payee	Transaction Date	Originating Account Holder	Country of Origination	Amount of Transaction
	5/31/2011	Leviathan Advisors Limited	Cyprus	$64,000
	11/15/2011	Global Highway Limited	Cyprus	$48,000
	12/17/2012	Lucicle Consultants Limited	Cyprus	$7,500
Vendor H Total				$520,440
Vendor I (Investment Company)	9/3/2013	Global Endeavour Inc.	Grenadines	$500,000
Vendor I Total				$500,000
Vendor J (Contractor in Florida)	11/15/2011	Global Highway Limited	Cyprus	$8,000
	12/5/2011	Leviathan Advisors Limited	Cyprus	$11,237
	12/21/2011	Black Sea View Limited	Cyprus	$20,000
	2/9/2012	Global Highway Limited	Cyprus	$51,000
	5/17/2012	Lucicle Consultants Limited	Cyprus	$68,000
	6/19/2012	Lucicle Consultants Limited	Cyprus	$60,000
	7/18/2012	Lucicle Consultants Limited	Cyprus	$32,250

	9/19/2012	Lucicle Consultants Limited	Cyprus	$112,000
	11/30/2012	Lucicle Consultants Limited	Cyprus	$39,700
	1/9/2013	Lucicle Consultants Limited	Cyprus	$25,600
	2/28/2013	Lucicle Consultants Limited	Cyprus	$4,700
Vendor J Total				$432,487
Vendor K (Landscaper in the Hamptons, New York)	12/5/2011	Leviathan Advisors Limited	Cyprus	$4,115
	3/1/2012	Global Highway Limited	Cyprus	$50,000
	6/6/2012	Lucicle Consultants Limited	Cyprus	$47,800
	6/25/2012	Lucicle Consultants Limited	Cyprus	$17,900
	6/27/2012	Lucicle Consultants Limited	Cyprus	$18,900
	2/12/2013	Lucicle Consultants Limited	Cyprus	$3,300
	7/15/2013	Pompolo Limited	United Kingdom	$13,325
	11/26/2013	Global Endeavour Inc.	Grenadines	$9,400
Vendor K Total				$164,740
Vendor L (Payments Relating to Three Range Rovers)	4/12/2012	Lucicle Consultants Limited	Cyprus	$83,525
	5/2/2012	Lucicle Consultants Limited	Cyprus	$12,525
	6/29/2012	Lucicle Consultants Limited	Cyprus	$67,655
Vendor L Total				$163,705
Vendor M	11/20/2	Lucicle Consultants	Cyprus	$45,000

	012	Limited		
	12/7/2012	Lucicle Consultants Limited	Cyprus	$21,000

Payee	Transaction Date	Originating Account Holder	Country of Origination	Amount of Transaction
(Contractor in Virginia)	12/17/2012	Lucicle Consultants Limited	Cyprus	$21,000
	1/17/2013	Lucicle Consultants Limited	Cyprus	$18,750
	1/29/2013	Lucicle Consultants Limited	Cyprus	$9,400
	2/12/2013	Lucicle Consultants Limited	Cyprus	$10,500
Vendor M Total				$125,650
Vendor N (Audio, Video, and Control System Home Integration and Installation Company in the Hamptons, New York)	1/29/2009	Yiakora Ventures Limited	Cyprus	$10,000
	3/17/2009	Yiakora Ventures Limited	Cyprus	$21,725
	4/16/2009	Yiakora Ventures Limited	Cyprus	$24,650
	12/2/2009	Global Highway Limited	Cyprus	$10,000
	3/8/2010	Global Highway Limited	Cyprus	$20,300
	4/23/2010	Yiakora Ventures Limited	Cyprus	$8,500
	7/29/2010	Leviathan Advisors Limited	Cyprus	$17,650
Vendor N Total				$112,825

Vendor O (Purchase of Mercedes Benz)	10/5/2012	Lucicle Consultants Limited	Cyprus	$62,750
Vendor O Total				$62,750
Vendor P (Purchase of Range Rover)	12/30/2008	Yiakora Ventures Limited	Cyprus	$47,000
Vendor P Total				$47,000
Vendor Q (Property Management Company in South Carolina)	9/2/2010	Yiakora Ventures Limited	Cyprus	$10,000
	10/6/2010	Global Highway Limited	Cyprus	$10,000
	10/18/2010	Leviathan Advisors Limited	Cyprus	$10,000
	2/8/2011	Global Highway Limited	Cyprus	$13,500
	2/9/2012	Global Highway Limited	Cyprus	$2,500
Vendor Q Total				$46,000
Vendor R (Art Gallery in Florida)	2/9/2011	Global Highway Limited	Cyprus	$17,900
	2/14/2013	Lucicle Consultants Limited	Cyprus	$14,000
Vendor R Total				$31,900
Vendor S	9/26/2011	Leviathan Advisors Limited	Cyprus	$5,000
	9/19/2012	Lucicle Consultants Limited	Cyprus	$5,000

Payee	Transaction Date	Originating Account Holder	Country of Origination	Amount of Transaction

(Housekee ping in New York)	10/9/20 13	Global Endeavour Inc.		Grenad ines	$10,000
		Vendor S Total			$20,000

16.   In 2012, MANAFORT caused the following wires to be sent to the entities listed below to purchase the real estate also listed below. MANAFORT did not report the money used to make these purchases on his 2012 tax return.

Property Purchased	Payee	Date	Originatin g Account	Cou ntry of Origin	Amount
Howard Street Condominium (New York)	DMP Internati onal LLC	2/1/20 12	Peranova	Cyp rus	$1,500, 000
Union Street Brownstone, (New York)	Attorney Account Of [Real Estate Attorney]	11/29/ 2012	Actinet Trading Limited	Cyp rus	$1,800, 000
		11/29/ 2012	Actinet Trading Limited	Cyp rus	$1,200, 000
Arlington House (Virginia)	Real Estate Trust	8/31/2 012	Lucicle Consultants Limited	Cyp rus	$1,900, 000
				Tot al	$6,400, 000

17.   MANAFORT and GATES also disguised, as purported "loans," more than $10 million transferred from Cypriot entities, including the overseas MANAFORT–GATES entities, to domestic entities owned by MANAFORT. For example, a $1.5 million wire from Peranova to DMI that MANAFORT used to purchase real estate on Howard Street in Manhattan, New York, was recorded as a "loan" from Peranova to DMI, rather than as income. The following loans were shams designed to reduce fraudulently MANAFORT's reported taxable income.

Ye ar	Payor / Ostensible "Lender"	Payee / Ostensible		Count ry of	Total Amount of

		"Borrower"	Origin	"Loans"
2008	Yiakora Ventures Limited	Jesand Investment Corporation	Cyprus	$8,120,000
2008	Yiakora Ventures Limited	DMP	Cyprus	$500,000
2009	Yiakora Ventures Limited	DMP	Cyprus	$694,000
2009	Yiakora Ventures Limited	Daisy Manafort, LLC	Cyprus	$500,000
2012	Peranova	DMI	Cyprus	$1,500,000
2014	Telmar Investments Ltd.	DMI	Cyprus	$900,000
2015	Telmar Investments Ltd.	DMI	Cyprus	$1,000,000
			Total	$13,214,000

18. From 2010 to 2014, GATES caused the following wires, totaling more than $3,000,000, to be sent to entities and bank accounts of which he was a beneficial owner or he otherwise controlled. GATES did not report this income on his tax returns.

Payee	Transaction Date	Originating Account Holder	Country of Origination	Amount of Transaction
Richard Gates United Kingdom Bank Account A	3/26/2010	Serangon Holdings Limited	Cyprus	$85,000
	4/20/2010	Serangon Holdings Limited	Cyprus	$50,000
	5/6/2010	Serangon Holdings Limited	Cyprus	$150,000
Richard Gates United Kingdom Bank Account B	9/7/2010	Serangon Holdings Limited	Cyprus	$160,000
	10/13/2010	Serangon Holdings Limited	Cyprus	$15,000

110

Richard Gates United States Bank Account C	9/27/20 10	Global Highway Limited	Cyprus	$50,000
2010 Tax Year Total				$510,00 0
Jemina LLC United States Bank Account D	9/9/201 1	Peranova	Cyprus	$48,500
Richard Gates United Kingdom Bank Account B	12/16/2 011	Peranova	Cyprus	$100,43 5
2011 Tax Year Total				$148,93 5
Richard Gates United Kingdom Bank Account B	1/9/201 2	Global Highway Limited	Cyprus	$100,00 0
	1/13/201 2	Peranova	Cyprus	$100,43 5
	2/29/20 12	Global Highway Limited	Cyprus	$28,500
	3/27/20 12	Bletilla Ventures Limited	Cyprus	$18,745

Payee	Transaction Date	Originating Account Holder	Country of Origination	Amount of Transaction
	4/26/20 12	Bletilla Ventures Limited	Cyprus	$26,455
	5/30/20 12	Bletilla Ventures Limited	Cyprus	$15,000
	5/30/20 12	Lucicle Consultants Limited	Cyprus	$14,650
	6/27/20	Bletilla Ventures	Cyprus	$18,745

	12	Limited		
	8/2/2012	Bletilla Ventures Limited	Cyprus	$28,745
	8/30/2012	Bletilla Ventures Limited	Cyprus	$38,745
	9/27/2012	Bletilla Ventures Limited	Cyprus	$32,345
	10/31/2012	Bletilla Ventures Limited	Cyprus	$46,332
	11/20/2012	Bletilla Ventures Limited	Cyprus	$48,547
	11/30/2012	Bletilla Ventures Limited	Cyprus	$38,532
	12/21/2012	Bletilla Ventures Limited	Cyprus	$47,836
	12/28/2012	Bletilla Ventures Limited	Cyprus	$47,836
2012 Tax Year Total				$651,448
Richard Gates United Kingdom Bank Account B	1/11/2013	Bletilla Ventures Limited	Cyprus	$47,836
	1/22/2013	Bletilla Ventures Limited	Cyprus	$34,783
	1/30/2013	Bletilla Ventures Limited	Cyprus	$46,583
	2/22/2013	Bletilla Ventures Limited	Cyprus	$46,233
	2/28/2013	Bletilla Ventures Limited	Cyprus	$46,583
	3/1/2013	Bletilla Ventures Limited	Cyprus	$42,433
	3/15/2013	Bletilla Ventures Limited	Cyprus	$37,834
	4/15/2013	Bletilla Ventures Limited	Cyprus	$59,735
	4/26/2013	Bletilla Ventures Limited	Cyprus	$48,802
	5/17/2013	Olivenia Trading	Cyprus	$57,798

Payee	Transaction Date	Originating Account Holder	Country of Origination	Amount of Transaction
	3	Limited		
	5/30/2013	Actinet Trading Limited	Cyprus	$45,622
	6/13/2013	Lucicle Consultants Limited	Cyprus	$76,343
	8/7/2013	Pompolo Limited	United Kingdom	$250,784
	9/6/2013	Lucicle Consultants Limited	Cyprus	$68,500
	9/13/2013	Cypriot Agent	Cyprus	$179,216
Jemina LLC United States Bank Account D	7/8/2013	Marziola Holdings Limited	Cyprus	$72,500
	9/4/2013	Marziola Holdings Limited	Cyprus	$89,807
	10/22/2013	Cypriot Agent	Cyprus	$119,844
	11/12/2013	Cypriot Agent	Cyprus	$80,000
	12/20/2013	Cypriot Agent	Cyprus	$90,000
2013 Tax Year Total				$1,541,237
Jemina LLC United States Bank Account D	2/10/2014	Cypriot Agent	Cyprus	$60,044
	4/29/2014	Cypriot Agent	Cyprus	$44,068
	10/6/2014	Global Endeavour Inc.	Grenadines	$65,000

Payee	Transaction Date	Originating Account Holder	Country of Origination	Amount of Transaction
Bade LLC United States Bank Account E	11/25/2014	Global Endeavour Inc.	Grenadines	$120,000

2014 Tax Year Total	$289,11
	2

MANAFORT And GATES' Hiding Foreign Bank Accounts And False Filings

19.   United States citizens who have authority over certain foreign bank accounts—whether or not the accounts are set up in the names of nominees who act for their principals—have reporting obligations to the United States

20.   First, the Bank Secrecy Act and its implementing regulations require United States citizens to report to the Treasury any financial interest in, or signatory authority over, any bank account or other financial account held in foreign countries, for every calendar year in which the aggregate balance of all such foreign accounts exceeds $10,000 at any point during the year. This is commonly known as a foreign bank account report or "FBAR." The Bank Secrecy Act requires these reports because they have a high degree of usefulness in criminal, tax, or regulatory investigations or proceedings. The Treasury's Financial Crimes Enforcement Network (FinCEN) is the custodian for FBAR filings, and FinCEN provides access to its FBAR database to law enforcement entities, including the Federal Bureau of Investigation. The reports filed by individuals and businesses are used by law enforcement to identify, detect, and deter money laundering that furthers criminal enterprise activity, tax evasion, and other unlawful activities.

21.   Second, United States citizens also are obligated to report information to the IRS regarding foreign bank accounts. For instance, in 2010, Schedule B of IRS Form 1040 had a "Yes" or "No" box to record an answer to the question: "At any time during [the calendar year], did you have an interest in or a signature or other authority over a financial account in a foreign country, such bank account, securities account, or other financial account?" If the answer was "Yes," then the form required the taxpayer to enter the name of the foreign country in which the financial account was located.

22.   For each year in or about and between 2008 through at least 2014, MANAFORT had authority over foreign accounts that required an FBAR filing. Specifically, MANAFORT was required to report to the Treasury each foreign bank account held by the foreign MANAFORT– GATES entities noted above in paragraph 12 that bears the initials PM. No FBAR filings were made by MANAFORT for these accounts.

23.   For each year in or about and between 2010 through at least 2013, GATES had authority over foreign accounts that required an FBAR filing. Specifically, GATES was required to report to the United States Treasury each foreign bank account held by the foreign MANAFORT– GATES entities noted above in paragraph 12 that bears the initials RG, as well as United Kingdom Bank Accounts A and B noted

in paragraph 18. No FBAR filings were made by GATES for these accounts.

24. Furthermore, in each of MANAFORT's tax filings for 2008 through 2014, MANAFORT, with the assistance of GATES, represented falsely that he did not have authority over any foreign bank accounts. MANAFORT and GATES had repeatedly and falsely represented in writing to MANAFORT's tax preparer that MANAFORT had no authority over foreign bank accounts, knowing that such false representations would result in false tax filings in MANAFORT's name. For instance, on October 4, 2011, MANAFORT's tax preparer asked MANAFORT in writing: "At any time during 2010, did you [or your wife or children] have an interest in or a signature or other authority over a financial account in a foreign country, such as a bank account, securities account or other financial account?" On the same day, MANAFORT falsely responded "NO." MANAFORT responded the same way as recently as October 3, 2016, when MANAFORT's tax preparer again emailed the question in connection with the preparation of MANAFORT's tax returns: "Foreign bank accounts etc.?" MANAFORT responded on or about the same day: "NONE."

25. In each of GATES' tax filings for 2010 through 2013, GATES represented falsely that he did not have authority over any foreign bank accounts. GATES had repeatedly and falsely represented to his tax preparers that he had no authority over foreign bank accounts, knowing that such false representations would result in false tax filings. As recently as October 2017, in preparation for his amended 2013 tax filing, GATES was asked by his tax preparer: "Did you have any foreign assets/bank accounts during 2013 or 2014?" to which he responded "no."

IV. *The Financial Institution Scheme*

26. Between in or around 2015 and the present, both dates being approximate and inclusive, in the Eastern District of Virginia and elsewhere, MANAFORT, GATES, and others devised and intended to devise, and executed and attempted to execute, a scheme and artifice to defraud, and to obtain money and property, by means of false and fraudulent pretenses, representations, and promises, from banks and other financial institutions. As part of the scheme, MANAFORT and GATES repeatedly provided and caused to be provided false information to banks and other lenders, among others.

MANAFORT And GATES' Fraud To Access Offshore Money

27. When they were flush with Ukraine funds, MANAFORT, with the assistance of GATES, used their offshore accounts to purchase and improve real estate in the United States. When the income from Ukraine dwindled in 2014 and 2015, MANAFORT, with the assistance of GATES,

obtained millions of dollars in mortgages on the United States properties, thereby allowing MANAFORT to have the benefits of liquid income without paying taxes on it. MANAFORT and GATES defrauded the lenders in various ways, including by lying about MANAFORT's and DMI's income, lying about their debt, and lying about MANAFORT's use of the property and the loan proceeds. For example, MANAFORT and GATES submitted fabricated profit and loss statements (P&Ls) that inflated income, and they caused others to provide doctored financial documents.

The Loan From Lender A On The Union Street Property

28. In 2012, MANAFORT, through a corporate vehicle called "MC Brooklyn Holdings, LLC" owned by him and his family, bought a brownstone on Union Street in the Carroll Gardens section of Brooklyn, New York. He paid approximately $3,000,000 in cash for the property. All of that money came from a MANAFORT–GATES entity in Cyprus. After purchase of the property, MANAFORT began renovations to transform it from a multi-family dwelling into a single-family home. MANAFORT used proceeds of a 2015 loan obtained from a financial institution to make the renovations. In order to obtain that loan, MANAFORT falsely represented to the bank that he did not derive more than 50% of his income/wealth from a country outside the United States.

29. In late 2015 through early 2016, MANAFORT sought to borrow cash against the Union Street property from Lender A. Lender A provided greater loan amounts for "construction loans"—that is, loans that required the loan funds to be used to pay solely for construction on the property and thus increase the value of the property serving as the loan's collateral. The institution would thus loan money against the expected completed value of the property, which in the case of the Union Street property was estimated to be $8,000,000. In early 2016, MANAFORT was able to obtain a loan of approximately $5,000,000, after promising Lender A that approximately $1,400,000 of the loan would be used solely for construction on the Union Street property. MANAFORT never intended to limit use of the proceeds to construction as required by the loan contracts and never did. In December 2015, before the loan was made, MANAFORT wrote his tax preparer, among others, that the "construction mortgage will allow me to pay back [another Manafort apartment] mortgage in full. . . ." Further, when the construction loan closed, MANAFORT used hundreds of thousands of dollars for purposes unrelated to the construction of the property.

The Loan From Lender B On The Howard Street Property

30. In 2012, MANAFORT, through a corporate vehicle called "MC Soho Holdings, LLC" owned by him and his family, bought a condominium on Howard Street in the Soho neighborhood of Manhattan, New York. He paid approximately $2,850,000. All the money used to purchase the condominium came from

MANAFORT–GATES entities in Cyprus. MANAFORT used the property from at least January 2015 through at least August 2017 as an income-generating rental property, charging thousands of dollars a week on Airbnb, among other places. On his tax returns, MANAFORT took advantage of the beneficial tax consequences of owning this rental property.

31.   In late 2015 through early 2016, MANAFORT applied for a mortgage on the Howard Street condominium from Lender B for approximately $3.4 million. Because the bank would permit a greater loan amount if the property were owner-occupied, MANAFORT falsely represented to the lender and its agents that it was a secondary home used as such by his daughter and son-in-law and was not held as a rental property. In an email on January 6, 2016, MANAFORT noted: "[i]n order to have the maximum benefit, I am claiming Howard St. as a second home. Not an investment property." Later, on January 26, 2016, MANAFORT wrote to his son-in-law to advise him that when the bank appraiser came to assess the condominium, his son-in-law should "[r]emember, he believes that you and [MANAFORT's daughter] are living there."

32.   MANAFORT, with GATES' assistance, also made a series of false and fraudulent representations to the bank in order to secure the millions of dollars in financing. For example, MANAFORT falsely represented the amount of debt he had by failing to disclose on his loan application the existence of the Lender A mortgage on his Union Street property. That liability would have risked his qualifying for the loan. Through its own due diligence, Lender B found evidence of the existing mortgage on the Union Street property. As a result, Lender B wrote to MANAFORT and GATES that the "application has the following properties as being owned free & clear . . . Union Street," but "[b]ased on the insurance binders that we received last night, we are showing that there are mortgages listed on these properties, can you please clarify[?]"

33.   To cover up the falsity of the loan application, GATES, on MANAFORT's behalf, caused an insurance broker to provide Lender B false information, namely, an outdated insurance report that did not list the Union Street loan. MANAFORT and GATES knew such a representation was fraudulent. After GATES contacted the insurance broker and asked her to provide Lender B with false information, he updated MANAFORT by email on February 24, 2016. MANAFORT replied to GATES, on the same day: "good job on the insurance issues."

34.   MANAFORT and GATES submitted additional false and fraudulent statements to Lender B. For example, MANAFORT submitted 2014 DMI tax returns to support his 2016 loan application to Lender B. Those tax returns included as a purported liability a $1.5 million loan from Peranova. Peranova was a Cypriot entity controlled by MANAFORT and GATES. On or about February 1, 2012, Peranova transferred $1.5 million to a DMI account in the United States, denominating the

transfer as a loan so that MANAFORT would not have to declare the money as income. MANAFORT used the "loan" to acquire the Howard Street property.

35. When MANAFORT needed to obtain a loan from Lender B, the existence of the Peranova "loan" undermined his creditworthiness. As a result of the listed Peranova liability, Lender B was not willing to make the loan to MANAFORT. To circumvent this issue, MANAFORT and GATES caused MANAFORT's tax accountant to send to Lender B back-dated documentation that falsely stated that the $1.5 million Peranova loan had been forgiven in 2015, and falsely inflated income for 2015 to mask MANAFORT's 2015 drop in income.

36. In March 2016, Lender B approved the loan in the amount of approximately $3.4 million (the $3.4 million loan).

The Loan From Lender C

37. In approximately February 2016, MANAFORT applied for a business loan from Lender C. MANAFORT made a series of false statements to Lender C. For example, MANAFORT submitted a false statement of assets and liabilities that failed to disclosed the Lender A loan on the Union Street property and misrepresented, among other things, the amount of the mortgage on the Howard Street property.

38. Further, in approximately March 2016, MANAFORT and GATES submitted a doctored 2015 DMI P&L that overstated DMI's 2015 income by more than $4 million. GATES asked DMI's bookkeeper to send him a "Word Document version of the 2015 P&L for [DMI]" because MANAFORT wanted GATES "to add the accrual revenue which we have not received in order to send to [Lender C]." The bookkeeper said she could send a .pdf version of the P&L. GATES then asked the bookkeeper to increase the DMI revenue, falsely claiming that: "[w]e have $2.4m in accrued revenue that [MANAFORT] wants added to the [DMI] 2015 income. Can you make adjustments on your end and then just send me a new scanned version[?]" The bookkeeper refused since the accounting method DMI used did not permit recording income before it was actually received.

39. Having failed to secure a falsified P&L from the bookkeeper, GATES falsified the P&L. GATES wrote to MANAFORT and another conspirator, "I am editing Paul's 2015 P&L statement." GATES then sent the altered P&L to Lender C, which claimed approximately $4.45 million in net income, whereas the true P&L had less than $400,000 in net income.

The Loan From Lender B On The Union Street Property

40. In March 2016, MANAFORT, with the assistance of GATES and others, applied for a $5.5 million loan from Lender B on the Union Street property. As part of the loan process, MANAFORT submitted a false statement of assets and

liabilities that hid his prior loan from Lender A on the Union Street property, among other liabilities. In addition, another conspirator on MANAFORT's behalf submitted a falsified 2016 DMI P&L. The falsified 2016 DMI P&L overstated DMI's income by more than $2 million, which was the amount that Lender B told MANAFORT he needed to qualify for the loan. When the document was first submitted to Lender B, a conspirator working at Lender B replied: "Looks Dr'd. Can't someone just do a clean excel doc and pdf to me??" A subsequent version was submitted to the bank.

The Loans From Lender D On The Bridgehampton And Union Street Properties

41. In 2016, MANAFORT sought a mortgage on property in Bridgehampton, New York from a financial institution. In connection with his application, MANAFORT falsely represented to the bank that DMI would be receiving $2.4 million in income later in the year for work on a "democratic development consulting project." To support this representation, GATES, on MANAFORT's behalf, provided the bank with a fake invoice for $2.4 million, directed "To Whom It May Concern," for "[s]ervices rendered per the consultancy agreement pertaining to the parliamentary elections." The bank, unwilling to rely on the invoice to support MANAFORT's stated 2016 income, requested additional information. The bank was unable to obtain satisfactory support for the stated income, and the loan application was denied.

42. MANAFORT applied to a second bank, Lender D. Between approximately July 2016 and January 2017, MANAFORT, with the assistance of GATES, sought and secured approximately $16,000,000 in two loans from Lender D. MANAFORT used the Bridgehampton property as collateral for one loan, and the Union Street property for the other.

43. MANAFORT and GATES made numerous false and fraudulent representations to secure the loans. For example, MANAFORT provided the bank with doctored P&Ls for DMI for both 2015 and 2016, overstating its income by millions of dollars. The doctored 2015 DMI P&L submitted to Lender D was the same false statement previously submitted to Lender C, which overstated DMI's income by more than $4 million. The doctored 2016 DMI P&L was inflated by MANAFORT by more than $3.5 million. To create the false 2016 P&L, on or about October 21, 2016, MANAFORT emailed GATES a .pdf version of the real 2016 DMI P&L, which showed a loss of more than $600,000. GATES converted that .pdf into a "Word" document so that it could be edited, which GATES sent back to MANAFORT. MANAFORT altered that "Word" document by adding more than $3.5 million in income. He then sent this falsified P&L to GATES and asked that the "Word" document be converted back to a .pdf, which GATES did and returned to MANAFORT. MANAFORT then sent the falsified 2016 DMI P&L .pdf to Lender D.

44. In addition, Lender D questioned MANAFORT about a $300,000

delinquency on his American Express card, which was more than 90 days past due. The delinquency significantly affected MANAFORT's credit rating score. MANAFORT falsely represented to Lender D that he had lent his credit card to a friend, GATES, who had incurred the charges and had not reimbursed him. MANAFORT supplied Lender D a letter from GATES that falsely stated that GATES had borrowed MANAFORT's credit card tomake the purchases at issue and would pay him back by a date certain.

V. Statutory Allegations
COUNTS 1–5: Subscribing to False United States Individual Income Tax Returns For Tax Years '10 – '14

45.   Paragraphs 1 through 44 are incorporated here.

46.   On or about the dates specified below, in the Eastern District of Virginia and elsewhere, defendant PAUL J. MANAFORT, JR., willfully and knowingly did make and subscribe, and aid and abet and cause to be made and subscribed, United States Individual Income Tax Returns, Forms 1040 and Schedule B, for the tax years set forth below, which returns contained and were verified by the written declaration of MANAFORT that they were made under penalties of perjury, and which returns MANAFORT did not believe to be true and correct as to every material matter, in that the returns (a) claimed that MANAFORT did not have a financial interest in and signature and other authority over a financial account in a foreign country and (b) failed to report income, whereas MANAFORT then and there well knew and believed that he had a financial interest in, and signature and other authority over, bank accounts in a foreign country and had earned total income in excess of the reported amounts noted below:

CO UNT	TA X YEAR	APPROX. FILING DATE	FOREIGN ACCOUNT REPORTED (Sch. B, Line 7a)	TOTAL INCOME REPORTED (Line 22)
1	201 0	October 14, 2011	None	$504,744
2	201 1	October 15, 2012	None	$3,071,409
3	201 2	October 7, 2013	None	$5,361,007
4	201 3	October 6, 2014	None	$1,910,928
5	201 4	October 14, 2015	None	$2,984,210

(26 U.S.C. § 7206(1); 18 U.S.C. §§ 2 and 3551 et seq.)

COUNTS 6-10: Assisting in the Preparation of False United States Individual Income Tax Returns ('10-'14)

47.   Paragraphs 1 through 44 are incorporated here.

48.   On or about the dates specified below, in the Eastern District of Virginia and elsewhere, defendant RICHARD W. GATES III willfully and knowingly did aid and assist in, and procure, counsel, and advise the preparation and presentation to the Internal Revenue Service, of a United States Individual Income Tax Return, Form 1040 and Schedule B, of PAUL J. MANAFORT, JR., for the tax years set forth below, which returns were false and fraudulent as to a material matter, in that the returns (a) claimed that MANAFORT did not have a financial interest in, and signature and other authority over, a financial account in a foreign country and (b) failed to report income, whereas GATES then and there well knew and believed that MANAFORT had a financial interest in, and signature and other authority over, bank accounts in a foreign country and had earned total income in excess of the reported amounts noted below:

CO UNT	TA X YEAR	APPROX. FILING DATE	FOREIGN ACCOUNT REPORTED (Sch. B, Line 7a)	TOTAL INCOME REPORTED (Line 22)
6	201 0	October 14, 2011	None	$504,744
7	201 1	October 15, 2012	None	$3,071,409
8	201 2	October 7, 2013	None	$5,361,007
9	201 3	October 6, 2014	None	$1,910,928
10	201 4	October 14, 2015	None	$2,984,210

(26 U.S.C. § 7206(2); 18 U.S.C. § 3551 et seq.)

COUNTS 11-14: Failure To File Reports Of Foreign Bank And Financial Accounts For '11 - '14

49.   Paragraphs 1 through 44 are incorporated here.

50.   On the filing due dates listed below, in the Eastern District of Virginia and elsewhere, defendant PAUL J. MANAFORT, JR., unlawfully, willfully, and knowingly did fail to file with the Treasury an FBAR disclosing that he had a

financial interest in, and signature and other authority over, a bank, securities, and other financial account in a foreign country, which had an aggregate value of more than $10,000 in a 12-month period, during the years listed below:

COUNT	YEAR	DUE DATE TO FILE FBAR
11	2011	June 29, 2012
12	2012	June 30, 2013
13	2013	June 30, 2014
14	2014	June 30, 2015

(31 U.S.C. §§ 5314 and 5322(a); 18 U.S.C. §§ 2 and 3551 et seq.)

COUNTS 15-19: Subscribing to False United States Individual Income Tax Returns For '10 - '14

51.   Paragraphs 1 through 44 are incorporated here.

52.   On or about the dates specified below, in the Eastern District of Virginia and elsewhere, defendant RICHARD W. GATES III willfully and knowingly did make and subscribe, and aid and abet and cause to be made and subscribed, United States Individual Income Tax Returns, Forms 1040 and Schedule B, for the tax years set forth below, which returns contained and were verified by the written declaration of defendant GATES that they were made under penalties of perjury, and which returns defendant GATES did not believe to be true and correct as to every material matter, in that the returns (a) claimed that GATES did not have a financial interest in, and signature and other authority over, a financial account in a foreign country and (b) failed to report income, whereas GATES then and there well knew and believed that he had a financial interest in, and signature and other authority over, a financial account in a foreign country and had earned total income in excess of the reported amounts noted below:

COUNT	TAX YEAR	APPROX. FILING DATE	FOREIGN ACCOUNT REPORTED (Sch. B, Line 7a)	TOTAL INCOME REPORTED (Line 22)
15	2010	July 26, 2011	None	$194,257
16	2011	October 11, 2012	None	$250,307
17	2012	October 15, 2013	None	$365,646

| 18 | 2013 | October 15, 2014 | None | $307,363 |
| 19 | 2014 | October 14, 2015 | None | $292,892 |

(26 U.S.C. § 7206(1); 18 U.S.C. §§ 2 and 3551 et seq.)

COUNT 20: Subscribing to False Amended United States Individual Income Tax Returns For 2013

53. Paragraphs 1 through 44 are incorporated here.

54.. On or about October 25, 2017, in the Eastern District of Virginia and elsewhere, defendant RICHARD W. GATES III willfully and knowingly did make and subscribe, and aid and abet and cause another to make and subscribe, a United States Individual Income Tax Return, Form 1040X, for the 2013 tax year, which return contained and was verified by the written declaration of defendant GATES that it was made under penalties of perjury, and which return defendant GATES did not believe to be true and correct as to every material matter, in that the return failed to report income, whereas GATES then and there well knew and believed that he had earned adjusted gross income in excess of the reported amount on Line 1C, to wit: $292,055.

(26 U.S.C. § 7206(1); 18 U.S.C. §§ 2 and 3551 et seq.)

COUNTS 21-23: Failure To File Reports Of Foreign Bank Financial Accounts For Years '11 - '13

55. Paragraphs 1 through 44 are incorporated here.

56. On On the filing due dates listed below, in the Eastern District of Virginia and elsewhere, defendant RICHARD W. GATES III unlawfully, willfully, and knowingly did fail to file with the Treasury an FBAR disclosing that he had a financial interest in, and signature authority over, a bank, securities, and other financial account in a foreign country, which had an aggregate value of more than $10,000 in a 12-month period, during the years listed below:

COUNT	YEAR	DUE DATE TO FILE FBAR
21	2011	June 29, 2012
22	2012	June 30, 2013
23	2013	June 30, 2014

(31 U.S.C. §§ 5314 and 5322(a); 18 U.S.C. §§ 2 and 3551 et seq.)

COUNT 24: Bank Fraud Conspiracy / Lender B / $3.4 million loan

57. Paragraphs 1 through 44 are incorporated here.

58. On or about and between December 2015 and March 2016, both dates being approximate and inclusive, in the Eastern District of Virginia and elsewhere, defendants PAUL J. MANAFORT, JR., and RICHARD W. GATES III did knowingly and intentionally conspire to execute a scheme and artifice to defraud one or more financial institutions, to wit: Lender B, the deposits of which were insured by the Federal Deposit Insurance Corporation, and to obtain moneys, funds, and credits owned by and under the custody and control of such financial institution by means of materially false and fraudulent pretenses, representations, and promises, contrary to Title 18, United States Code, Section 1344.

(18 U.S.C. §§ 1349 and 3551 et seq.)

COUNT 25: Bank Fraud / Lender B / $3.4 million loan

59. Paragraphs 1 through 44 are incorporated here.

60. On or about and between December 2015 and March 2016, both dates being approximate and inclusive, in the Eastern District of Virginia and elsewhere, defendants PAUL J. MANAFORT, JR., and RICHARD W. GATES III did knowingly and intentionally execute and attempt to execute a scheme and artifice to defraud one or more financial institutions, to wit: Lender B, the deposits of which were insured by the Federal Deposit Insurance Corporation, and to obtain moneys, funds, and credits owned by and under the custody and control of such financial institution by means of materially false and fraudulent pretenses, representations, and promises.

(18 U.S.C. §§ 1344, 2, and 3551 et seq.)

COUNT 26: Bank Fraud Conspiracy / Lender C / $1 million loan

61. Paragraphs 1 through 44 are incorporated here.

62. On or about and between March 2016 and May 2016, both dates being approximate and inclusive, in the Eastern District of Virginia and elsewhere, defendants PAUL J. MANAFORT, JR., and RICHARD W. GATES III did knowingly and intentionally conspire to execute a scheme and artifice to defraud one or more financial institutions, to wit: Lender C, the deposits of which were insured by the Federal Deposit Insurance Corporation, and to obtain moneys, funds, and credits owned by and under the custody and control of such financial institution by means of materially false and fraudulent pretenses, representations, and promises, contrary to Title 18, United States Code, Section 1344.

(18 U.S.C. §§ 1349 and 3551 et seq.)

COUNT 27:Bank Fraud / Lender C / $1 million loan

63.   Paragraphs 1 through 44 are incorporated here.

64.   On or about and between December 2015 and March 2016, both dates being approximate and inclusive, in the Eastern District of Virginia and elsewhere, defendants PAUL J. MANAFORT, JR., and RICHARD W. GATES III did knowingly and intentionally execute and attempt to execute a scheme and artifice to defraud one or more financial institutions, to wit: Lender C, the deposits of which were insured by the Federal Deposit Insurance Corporation, and to obtain moneys, funds, and credits owned by and under the custody and control of such financial institution by means of materially false and fraudulent pretenses, representations, and promises.

(18 U.S.C. §§ 1344, 2, and 3551 et seq.)

COUNT 28: Bank Fraud Conspiracy / Lender B / $5.5 million loan

65.   Paragraphs 1 through 44 are incorporated here.

66.   On or about and between March 2016 and August 2016, both dates being approximate and inclusive, in the Eastern District of Virginia and elsewhere, defendants PAUL J. MANAFORT, JR., and RICHARD W. GATES III did knowingly and intentionally conspire to execute a scheme and artifice to defraud one or more financial institutions, to wit: Lender B, the deposits of which were insured by the Federal Deposit Insurance Corporation, and to obtain moneys, funds, and credits owned by and under the custody and control of such financial institution by means of materially false and fraudulent pretenses, representations, and promises, contrary to Title 18, United States Code, Section 1344.

(18 U.S.C. §§ 1349 and 3551 et seq.)

COUNT 29: Bank Fraud Conspiracy / Lender D / $9.5 million loan

67.   Paragraphs 1 through 44 are incorporated here.

68.   On or about and between April 2016 and November 2016, both dates being approximate and inclusive, in the Eastern District of Virginia and elsewhere, defendants PAUL J. MANAFORT, JR., and RICHARD W. GATES III did knowingly and intentionally conspire to execute a scheme and artifice to defraud one or more financial institutions, to wit: Lender D, the deposits of which were insured by the Federal Deposit Insurance Corporation, and to obtain moneys, funds, and credits owned by and under the custody and control of such financial institution by means of materially false and fraudulent pretenses, representations, and promises, contrary to Title 18, United States Code, Section 1344.

(18 U.S.C. §§ 1349 and 3551 et seq.)

COUNT 30: Bank Fraud / Lender D / $9.5 million loan

69. Paragraphs 1 through 44 are incorporated here.

70. On or about and between April 2016 and November 2016, both dates being approximate and inclusive, in the Eastern District of Virginia and elsewhere, defendants PAUL J. MANAFORT, JR., and RICHARD W. GATES III did knowingly and intentionally execute and attempt to execute a scheme and artifice to defraud one or more financial institutions, to wit: Lender D, the deposits of which were insured by the Federal Deposit Insurance Corporation, and to obtain moneys, funds, and credits owned by and under the custody and control of such financial institution by means of materially false and fraudulent pretenses, representations, and promises.

(18 U.S.C. § 1344, 2, and 3551 et seq.)

COUNT 31: Bank Fraud / Lender D / $6.5 million loan

71. Paragraphs 1 through 44 are incorporated here.

72. On or about and between April 2016 and January 2017, both dates being approximate and inclusive, in the Eastern District of Virginia and elsewhere, defendants PAUL J. MANAFORT, JR., and RICHARD W. GATES III did knowingly and intentionally conspire to execute a scheme and artifice to defraud one or more financial institutions, to wit: Lender D, the deposits of which were insured by the Federal Deposit Insurance Corporation, and to obtain moneys, funds, and credits owned by and under the custody and control of such financial institution by means of materially false and fraudulent pretenses, representations, and promises, contrary to Title 18, United States Code, Section 1344.

(18 U.S.C. §§ 1349 and 3551 et seq.)

COUNT 32: Bank Fraud / Lender D / $6.5 million loan

73. Paragraphs 1 through 44 are incorporated here.

74. On or about and between April 2016 and January 2017, both dates being approximate and inclusive, in the Eastern District of Virginia and elsewhere, defendants PAUL J. MANAFORT, JR., and RICHARD W. GATES III did knowingly and intentionally execute and attempt to execute a scheme and artifice to defraud one or more financial institutions, to wit: Lender D, the deposits of which were insured by the Federal Deposit Insurance Corporation, and to obtain moneys, funds, and credits owned by and under the custody and control of such financial institution by means of materially false and fraudulent pretenses, representations, and promises.

(18 U.S.C. §§ 1344, 2, and 3551 et seq.)

FORFEITURE NOTICE

75. Pursuant to Fed. R. Crim. P. 32.2, notice is hereby given to the defendants that the United States will seek forfeiture as part of any sentence in accordance with Title 18, United States Code, Section 982(a)(2), in the event of the defendants' convictions under Counts Twenty-Four through Thirty-Two of this Superseding Indictment. Upon conviction of the offenses charged in Counts Twenty-Four through Thirty-Two, defendants PAUL J. MANAFORT, JR., and RICHARD W. GATES III shall forfeit to the United States any property constituting, or derived from, proceeds obtained, directly or indirectly, as a result of such violation(s). Notice is further given that, upon conviction, the United States intends to seek a judgment against each defendant for a sum of money representing the property described in this paragraph, as applicable to each defendant (to be offset by the forfeiture of any specific property).

76. The grand jury finds probable cause to believe that the property subject to forfeiture by PAUL J. MANAFORT, JR., includes, but is not limited to, the following listed assets:

   a. All funds held in account number XXXXXX0969 at Lender D, and any property traceable thereto.

Substitute Assets

77. If any of the property described above as being subject to forfeiture, as a result of any act or omission of any defendant:

   a. cannot be located upon the exercise of due diligence;
   b. has been transferred or sold to, or deposited with, a third party;
   c. has been placed beyond the jurisdiction of the court;
   d. has been substantially diminished in value; or
   e. has been commingled with other property that cannot be subdivided without difficulty;

...it is the intent of the United States of America, pursuant to Title 18, United States Code, Section 982(b) and Title 28, United States Code, Section 2461(c), incorporating Title 21, United States Code, Section 853, to seek forfeiture of any other property of said defendant.

(18 U.S.C. § 982)

Signed: Robert S. Mueller, III
Special Counsel

CHAPTER 8: MICHAEL COHEN, AUGUST 21, 2018

UNITED STATES v. MICHAEL COHEN

PLEA AGREEMENTS FILED: August 21, 2018 in the U.S. District Court for the Southern District of New York & November 29, 2018 in the U.S. District Court for the District of Columbia

Editor's note: Michael Cohen was Trump's longtime personal attorney and was named deputy finance chair of the Republican National Committee.

Statement of the Offense

The Special Counsel charges:

Background

I.   *The Defendant*

1.   From in or around 2007 through in or around January 2017, MICHAEL COHEN, the defendant, was an attorney and employee of a Manhattan-based real estate company (the "Company").COHEN held the title of "Executive Vice President" and "Special Counsel" to the owner of the Company ("Individual 1").

II.   *False Statements to the U.S. Congress*

2.   On or about January 13, 2017, the U.S. Senate Select Committee on Intelligence ("SSCI") announced that it would conduct an investigation into Russian election interference and possible links between Russia and individuals associated with political campaigns. On or about January 25, 2017, the House of Representatives Permanent Select Committee on Intelligence ("HPSCI") announced that it also was conducting an investigation into Russian election interference and possible links between Russia and individuals associated with political campaigns.

3.   On or about August 28, 2017, COHEN caused a two-page letter to be sent on his behalf to SSCI and HPSCI. The letter addressed his efforts at the Company to pursue a branded property in Moscow, Russia (the "Moscow Project"). COHEN stated the purpose of the letter was "to provide the Committee with additional information regarding the proposal," referring to the Moscow Project .

4.   In the letter to SSCI and HPSCI, COHEN knowingly and deliberately

made the following false representations

    a.   The Moscow Project ended in January 2016 and was not discussed extensively with others in the Company. "The proposal was under consideration at the [Company] from September 2015 until the end of January 2016. By the end of January 2016, I determined that the proposal was not feasible for a variety of business reasons and should not be pursued further. Based on my business determinations , the [Company] abandoned the [Moscow Project] proposal. To the best of my knowledge, [Individual 1] was never in contact with anyone about this proposal other than me on three occasions. I did not ask or brief [Individual 1], or any of his family, before I made the decision to terminate further work on the proposal."

b.   COHEN never agreed to travel to Russia in connection with the Moscow Project and "never considered" asking Individual 1 to travel for the project. "I primarily development communicated with the Moscow-based company through a U.S. citizen third-party intermediary, [Individual 2]. [Individual 2] constantly asked me to travel to Moscow as part of his efforts to push forward the discussion of the proposal. I ultimately determined that the proposal was not feasible and never agreed to make a trip to Russia. Despite overtures by [Individual 2], I never considered asking [Individual 1] to travel to Russia in connection with this proposal."

c.   COHEN did not recall any Russian government response or contact about the Moscow Project. "In mid-January 2016, [Individual 2] suggested that I send an email to [Russian Official 1], the Press Secretary for the President of Russia, since the proposal would require approvals within the Russian government that had not been issued. Those permissions were never provided. I decided to abandon the proposal less than two weeks ;ater for business reasons and do not recall any response to my email, nor any other contacts by me with [Russian Official 1] or other Russian government officials about the proposal."

5.   On or about September 19, 2017, COHEN was scheduled to appear before SSCI accompanied by counsel. In prepared remarks released to the public, COHEN stated, "I assume we will discuss the rejected proposal to build a (Company-branded] property in Moscow that was terminated in January of 2016; which occurred before the Iowa caucus and months before the very first primary. This was solely a real estate deal and nothing more. I was doing my job. I would ask that the two-page statement about the Moscow proposal that I sent to the Committee in August be incorporated into and attached to this transcript."

6.   On or about October 25, 2017, COHEN gave testimony to SSCI, which included testimony about the Moscow Project consistent with his prepared remarks and his two-page statement.

7.   In truth and in fact, and as COHEN well knew, COHEN's representations about the Moscow Project he made to SSCI and HPSCI were false and misleading. COHEN made the false statements to (1) minimize links between the Moscow Project and Individual 1 and (2) give the false impression that the Moscow Project ended before "the Iowa caucus and . the very first primary," in hopes of limiting the ongoing Russia investigations. COHEN attempted to conceal or minimize through his false statements the following facts:

a . The Moscow Project was discussed multiple times within the Company and did not end in January 2016. Instead, as late as approximately June 2016, COHEN and Individual 2 discussed efforts to obtain Russian governmental approval for the Moscow Project. COHEN discussed the status and progress of the Moscow Project with Indivictual 1 on more than the three occasions COHEN claimed to the Committee, and he briefed family members of Individual 1 within the Company about the project.

    b.   COHEN agreed to travel to Russia in connection with the Moscow Project and took steps in contemplation of Individual 1's possible travel to Russia. COHEN and Individual 2 discussed on multiple occasions traveling to Russia to pursue the Moscow Project.

    i.   COHEN asked Individual 1 about the possibility of Individual 1 traveling to Russia in connection with the Moscow Project, and asked a senior campaign official about potential business travel to Russia.

    ii.   On or about May 4, 2016, Individual 2 wrote to COHEN, "I had a chat with Moscow. ASSUMING the trip does happen the question is before or after the convention . Obviously the pre-meeting trip (you only) can happen anytime you want but the 2 big guys where [sic] the question. I said I would confirm and revert." COHEN responded, "My trip before Cleveland. [Individual 1] once he becomes the nominee after the convention."

    iii.   On or about May 5, 2016, Individual 2 followed up with COHEN and wrote, "[Russian Official 1] would like to invite you as his guest to the St. Petersburg Forum which is Russia's Davos it's June 16-19. He wants to meet there with you and possibly introduce you to either [the President of Russia] or [the Prime Minister of Russia], as they are not sure if 1 or both will be there. He said anything you want to discuss including dates and subjects are on the table to discuss."

    iv.   On or about May 6, 2016, Individual 2 asked COHEN to confirm those dates would work for him to travel. COHEN wrote back, "Works for me."

    v.   From on or about June 9 to June 14, 2016, Indivictual 2 sent numerous messages to COHEN about the travel, including forms for COHEN to complete. However, on or about June 14, 2016, COHEN met Indivictual 2 in the lobby of the Company's headquarters to inform Individual 2 he would not be traveling at that time.

    b.   COHEN did recall that in or around January 2016, COHEN received a response from the office of Russian Official 1, the Press Secretary for the President of Russia, and spoke to a member of that office about the Moscow Project.

    i.   On or about January 14, 2016, COHEN emailed Russian Official 1's office asking for assistance in connection with the Moscow

Project. On or about January 16, 2016, COHEN emailed Russian Official 1's office again, said he was trying to reach another high-level Russian official, and asked for someone who spoke English to contact him.

        ii.   On or about January 20, 2016, COHEN received an email from the personal assistant to Russian Official 1 ("Assistant 1"), stating that she had been trying to reach COHEN and requesting that he call her using a Moscow-based phone number she provided.

        iii.   Shortly after receiving the email, COHEN called Assistant 1 and spoke to her for approximately 20 minutes. On that call, COHEN described his position at the Company and outlined the proposed Moscow Project, including the Russian development company with which the Company had partnered. COHEN requested assistance in moving the project forward, both in securing land to build the proposed tower and financing the construction. Assistant 1 asked detailed questions and took notes, stating that she would follow up with others in Russia.

        iv.   The day after COHEN's call with Assistant 1, Individual 2 contacted him, asking for a call. Individual 2 wrote to COHEN, "It's about [the President of Russia] they called today."

Plea Information

COUNT 1: Making False Statements (Lying Under Oath to Congress) (18 U.S.C. § 1001)

      8.   Paragraphs 1 through 7 of this Information are re- alleged and incorporated by reference as if fully set forth herein.

      9.   On or about August 28, 2017, the defendant MICHAEL COHEN, in the District of Columbia and elsewhere, in a matter within the jurisdiction of the legislative branch of the Government of the United States, knowingly and willfully made a materially false, fictitious, and fraudulent statement and representation, to wit, COHEN caused to be submitted a written statement to SSCI containing material false statements about the Moscow Project, including false statements about the timing of the Moscow Project, discussions with people in the Company and in Russia about the Moscow Project, and contemplated travel to Russia in connection with the Moscow Project.

    (Title 18, United States Code, Section 1001(a)(2).)

SENTENCE: Three months in prison to be served concurrently with the three years in prison that COHEN received in August 2018 after pleading guilty in a New York federal court to eight counts including bank fraud, tax evasion and campaign finance violations in another case stemming from President Trump's 2016 campaign (but unrelated to the Special Counsel's inquiry into Russian election interference) as well as COHEN's personal business dealings. The New York case was referred to investigators there by the special counsel's office.

Signed: Robert S. Mueller, III

Special Counsel

Prepared By: Jeannie S. Rhee, Andrew D. Goldstein & L. Rush Atkinson

Senior/Assistant Special Counsels

CHAPTER 9: MANAFORT & KILIMNIK, JUNE 8, 2018

UNITED STATES v. PAUL J. MANAFORT, JR. & KONSTANTIN KILIMNIK

FILED: June 8, 2018 in the United States District Court for the District of Columbia

Editor's Note: This indictment added further detail to what we already knew about Paul Manafort's manifold misdeeds and brings to our attention another one of his co-conspirators, Konstantin Kilimnik. It also begins to show the lengths to which Manafort went in an attempt to stymie federal investigators and keep secret his many trespasses against the government of the United States.

Superseding Indictment

The Grand Jury for the District of Columbia charges:

I.   Introduction

At all times relevant to this Superseding Indictment:

1.   Defendant PAUL J. MANAFORT, JR. (MANAFORT) served for years as a political consultant and lobbyist. Between at least 2006 and 2015, MANAFORT, through companies he ran, acted as an unregistered agent of a foreign government and foreign political parties. Specifically, he represented the Government of Ukraine, the President of Ukraine (Viktor Yanukovych, who was President from 2010 to 2014), the Party of Regions (a Ukrainian political party led by Yanukovych), and the Opposition Bloc (a successor to the Party of Regions after Yanukovych fled to Russia in 2014).

2.   MANAFORT generated tens of millions of dollars in income as a result of his Ukraine work. From approximately 2006 through 2017, MANAFORT, along with others including Richard W. Gates III (Gates), engaged in a scheme to hide the Ukraine income from United States authorities, while enjoying the use of the money. From approximately 2006 to 2015, when MANAFORT was generating tens of millions of dollars in income from his Ukraine activities, MANAFORT, with the assistance of Gates, avoided paying taxes by disguising tens of millions of dollars

in income as alleged "loans" from nominee offshore corporate entities and by making millions of dollars in unreported payments from foreign accounts to bank accounts they controlled and United States vendors. MANAFORT also used the offshore accounts to purchase real estate in the United States, and MANAFORT used the undisclosed income to make improvements to and refinance his United States properties.

3.   In furtherance of the scheme, MANAFORT, with the assistance of Gates, funneled millions of dollars in payments into numerous foreign nominee companies and bank accounts, opened by them and their accomplices in nominee names and in various foreign countries, including Cyprus, Saint Vincent & the Grenadines (Grenadines), and the Seychelles. MANAFORT concealed the existence and ownership of the foreign companies and bank accounts, falsely and repeatedly reporting to his tax preparers and to the United States that he had no foreign bank accounts.

4.   In furtherance of the scheme, MANAFORT, with the assistance of Gates, concealed from the United States his work as an agent of, and millions of dollars in payments from, Ukraine and its political parties and leaders. Because MANAFORT, among other things, participated in a campaign to lobby United States officials on behalf of the Government of Ukraine, the President of Ukraine, and the Party of Regions, he was required by law to report to the United States his work and fees. MANAFORT did not do so. Instead, when the Department of Justice sent inquiries to MANAFORT and Gates in 2016 about their activities, MANAFORT and Gates responded with a series of false and misleading statements.

5.   In furtherance of the scheme, MANAFORT used his hidden overseas wealth to enjoy a lavish lifestyle in the United States, without paying taxes on that income. MANAFORT, without reporting the income to his tax preparer or the United States, spent millions of dollars on luxury goods and services for himself and his extended family through payments wired from offshore nominee accounts to United States vendors. MANAFORT also used these offshore accounts to purchase multi-million dollar properties in the United States and to improve substantially another property owned by his family.

6.   In total, more than $75,000,000 flowed through these offshore accounts. MANAFORT, with the assistance of Gates, laundered more than $30,000,000, income that he concealed from the United States Department of the Treasury (Treasury), the Department of Justice, and others.

II.   *Relevant Individuals And Entities*

7.   MANAFORT was a United States citizen. He resided in homes in Virginia, Florida, and Long Island, New York.

8.   In 2005, MANAFORT and another partner created Davis Manafort Partners, Inc. (DMP) to engage principally in political consulting. DMP had staff in the United States, Ukraine, and Russia. In 2011, MANAFORT created DMP International, LLC (DMI) to engage in work for foreign clients, in particular political consulting, lobbying, and public relations for the Government of Ukraine, the Party of Regions, and members of the Party of Regions. DMI was a partnership solely owned by MANAFORT and his spouse. Gates worked for both DMP and DMI and served as MANAFORT's right-hand man. Defendant KONSTANTIN KILIMNIK (KILIMNIK) worked for DMI and oversaw its Kiev office.

9.   The Party of Regions was a pro-Russia political party in Ukraine. Beginning in approximately 2006, it retained MANAFORT, through DMP and then DMI, to advance its interests in Ukraine, the United States, and elsewhere, including the election of its Ukrainian slate of candidates. In 2010, its candidate for President, Yanukovych, was elected President of Ukraine. In 2014, Yanukovych fled Ukraine for Russia in the wake of popular protests of widespread government corruption. Yanukovych, the Party of Regions, and the Government of Ukraine were MANAFORT, DMP, and DMI clients.

10.   The European Centre for a Modern Ukraine (the Centre) was created in or about 2012 in Belgium as a mouthpiece for Yanukovych and the Party of Regions. It reported to the Ukraine First Vice Prime Minister. The Centre was used by MANAFORT, Gates, and others in order to lobby and conduct a public relations campaign in the United States and Europe on behalf of the existing Ukraine regime. The Centre effectively ceased to operate upon the downfall of Yanukovych in 2014.

11.   MANAFORT, with the assistance of Gates, owned or controlled the following entities, which were used in the scheme (the MANAFORT entities):

Domestic Entities

Entity Name	Date Created	Incorporation Location
Daisy Manafort, LLC (PM)	August 2008	Virginia
	March 2011	Florida
Davis Manafort International LLC (PM)	March 2007	Delaware
DMP (PM)	March 2005	Virginia
	March 2011	Florida
Davis Manafort, Inc. (PM)	October 1999	Delaware
	November 1999	Virginia
DMI (PM)	June 2011	Delaware
	March 2012	Florida
Global Sites LLC (PM, RG)	July 2008	Delaware

Entity Name	Date Created	Incorporation Location
Jesand Investment Corporation (PM)	April 2002	Virginia
Jesand Investments Corporation (PM)	March 2011	Florida
John Hannah, LLC (PM)	April 2006	Virginia
	March 2011	Florida
Lilred, LLC (PM)	December 2011	Florida

LOAV Ltd. (PM)	April 1992	Delaware
MC Brooklyn Holdings, LLC (PM)	November 2012	New York
MC Soho Holdings, LLC (PM)	January 2012	Florida
	April 2012	New York
Smythson LLC (also known as Symthson LLC) (PM, RG)	July 2008	Delaware

Cypriot Entities

Entity Name	Date Created	Incorporation Location
Actinet Trading Limited (PM, RG)	May 2009	Cyprus
Black Sea View Limited (PM, RG)	August 2007	Cyprus
Bletilla Ventures Limited (PM, RG)	October 2010	Cyprus
Global Highway Limited (PM, RG)	August 2007	Cyprus
Leviathan Advisors Limited (PM, RG)	August 2007	Cyprus
LOAV Advisors Limited (PM, RG)	August 2007	Cyprus
Lucicle Consultants Limited (PM, RG)	December 2008	Cyprus
Marziola Holdings Limited (PM)	March 2012	Cyprus
Olivenia Trading Limited (PM, RG)	March 2012	Cyprus

Entity Name	Date Created	Incorporation Location
Peranova Holdings Limited (Peranova) (PM, RG)	June 2007	Cyprus
Serangon Holdings Limited (PM, RG)	January 2008	Cyprus
Yiakora Ventures Limited (PM)	February 2008	Cyprus

Other Foreign Entities

Entity Name	Date Created	Incorporation Location
Global Endeavour Inc. (also known as Global Endeavor Inc.) (PM)	Unknown	Grenadines
Jeunet Ltd. (PM)	August 2011	Grenadines
Pompolo Limited (PM, RG)	April 2013	United Kingdom

12. The Internal Revenue Service (IRS) was a bureau in the Treasury responsible for administering the tax laws of the United States and collecting taxes owed to the Treasury.

III. *The Scheme*

13. Between in or around 2006 and 2017, both dates being approximate and inclusive, in the District of Columbia and elsewhere, MANAFORT and others devised and intended to devise, and executed and attempted to execute, a scheme and artifice to defraud, and to obtain money and property by means of false and fraudulent pretenses, representations, and promises from the United States and others. As part of the scheme, MANAFORT repeatedly provided and caused to be provided false information to financial bookkeepers, tax accountants, and legal counsel, among others.

MANAFORT's Wiring Money From Offshore Accounts Into The United States

14.   In order to use the money in the offshore nominee accounts of the MANAFORT entities without paying taxes on it, MANAFORT caused millions of dollars in wire transfers from these accounts to be made for goods, services, and real estate. He did not report these transfers as income.

15.   From 2008 to 2014, MANAFORT caused the following wires, totaling over $12,000,000, to be sent to the vendors listed below for personal items. MANAFORT did not pay taxes on this income, which was used to make the purchases.

Payee	Transaction Date	Originating Account Holder	Country of Origination	Amount of Transaction
Vendor A (Home Improvement Company in the Hamptons, New York)	6/10/2008	LOAV Advisors Limited	Cyprus	$107,000
	6/25/2008	LOAV Advisors Limited	Cyprus	$23,500
	7/7/2008	LOAV Advisors Limited	Cyprus	$20,000
	8/5/2008	Yiakora Ventures Limited	Cyprus	$59,000
	9/2/2008	Yiakora Ventures Limited	Cyprus	$272,000
	10/6/2008	Yiakora Ventures Limited	Cyprus	$109,000
	10/24/2008	Yiakora Ventures Limited	Cyprus	$107,800
	11/20/2008	Yiakora Ventures Limited	Cyprus	$77,400
	12/22/2008	Yiakora Ventures Limited	Cyprus	$100,000
	1/14/2009	Yiakora Ventures Limited	Cyprus	$9,250
	1/29/2009	Yiakora Ventures Limited	Cyprus	$97,670
	2/25/2009	Yiakora Ventures Limited	Cyprus	$108,100

4/16/2009	Yiakora Ventures Limited	Cyprus	$94,394	
5/7/2009	Yiakora Ventures Limited	Cyprus	$54,000	
5/12/2009	Yiakora Ventures Limited	Cyprus	$9,550	
6/1/2009	Yiakora Ventures Limited	Cyprus	$86,650	
6/18/2009	Yiakora Ventures Limited	Cyprus	$34,400	
7/31/2009	Yiakora Ventures Limited	Cyprus	$106,000	
8/28/2009	Yiakora Ventures Limited	Cyprus	$37,000	
9/23/2009	Yiakora Ventures Limited	Cyprus	$203,500	
10/26/2009	Yiakora Ventures Limited	Cyprus	$38,800	
11/18/2009	Global Highway Limited	Cyprus	$130,906	
3/8/2010	Global Highway Limited	Cyprus	$124,000	

Payee	Transaction Date	Originating Account Holder	Country of Origination	Amount of Transaction
	5/11/2010	Global Highway Limited	Cyprus	$25,000
	7/8/2010	Global Highway Limited	Cyprus	$28,000
	7/23/2010	Leviathan Advisors Limited	Cyprus	$26,500
	8/12/2010	Leviathan Advisors Limited	Cyprus	$138,900
	9/2/2010	Yiakora Ventures Limited	Cyprus	$31,500

	10/6/2010	Global Highway Limited	Cyprus	$67,600
	10/14/2010	Yiakora Ventures Limited	Cyprus	$107,600
	10/18/2010	Leviathan Advisors Limited	Cyprus	$31,500
	12/16/2010	Global Highway Limited	Cyprus	$46,160
	2/7/2011	Global Highway Limited	Cyprus	$36,500
	3/22/2011	Leviathan Advisors Limited	Cyprus	$26,800
	4/4/2011	Leviathan Advisors Limited	Cyprus	$195,000
	5/3/2011	Global Highway Limited	Cyprus	$95,000
	5/16/2011	Leviathan Advisors Limited	Cyprus	$6,500
	5/31/2011	Leviathan Advisors Limited	Cyprus	$70,000
	6/27/2011	Leviathan Advisors Limited	Cyprus	$39,900
	7/27/2011	Leviathan Advisors Limited	Cyprus	$95,000
	10/24/2011	Global Highway Limited	Cyprus	$22,000
	10/25/2011	Global Highway Limited	Cyprus	$9,300
	11/15/2011	Global Highway Limited	Cyprus	$74,000
	11/23/2011	Global Highway Limited	Cyprus	$22,300
	11/29/2011	Global Highway Limited	Cyprus	$6,100
	12/12/2011	Leviathan Advisors Limited	Cyprus	$17,800
	1/17/2012	Global Highway Limited	Cyprus	$29,800

	Transaction Date	Originating Account Holder	Country of Origination	Amount of Transaction
	1/20/2012	Global Highway Limited	Cyprus	$42,600
	2/9/2012	Global Highway Limited	Cyprus	$22,300
	2/23/2012	Global Highway Limited	Cyprus	$75,000
	2/28/2012	Global Highway Limited	Cyprus	$22,300
	3/28/2012	Peranova	Cyprus	$37,500
	4/18/2012	Lucicle Consultants Limited	Cyprus	$50,000
	5/15/2012	Lucicle Consultants Limited	Cyprus	$79,000
	6/5/2012	Lucicle Consultants Limited	Cyprus	$45,000
	6/19/2012	Lucicle Consultants Limited	Cyprus	$11,860
	7/9/2012	Lucicle Consultants Limited	Cyprus	$10,800
	7/18/2012	Lucicle Consultants Limited	Cyprus	$88,000
	8/7/2012	Lucicle Consultants Limited	Cyprus	$48,800
	9/27/2012	Lucicle Consultants Limited	Cyprus	$100,000
	11/20/2012	Lucicle Consultants Limited	Cyprus	$298,000

Payee	Transaction Date	Originating Account Holder	Country of Origination	Amount of Transaction
	12/20/2012	Lucicle Consultants Limited	Cyprus	$55,000
	1/29/2013	Lucicle Consultants Limited	Cyprus	$149,000

	3/12/2013	Lucicle Consultants Limited	Cyprus	$375,000
	8/29/2013	Global Endeavour Inc.	Grenadines	$200,000
	11/13/2013	Global Endeavour Inc.	Grenadines	$75,000
	11/26/2013	Global Endeavour Inc.	Grenadines	$80,000
	12/6/2013	Global Endeavour Inc.	Grenadines	$130,000
	12/12/2013	Global Endeavour Inc.	Grenadines	$90,000
	4/22/2014	Global Endeavour Inc.	Grenadines	$56,293
	8/18/2014	Global Endeavour Inc.	Grenadines	$34,660
Vendor A Total				$5,434,793
Vendor B (Home Automation, Lighting, and Home Entertainment Company in Florida)	3/22/2011	Leviathan Advisors Limited	Cyprus	$12,000
	3/28/2011	Leviathan Advisors Limited	Cyprus	$25,000
	4/27/2011	Leviathan Advisors Limited	Cyprus	$12,000
	5/16/2011	Leviathan Advisors Limited	Cyprus	$25,000
	11/15/2011	Global Highway Limited	Cyprus	$17,006
	11/23/2011	Global Highway Limited	Cyprus	$11,000
	2/28/2012	Global Highway Limited	Cyprus	$6,200
	10/31/2012	Lucicle Consultants Limited	Cyprus	$290,000
	12/17/2012	Lucicle Consultants Limited	Cyprus	$160,600
	1/15/2013	Lucicle Consultants Limited	Cyprus	$194,000

	1/24/2013	Lucicle Consultants Limited	Cyprus	$6,300
	2/12/2013	Lucicle Consultants Limited	Cyprus	$51,600
	2/26/2013	Lucicle Consultants Limited	Cyprus	$260,000
	7/15/2013	Pompolo Limited	United Kingdom	$175,575
	11/5/2013	Global Endeavour Inc.	Grenadines	$73,000
Vendor B Total				$1,319,281
Vendor C (Antique Rug Store in Alexandria, Virginia)	10/7/2008	Yiakora Ventures Limited	Cyprus	$15,750
	3/17/2009	Yiakora Ventures Limited	Cyprus	$46,200
	4/16/2009	Yiakora Ventures Limited	Cyprus	$7,400
	4/27/2009	Yiakora Ventures Limited	Cyprus	$65,000
	5/7/2009	Yiakora Ventures Limited	Cyprus	$210,000
	7/15/2009	Yiakora Ventures Limited	Cyprus	$200,000
	3/31/2010	Yiakora Ventures Limited	Cyprus	$140,000
	6/16/2010	Global Highway Limited	Cyprus	$250,000
Vendor C Total				$934,350

Payee	Transaction Date	Originating Account Holder	Country of Origination	Amount of Transaction
Vendor D (Related to Vendor C)	2/28/2012	Global Highway Limited	Cyprus	$100,000
Vendor D Total				$100,000
Vendor E (Men's Clothing Store in New York)	11/7/2008	Yiakora Ventures Limited	Cyprus	$32,000
	2/5/2009	Yiakora Ventures Limited	Cyprus	$22,750
	4/27/2009	Yiakora Ventures Limited	Cyprus	$13,500
	10/26/2009	Yiakora Ventures Limited	Cyprus	$32,500
	3/30/2010	Yiakora Ventures Limited	Cyprus	$15,000
	5/11/2010	Global Highway Limited	Cyprus	$39,000
	6/28/2010	Leviathan Advisors Limited	Cyprus	$5,000
	8/12/2010	Leviathan Advisors Limited	Cyprus	$32,500
	11/17/2010	Global Highway Limited	Cyprus	$11,500
	2/7/2011	Global Highway Limited	Cyprus	$24,000
	3/22/2011	Leviathan Advisors Limited	Cyprus	$43,600
	3/28/2011	Leviathan Advisors Limited	Cyprus	$12,000
	4/27/2011	Leviathan Advisors Limited	Cyprus	$3,000
	6/30/2011	Global Highway Limited	Cyprus	$24,500

9/26/2011	Leviathan Advisors Limited	Cyprus	$12,000
11/2/2011	Global Highway Limited	Cyprus	$26,700
12/12/2011	Leviathan Advisors Limited	Cyprus	$46,000
2/9/2012	Global Highway Limited	Cyprus	$2,800
2/28/2012	Global Highway Limited	Cyprus	$16,000
3/14/2012	Lucicle Consultants Limited	Cyprus	$8,000
4/18/2012	Lucicle Consultants Limited	Cyprus	$48,550
5/15/2012	Lucicle Consultants Limited	Cyprus	$7,000
6/19/2012	Lucicle Consultants Limited	Cyprus	$21,600
8/7/2012	Lucicle Consultants Limited	Cyprus	$15,500
11/20/2012	Lucicle Consultants Limited	Cyprus	$10,900
12/20/2012	Lucicle Consultants Limited	Cyprus	$7,500
1/15/2013	Lucicle Consultants Limited	Cyprus	$37,000
2/12/2013	Lucicle Consultants Limited	Cyprus	$7,000
2/26/2013	Lucicle Consultants Limited	Cyprus	$39,000
9/3/2013	Global Endeavour Inc.	Grenadines	$81,500
10/15/2013	Global Endeavour Inc.	Grenadines	$53,000
11/26/2013	Global Endeavour Inc.	Grenadines	$13,200
4/24/2014	Global Endeavour Inc.	Grenadines	$26,680

	9/11/2014	Global Endeavour Inc.	Grenadines	$58,435

Payee	Transaction Date	Originating Account Holder	Country of Origination	Amount of Transaction
Vendor E Total		$849,215		
Vendor F (Landscaper in the Hamptons, New York)	4/27/2009	Yiakora Ventures Limited	Cyprus	$34,000
	5/12/2009	Yiakora Ventures Limited	Cyprus	$45,700
	6/1/2009	Yiakora Ventures Limited	Cyprus	$21,500
	6/18/2009	Yiakora Ventures Limited	Cyprus	$29,000
	9/21/2009	Yiakora Ventures Limited	Cyprus	$21,800
	5/11/2010	Global Highway Limited	Cyprus	$44,000
	6/28/2010	Leviathan Advisors Limited	Cyprus	$50,000
	7/23/2010	Leviathan Advisors Limited	Cyprus	$19,000
	9/2/2010	Yiakora Ventures Limited	Cyprus	$21,000
	10/6/2010	Global Highway Limited	Cyprus	$57,700
	10/18/2010	Leviathan Advisors Limited	Cyprus	$26,000
	12/16/2010	Global Highway Limited	Cyprus	$20,000
	3/22/2011	Leviathan Advisors Limited	Cyprus	$50,000
	5/3/2011	Global Highway Limited	Cyprus	$40,000
	6/1/2011	Leviathan Advisors Limited	Cyprus	$44,000

	7/27/20 11	Leviathan Advisors Limited	Cyprus	$27,000
	8/16/20 11	Leviathan Advisors Limited	Cyprus	$13,450
	9/19/20 11	Leviathan Advisors Limited	Cyprus	$12,000
	10/24/2 011	Global Highway Limited	Cyprus	$42,000
	11/2/201 1	Global Highway Limited	Cyprus	$37,350
Vendor F Total				$655,50 0
Vendor G (Antique Dealer in New York)	9/2/201 0	Yiakora Ventures Limited	Cyprus	$165,00 0
	10/18/2 010	Leviathan Advisors Limited	Cyprus	$165,00 0
	2/28/20 12	Global Highway Limited	Cyprus	$190,60 0
	3/14/201 2	Lucicle Consultants Limited	Cyprus	$75,000
	2/26/20 13	Lucicle Consultants Limited	Cyprus	$28,310
Vendor G Total				$623,91 0
Vendor H (Clothing Store in Beverly Hills, California)	6/25/20 08	LOAV Advisors Limited	Cyprus	$52,000
	12/16/2 008	Yiakora Ventures Limited	Cyprus	$49,00 0
	12/22/2 008	Yiakora Ventures Limited	Cyprus	$10,260
	8/12/20 09	Yiakora Ventures Limited	Cyprus	$76,400
	5/11/201 0	Global Highway Limited	Cyprus	$85,000
	11/17/20 10	Global Highway Limited	Cyprus	$128,28 0
	5/31/201 1	Leviathan Advisors Limited	Cyprus	$64,00 0

	11/15/2011	Global Highway Limited	Cyprus	$48,000
	12/17/2012	Lucicle Consultants Limited	Cyprus	$7,500
Vendor H Total				$520,440

Payee	Transaction Date	Originating Account Holder	Country of Origination	Amount of Transaction
Vendor I (Investment Company)	9/3/2013	Global Endeavour Inc.	Grenadines	$500,000
Vendor I Total				$500,000
Vendor J (Contractor in Florida)	11/15/2011	Global Highway Limited	Cyprus	$8,000
	12/5/2011	Leviathan Advisors Limited	Cyprus	$11,237
	12/21/2011	Black Sea View Limited	Cyprus	$20,000
	2/9/2012	Global Highway Limited	Cyprus	$51,000
	5/17/2012	Lucicle Consultants Limited	Cyprus	$68,000
	6/19/2012	Lucicle Consultants Limited	Cyprus	$60,000
	7/18/2012	Lucicle Consultants Limited	Cyprus	$32,250
	9/19/2012	Lucicle Consultants Limited	Cyprus	$112,000
	11/30/2012	Lucicle Consultants Limited	Cyprus	$39,700
	1/9/2013	Lucicle Consultants Limited	Cyprus	$25,600
	2/28/20	Lucicle Consultants	Cyprus	$4,700

	13	Limited		
		Vendor J Total		$432,48 7
Vendor K (Landscaper in the Hamptons, New York)	12/5/201 1	Leviathan Advisors Limited	Cyprus	$4,115
	3/1/2012	Global Highway Limited	Cyprus	$50,000
	6/6/201 2	Lucicle Consultants Limited	Cyprus	$47,800
	6/25/20 12	Lucicle Consultants Limited	Cyprus	$17,900
	6/27/20 12	Lucicle Consultants Limited	Cyprus	$18,900
	2/12/201 3	Lucicle Consultants Limited	Cyprus	$3,300
	7/15/201 3	Pompolo Limited	United Kingdom	$13,325
	11/26/2 013	Global Endeavour Inc.	Grenad ines	$9,400
		Vendor K Total		$164,74 0
Vendor L (Payments Relating to Three Range Rovers)	4/12/20 12	Lucicle Consultants Limited	Cyprus	$83,525
	5/2/201 2	Lucicle Consultants Limited	Cyprus	$12,525
	6/29/20 12	Lucicle Consultants Limited	Cyprus	$67,655
		Vendor L Total		$163,70 5
Vendor M (Contractor in Virginia)	11/20/2 012	Lucicle Consultants Limited	Cyprus	$45,000
	12/7/201 2	Lucicle Consultants Limited	Cyprus	$21,000
	12/17/20 12	Lucicle Consultants Limited	Cyprus	$21,000
	1/17/201 3	Lucicle Consultants Limited	Cyprus	$18,750

| | 1/29/20 13 | Lucicle Consultants Limited | Cyprus | $9,400 |
| | 2/12/201 3 | Lucicle Consultants Limited | Cyprus | $10,500 |

Payee	Transac tion Date	Originating Account Holder	Countr y of Origina tion	Amount of Transac tion
Vendor M Total				$125,65 0
Vendor N (Audio, Video, and Control System Home Integration and Installation Company in the Hamptons, New York)	1/29/20 09	Yiakora Ventures Limited	Cyprus	$10,000
	3/17/20 09	Yiakora Ventures Limited	Cyprus	$21,725
	4/16/20 09	Yiakora Ventures Limited	Cyprus	$24,650
	12/2/20 09	Global Highway Limited	Cyprus	$10,000
	3/8/201 0	Global Highway Limited	Cyprus	$20,300
	4/23/20 10	Yiakora Ventures Limited	Cyprus	$8,500
	7/29/20 10	Leviathan Advisors Limited	Cyprus	$17,650
Vendor N Total				$112,82 5
Vendor O (Purchase of Mercedes Benz)	10/5/20 12	Lucicle Consultants Limited	Cyprus	$62,750
Vendor O Total				$62,750
Vendor P (Purchase of Range Rover)	12/30/2 008	Yiakora Ventures Limited	Cyprus	$47,000

Vendor P Total				$47,000
Vendor Q (Property Management Company in South Carolina)	9/2/2010	Yiakora Ventures Limited	Cyprus	$10,000
	10/6/2010	Global Highway Limited	Cyprus	$10,000
	10/18/2010	Leviathan Advisors Limited	Cyprus	$10,000
	2/8/2011	Global Highway Limited	Cyprus	$13,500
	2/9/2012	Global Highway Limited	Cyprus	$2,500
Vendor Q Total				$46,000
Vendor R (Art Gallery in Florida)	2/9/2011	Global Highway Limited	Cyprus	$17,900
	2/14/2013	Lucicle Consultants Limited	Cyprus	$14,000
Vendor R Total				$31,900
Vendor S (Housekeeping in New York)	9/26/2011	Leviathan Advisors Limited	Cyprus	$5,000
	9/19/2012	Lucicle Consultants Limited	Cyprus	$5,000
	10/9/2013	Global Endeavour Inc.	Grenadines	$10,000
Vendor S Total				$20,000

16.   In 2012, MANAFORT caused the following wires to be sent to the entities listed below to purchase the real estate also listed below. MANAFORT did not report the money used to make these purchases on his 2012 tax return.

Property Purchased	Payee	Date	Originating Account	Country of Origination	Amount
Howard Street Condominium (New York)	DMP International LLC	2/1/2012	Peranova	Cyprus	$1,500,000

Union Street Brownstone, (New York)	Attorney Account Of [Real Estate Attorney]	11/29/2012	Actinet Trading Limited	Cyprus	$1,800,000
		11/29/2012	Actinet Trading Limited	Cyprus	$1,200,000
Arlington House (Virginia)	Real Estate Trust	8/31/2012	Lucicle Consultants Limited	Cyprus	$1,900,000
Total					$6,400,000

17.   MANAFORT also disguised, as purported "loans," more than $10 million from Cypriot entities, including the overseas MANAFORT entities, to domestic entities owned by MANAFORT. For example, a $1.5 million wire from Peranova to DMI that MANAFORT used to purchase real estate on Howard Street in Manhattan, New York, was recorded as a "loan" from Peranova to DMI, rather than as income. The following loans were shams designed to reduce fraudulently MANAFORT's reported taxable income.

Year	Payor / Ostensible "Lender"	Payee / Ostensible "Borrower"	Country of Origination	Total Amount of "Loans"
2008	Yiakora Ventures Limited	Jesand Investment Corporation	Cyprus	$8,120,000
2008	Yiakora Ventures Limited	DMP	Cyprus	$500,000
2009	Yiakora Ventures Limited	DMP	Cyprus	$694,000
2009	Yiakora Ventures Limited	Daisy Manafort, LLC	Cyprus	$500,000
2012	Peranova	DMI	Cyprus	$1,500,000

Year	Payor / Ostensible "Lender"	Payee / Ostensible "Borrower"	Country of Origination	Total Amount of "Loans"
2014	Telmar Investments Ltd.	DMI	Cyprus	$900,000
2015	Telmar Investments Ltd.	DMI	Cyprus	$1,000,000
Total				$13,214,000

18.   From 2010 to 2014, Gates caused the following wires, totaling more than $3,000,000, to be sent to entities and bank accounts of which he was a beneficial owner or he otherwise controlled.

Payee	Transaction Date	Originating Account Holder	Country of Origination	Amount of Transaction
Richard Gates United Kingdom Bank Account A	3/26/2010	Serangon Holdings Limited	Cyprus	$85,000
	4/20/2010	Serangon Holdings Limited	Cyprus	$50,000
	5/6/2010	Serangon Holdings Limited	Cyprus	$150,000
Richard Gates United Kingdom Bank Account B	9/7/2010	Serangon Holdings Limited	Cyprus	$160,000
	10/13/2010	Serangon Holdings Limited	Cyprus	$15,000
Richard Gates United States Bank Account C	9/27/2010	Global Highway Limited	Cyprus	$50,000
2010 Tax Year Total				$510,000
Jemina LLC United	9/9/2011	Peranova	Cyprus	$48,500

States Bank Account D				
Richard Gates United Kingdom Bank Account B	12/16/2011	Peranova	Cyprus	$100,435
2011 Tax Year Total				$148,935
Richard Gates United Kingdom Bank Account B	1/9/2012	Global Highway Limited	Cyprus	$100,000
	1/13/2012	Peranova	Cyprus	$100,435
	2/29/2012	Global Highway Limited	Cyprus	$28,500
	3/27/2012	Bletilla Ventures Limited	Cyprus	$18,745
	4/26/2012	Bletilla Ventures Limited	Cyprus	$26,455
	5/30/2012	Bletilla Ventures Limited	Cyprus	$15,000
	5/30/2012	Lucicle Consultants Limited	Cyprus	$14,650
	6/27/2012	Bletilla Ventures Limited	Cyprus	$18,745
	8/2/2012	Bletilla Ventures Limited	Cyprus	$28,745
	8/30/2012	Bletilla Ventures Limited	Cyprus	$38,745
	9/27/2012	Bletilla Ventures Limited	Cyprus	$32,345
	10/31/2012	Bletilla Ventures Limited	Cyprus	$46,332

Payee	Transaction Date	Originating Account Holder	Country of Origination	Amount of Transaction
	11/20/2012	Bletilla Ventures Limited	Cyprus	$48,547
	11/30/2012	Bletilla Ventures Limited	Cyprus	$38,532
	12/21/2012	Bletilla Ventures Limited	Cyprus	$47,836
	12/28/2012	Bletilla Ventures Limited	Cyprus	$47,836
2012 Tax Year Total				$651,448
Richard Gates United Kingdom Bank Account B	1/11/2013	Bletilla Ventures Limited	Cyprus	$47,836
	1/22/2013	Bletilla Ventures Limited	Cyprus	$34,783
	1/30/2013	Bletilla Ventures Limited	Cyprus	$46,583
	2/22/2013	Bletilla Ventures Limited	Cyprus	$46,233
	2/28/2013	Bletilla Ventures Limited	Cyprus	$46,583
	3/1/2013	Bletilla Ventures Limited	Cyprus	$42,433
	3/15/2013	Bletilla Ventures Limited	Cyprus	$37,834
	4/15/2013	Bletilla Ventures Limited	Cyprus	$59,735
	4/26/2013	Bletilla Ventures Limited	Cyprus	$48,802
	5/17/2013	Olivenia Trading Limited	Cyprus	$57,798
	5/30/2013	Actinet Trading Limited	Cyprus	$45,622
	6/13/2013	Lucicle Consultants Limited	Cyprus	$76,343

	8/7/2013	Pompolo Limited	United Kingdom	$250,784
	9/6/2013	Lucicle Consultants Limited	Cyprus	$68,500
	9/13/2013	Cypriot Agent	Cyprus	$179,216
Jemina LLC United States Bank Account D	7/8/2013	Marziola Holdings Limited	Cyprus	$72,500
	9/4/2013	Marziola Holdings Limited	Cyprus	$89,807
	10/22/2013	Cypriot Agent	Cyprus	$119,844
	11/12/2013	Cypriot Agent	Cyprus	$80,000
	12/20/2013	Cypriot Agent	Cyprus	$90,000
2013 Tax Year Total				$1,541,237
Jemina LLC United States Bank Account D	2/10/2014	Cypriot Agent	Cyprus	$60,044
	4/29/2014	Cypriot Agent	Cyprus	$44,068
	10/6/2014	Global Endeavour Inc.	Grenadines	$65,000
Bade LLC United States Bank Account E	11/25/2014	Global Endeavour Inc.	Grenadines	$120,000
2014 Tax Year Total				$289,112

MANAFORT And Gates' Hiding Ukraine Lobbying And Public Relations Work

19.   It is illegal to act as an agent of a foreign principal engaged in certain United States influence activities without registering the affiliation. Specifically, a person who engages in lobbying or public relations work in the United States (hereafter collectively referred to as lobbying) for a foreign principal, such as the Government of Ukraine or the Party of Regions, is required to provide a detailed written registration statement to the United States Department of Justice. The filing,

made under oath, must disclose the name of the foreign principal, the financial payments to the lobbyist, and the measures undertaken for the foreign principal, among other information. A person required to make such a filing must further include in all lobbying material a "conspicuous statement" that the materials are distributed on behalf of the foreign principal, among other things. The filing thus permits public awareness and evaluation of the activities of a lobbyist who acts as an agent of a foreign power or foreign political party in the United States.

20. In furtherance of the scheme, from 2006 until 2014, both dates being approximate and inclusive, MANAFORT, with the assistance of Gates, KILIMNIK, and others, engaged in a multi- million dollar lobbying campaign in the United States at the direction of Yanukovych, the Party of Regions, and the Government of Ukraine. MANAFORT did so without registering and providing the disclosures required by law.

21. As one part of the scheme, in February 2012, MANAFORT, with the assistance of Gates, solicited two Washington, D.C., firms (Company A and Company B) to lobby in the United States on behalf of Yanukovych, the Party of Regions, and the Government of Ukraine. For instance, Gates wrote to Company A that it would be "representing the Government of Ukraine in [Washington,] DC."

22. MANAFORT repeatedly communicated in person and in writing with Yanukovych, and Gates passed on directions to Company A and Company B. For instance, MANAFORT wrote Yanukovych a memorandum dated April 8, 2012, in which he provided Yanukovych an update on the lobbying firms' activities "since the inception of the project a few weeks ago. It is my intention to provide you with a weekly update moving forward." Toward the end of that first year, in November 2012, Gates wrote to Company A and Company B that the firms needed to prepare an assessment of their past and prospective lobbying efforts so the "President" could be briefed by "Paul" "on what Ukraine has done well and what it can do better as we move into 2013."

23. At the direction of MANAFORT and Gates, Company A and Company B engaged in extensive lobbying. Among other things, they lobbied multiple Members of Congress and their staffs about Ukraine sanctions, the validity of Ukraine elections, and the propriety of Yanukovych's imprisoning his presidential rival, Yulia Tymoshenko. In addition, with the assistance of Company A, MANAFORT directly lobbied a Member of Congress who had Ukraine within his subcommittee's purview, and reported in writing that lobbying effort to senior Government of Ukraine leadership.

24. To minimize public disclosure of their lobbying campaign and distance their work from the Government of Ukraine, MANAFORT, Gates, and others arranged for the Centre to be the nominal client of Company A and Company B, even though in fact the Centre was under the ultimate direction of the Government of

Ukraine, Yanukovych, and the Party of Regions. For instance, MANAFORT and Gates selected Company A and Company B, and only thereafter did the Centre sign contracts with the lobbying firms without ever meeting either company. Company A and Company B were paid for their services not by their nominal client, the Centre, but solely through offshore accounts associated with the MANAFORT entities, namely Bletilla Ventures Limited (in Cyprus) and Jeunet Ltd. and Global Endeavour Inc. (in Grenadines). In total, Company A and Company B were paid more than $2 million from these accounts between 2012 and 2014. Indeed, various employees of Company A and Company B viewed the Centre as a fig leaf. As a Company A employee noted to another employee: Gates was lobbying for the Centre "in name only. [Y]ou've gotta see through the nonsense of that[.]"Neither Company A nor Company B registered as required with the United States Department of Justice. In order to avoid such registration, Gates provided the companies a false and misleading signed statement from the Centre, stating that it was not "directly or indirectly supervised, directed, controlled, financed, or subsidized in whole or in part by a government of a foreign country or a foreign political party." In fact, the Centre took direction from Yanukovych and the Party of Regions, as MANAFORT and Gates knew.

  25. To conceal the scheme, MANAFORT and Gates developed a false and misleading cover story that would distance themselves and the Government of Ukraine, Yanukovych, and the Party of Regions from the Centre, Company A, and Company B. For instance, in the wake of extensive press reports on MANAFORT and his connections with Ukraine, on August 16, 2016, Gates communicated false and misleading talking points to Company B in writing, including:

    a. Q: "Can you describe your initial contact with [Company B] and the lobbying goals he discussed with them?" A: "We provided an introduction between the [Centre] and [Company B/Company A] in 2012. The [Centre] was seeking to retain representation in Washington, DC to support the mission of the NGO."

    b. A: "Our [MANAFORT and Gates'] task was to assist the [Centre to] find representation in Washington, but at no time did our firm or members provide any direct lobbying support."

    c. A: "The structure of the arrangement between the [Centre] and [Company A / Company B] was worked out by the two parties."

    d. Q: "Can you say where the funding from for [sic] the [Centre] came from? (this amounted to well over a million dollars between 2012 and 2014)." A: "This is a question better asked of the [Centre] who contracted with the two firms."

    e. Q: "Can you describe the lobbying work specifically undertaken by [Company B] on behalf of the Party of Regions/the [Centre]?" A: "This is a question better asked to [Company B] and/or the [Centre] as the agreement was between the parties. Our firm did not play a role in the structure, nor were we registered lobbyists."

26. Company B through a principal replied to Gates the same day that "there's a lot of email traffic that has you much more involved than this suggests[.] We will not disclose that but heaven knows what former employees of [Company B] or [Company A] might say."

27. In September 2016, after numerous recent press reports concerning MANAFORT, the Department of Justice informed MANAFORT, Gates, and DMI that it sought to determine whether they had acted as agents of a foreign principal under the Foreign Agents Registration Act (FARA), without registering. In November 2016 and February 2017, MANAFORT, Gates, and DMI caused false and misleading letters to be submitted to the Department of Justice, which mirrored the false cover story set out above. The letters, both of which were approved by MANAFORT and Gates before they were submitted, represented, among other things, that:

a. DMI's "efforts on behalf of the Party of Regions" "did not include meetings or outreach within the U.S.";

b. MANAFORT and Gates did not "recall meeting with or conducting outreach to U.S. government officials or U.S. media outlets on behalf of the [Centre], nor do they recall being party to, arranging, or facilitating any such communications. Rather, it is the recollection and understanding of Messrs. Gates and Manafort that such communications would have been facilitated and conducted by the [Centre's] U.S. consultants, as directed by the [Centre],";

c. MANAFORT and Gates had merely served as a means of introduction of Company A and Company B to the Centre and provided the Centre with a list of "potential U.S.-based consultants—including [Company A] and [Company B]—for the [Centre's] reference and further consideration."

d. DMI "does not retain communications beyond thirty days" and as a result of this policy, a "search has returned no responsive documents." The November 2016 letter attached a one-page, undated document that purported to be a DMI "Email Retention Policy."

28. In fact, MANAFORT and Gates had: selected Company A and Company B; engaged in weekly scheduled calls and frequent emails with Company A and Company B to provide them directions as to specific lobbying steps that should be taken; sought and received detailed oral and written reports from these firms on the lobbying work they had performed; communicated with Yanukovych to brief him on their lobbying efforts; both congratulated and reprimanded Company A and

Company B on their lobbying work; communicated directly with United States officials in connection with this work; and paid the lobbying firms over $2 million from offshore accounts they controlled, among other things. In addition, court-authorized searches of MANAFORT and Gates' DMI email accounts in 2017 and a search of MANAFORT's Virginia residence in July 2017 revealed numerous documents, including documents related to lobbying, which were more than thirty-days old at the time of the November 2016 letter to the Department of Justice.

29. As a second part of the lobbying scheme, in 2012, MANAFORT, with the assistance of Gates, on behalf of Yanukovych and the Government of Ukraine's Ministry of Justice, retained a United States law firm to write a report on the trial of Tymoshenko, among other things. The treatment of Tymoshenko was condemned by the United States and was viewed as a major hurdle to normalization of relations with Ukraine. MANAFORT and Gates used one of their offshore accounts to funnel $4 million to pay for the report, a fact that was not disclosed in the report or to the public. They also retained a public relations firm (Company C) to create and implement a roll- out plan for the report. MANAFORT and Gates again secretly used one of their offshore accounts to pay Company C, funneling the equivalent of more than $1 million to pay for the work. MANAFORT, Gates, and their conspirators developed detailed written lobbying plans in connection with the dissemination of the law firm's report, including outreach to United States politicians and press. MANAFORT reported on the law firm's work and the lobbying plan to representatives of the Government of Ukraine, including President Yanukovych. For instance, a July 27, 2012, memorandum from MANAFORT noted: "[t]his document will address the global rollout strategy for the [law firm's] legal report, and provide a detailed plan of action[]." The plans included lobbying in the United States.

30. As a third part of the lobbying scheme, in or about 2012, MANAFORT, with the assistance of Gates and KILIMNIK, on behalf of Yanukovych and the Party of Regions, secretly retained a group of former senior European politicians to take positions favorable to Ukraine, including by lobbying in the United States. The plan was for the former politicians, informally called the "Hapsburg group," to appear to be providing their independent assessments of Government of Ukraine actions, when in fact they were paid lobbyists for Ukraine. In 2012 and 2013, MANAFORT used at least four offshore accounts to wire more than 2 million euros to pay the group of former politicians.

31. MANAFORT explained in an "EYES ONLY" memorandum created in or about June 2012 that the purpose of the "SUPER VIP" effort would be to "assemble a small group of high-level european highly influencial [sic] champions and politically credible friends who can act informally and without any visible relationship with the Government of Ukraine." Yanukovych and the Party of Regions through MANAFORT retained an additional group of lobbyists (Company D and

Persons D1 and D2, among others) to serve as intermediaries with the Hapsburg group and to engage in other lobbying for Ukraine. The Hapsburg group was led by a former European Chancellor, Foreign Politician A, who coordinated with MANAFORT, KILIMNIK, and Person D1. As explained by MANAFORT, a nongovernmental agency would be created to retain this group, but it would act "at our quiet direction." In or about 2013, Foreign Politician A and other former politicians from the group lobbied United States Members of Congress, officials in the Executive Branch, and their staffs in coordination with MANAFORT, Gates, KILIMNIK, Persons D1 and D2, Company A, and Company B, among others.

MANAFORT's Hiding Foreign Bank Accounts And False Filings

32.　United States citizens who have authority over certain foreign bank accounts—whether or not the accounts are set up in the names of nominees who act for their principals—have reporting obligations to the United States.

33.　First, the Bank Secrecy Act and its implementing regulations require United States citizens to report to the Treasury any financial interest in, or signatory authority over, any bank account or other financial account held in foreign countries, for every calendar year in which the aggregate balance of all such foreign accounts exceeds $10,000 at any point during the year. This is commonly known as a foreign bank account report or "FBAR." The Bank Secrecy Act requires these reports because they have a high degree of usefulness in criminal, tax, or regulatory investigations or proceedings. The Treasury's Financial Crimes Enforcement Network (FinCEN) is the custodian for FBAR filings, and FinCEN provides access to its FBAR database to law enforcement entities, including the Federal Bureau of Investigation. The reports filed by individuals and businesses are used by law enforcement to identify, detect, and deter money laundering that furthers criminal enterprise activity, tax evasion, and other unlawful activities.

34.　Second, United States citizens are also obligated to report information to the IRS regarding foreign bank accounts. For instance, in 2010, Schedule B of IRS Form 1040 had a "Yes" or "No" box to record an answer to the question: "At any time during [the calendar year], did you have an interest in or a signature or other authority over a financial account in a foreign country, such as a bank account, securities account, or other financial account?" If the answer was "Yes," then the form required the taxpayer to enter the name of the foreign country in which the financial account was located.

35.　For each year in or about and between 2008 through at least 2014, MANAFORT had authority over foreign accounts that required an FBAR filing. Specifically, MANAFORT was required to report to the Treasury each foreign bank account held by the foreign MANAFORT entities noted above in paragraph 11 that bears the initials PM. No FBAR reports were made by MANAFORT for these accounts.

36. In each of MANAFORT's tax filings for 2008 through 2014, MANAFORT, with the assistance of Gates, represented falsely that he did not have authority over any foreign bank accounts. MANAFORT and Gates had repeatedly and falsely represented in writing to MANAFORT's tax preparer that MANAFORT had no authority over foreign bank accounts, knowing that such false representations would result in false tax filings in MANAFORT's name. For instance, on October 4, 2011, MANAFORT's tax preparer asked MANAFORT in writing: "At any time during 2010, did you [or your wife or children] have an interest in or a signature or other authority over a financial account in a foreign country, such as a bank account, securities account or other financial account?" On the same day, MANAFORT falsely responded "NO." MANAFORT responded the same way as recently as October 3, 2016, when MANAFORT's tax preparer again emailed the question in connection with the preparation of MANAFORT's tax returns: "Foreign bank accounts etc.?" MANAFORT responded on or about the same day: "NONE."

IV.   *Statutory Allegations*

COUNT ONE: *Conspiracy Against The United States (18 U.S.C. §§ 371 and 3551 et seq.)*

37. Paragraphs 1 through 36 are incorporated here.

38. From in or about and between 2006 and 2017, both dates being approximate and inclusive, in the District of Columbia and elsewhere, the defendant PAUL J. MANAFORT, JR., together with others, knowingly and intentionally conspired to defraud the United States by impeding, impairing, obstructing, and defeating the lawful governmental functions of a government agency, namely the Department of Justice and the Treasury, and to commit offenses against the United States, to wit: the violations of law charged in Counts Three, Four, and Five, and to unlawfully, willfully, and knowingly fail to file with the Treasury an FBAR disclosing a financial interest in, and signature and other authority over, a bank, securities, and other financial account in a foreign country, which had an aggregate value of more than $10,000 in a 12-month period, in violation of 31 U.S.C. §§ 5314 and 5322(a).

39. In furtherance of the conspiracy and to effect its illegal object, MANAFORT and his conspirators committed the overt acts noted in Count Four and the overt acts, among others, in the District of Columbia and elsewhere, set forth in paragraphs 8–11,14–18, 20–31, and 35–36, which are incorporated herein.

COUNT TWO: *Conspiracy To Launder Money (18 U.S.C. §§ 1956(h) and 3551 et seq.)*

40. Paragraphs 1 through 36 are incorporated here.

In or around and between 2006 and 2016, both dates being approximate and inclusive, within the District of Columbia and elsewhere, the defendant PAUL J. MANAFORT, JR., together with others, did knowingly and intentionally conspire to:

a.   transport, transmit, and transfer monetary instruments and funds from places outside the United States to and through places in the United States and from places in the United States to and through places outside the United States, with the intent to promote the carrying on of specified unlawful activity, to wit: a felony violation of FARA, in violation of Title 22, United States Code, Sections 612 and 618 (the "Specified Unlawful Activity"), contrary to Title 18, United States Code, Section 1956(a)(2)(A); and

b.   conduct financial transactions, affecting interstate and foreign commerce, knowing that the property involved in the financial transactions would represent the proceeds of some form of unlawful activity, and the transactions in fact would involve the proceeds of the Specified Unlawful Activity, knowing that such financial transactions were designed in whole and in part (i) to engage in conduct constituting a violation of sections 7201 and 7206 of the Internal Revenue Code of 1986, and (ii) to conceal and disguise the nature, location, source, ownership, and control of the proceeds of the Specified Unlawful Activity, contrary to Title 18, United States Code, Section 1956(a)(1)(A)(ii) and 1956(a)(1)(B)(i).

COUNT THREE: Unregistered Agent Of A Foreign Principal (22 U.S.C. §§ 612 & 618(a)(1); 18 U.S.C. §§ 2 & 3551 et seq.)

41.   Paragraphs 1 through 36 are incorporated here.

42.   From in or about and between 2008 and 2014, both dates being approximate and inclusive, within the District of Columbia and elsewhere, the defendant PAUL J. MANAFORT, JR., knowingly and willfully acted as an agent of a foreign principal, and caused and aided and abetted Companies A, B, and C, and others, including former senior foreign politicians, to act as agents of a foreign principal, to wit, the Government of Ukraine, the Party of Regions, and Yanukovych, without registering with the Attorney General as required by law.

COUNT FOUR: False and Misleading FARA Statements (22 U.S.C. §§ 612 & 618(a)(2); 18 U.S.C. §§ 2 & 3551 et seq.)

43.   Paragraphs 1 through 36 are incorporated here.

44.   On or about November 23, 2016, and February 10, 2017, within the District of Columbia and elsewhere, the defendant PAUL J. MANAFORT, JR., knowingly and willfully caused to be made a false statement of a material fact, and omitted a material fact necessary to make the statements therein not misleading, in

a document filed with and furnished to the Attorney General under the provisions of FARA, to wit, the underlined statements:

> a. "[DMI]'s efforts on behalf of the Party of Regions and Opposition Bloc did not include meetings or outreach within the U.S."

> b. "[N]either [DMI] nor Messrs. Manafort or Gates had any agreement with the [Centre] to provide services."

> c. "[DMI] did provide the [Centre], at the request of members of the Party of Regions, with a list of potential U.S.-based consultants—including [Company A and Company B]—for the [Centre]'s reference and further consideration. [The Centre] then contracted directly with [Company A and Company B] to provide services within the United States for which these entities registered under the Lobbying Disclosure Act."

> d. "Although Gates recalls interacting with [the Centre]'s consultants regardingefforts in the Ukraine and Europe, neither Gates nor Mr. Manafort recall meeting with or conducting outreach to U.S. government officials or U.S. media outlets on behalf of the [the Centre], nor do they recall being party to, arranging, or facilitating any such communications. Rather, it is the recollection and understanding of Messrs. Gates and Manafort that such communications would have been facilitated and conducted by the [Centre]'s U.S. consultants, as directed by the [Centre], pursuant to the agreement reached between those parties (to which [DMI] was not a party)."

> e. "[A] search has been conducted for correspondence containing additional information related to the matters described in [the government's] Letters. However, as a result of [DMI's] Email Retention Policy, which does not retain communications beyond thirty days, the search has returned no responsive communications."

COUNT FIVE: Making False Statements to Investigators (18 U.S.C. §§ 2, 1001(a), and 3551 et seq.)

45. Paragraphs 1 through 36 and paragraph 45 are incorporated here.

46. On or about November 23, 2016, and February 10, 2017, within the District of Columbia and elsewhere, in a matter within the jurisdiction of the executive branch of the Government of the United States, the defendant PAUL J. MANAFORT, JR., knowingly and willfully did cause another: to falsify, conceal, and cover up by a scheme and device a material fact; to make a materially false, fictitious, and fraudulent statement and representation; and to make and use a false writing and document knowing the same to contain a materially false, fictitious, and fraudulent statement, to wit, the statements in the November 23, 2016, and February 10, 2017, submissions to the Department of Justice quoted in paragraph 45.

COUNT SIX: Obstruction Of Justice (18 U.S.C. §§ 2, 1512(b)(1), and 3551 et seq.)

47. Paragraphs 1 through 36 are incorporated here.

48. From in or about and between February 23, 2018, and April 2018, both dates being approximate and inclusive, within the District of Columbia and elsewhere, the defendants PAUL J. MANAFORT, JR., and KONSTANTIN KILIMNIK knowingly and intentionally attempted to corruptly persuade another person, to wit: Persons D1 and D2, with intent to influence, delay, and prevent the testimony of any person in an official proceeding.

COUNT SEVEN: Conspiracy to Obstruct Justice (18 U.S.C. §§ 1512(k) and 3551 et seq.)

49. Paragraphs 1 through 36 are incorporated here.

50. From in or about and between February 23, 2018, and April 2018, both dates being approximate and inclusive, within the District of Columbia and elsewhere, the defendants PAUL J. MANAFORT, JR., and KONSTANTIN KILIMNIK knowingly and intentionally conspired to corruptly persuade another person, to wit: Persons D1 and D2, with intent to influence, delay, and prevent the testimony of any person in an official proceeding, in violation of 18 U.S.C. § 1512(b)(1).

FORFEITURE ALLEGATION

52. Pursuant to Fed. R. Crim. P. 32.2, notice is hereby given to the defendants that the United States will seek forfeiture as part of any sentence in accordance with Title 18, United States Code, Sections 981(a)(1)(C) and 982(a)(1), and Title 28, United States Code, Section 2461(c), in the event of the defendants' conviction. Upon conviction of the offense charged in Count Two, the defendant PAUL J. MANAFORT, JR., shall forfeit to the United States any property, real or personal, involved in such offense, and any property traceable to such property. Upon conviction of the offenses charged in Counts One, Three, Four, Six, and Seven, the defendants PAUL J. MANAFORT, JR., and KONSTANTIN KILIMNIK (as to Counts Six and Seven) shall forfeit to the United States any property, real or personal, which constitutes or is derived from proceeds traceable to the offense(s) of conviction. Notice is further given that, upon conviction, the United States intends to seek a judgment against the defendants for a sum of money representing the property described in this paragraph (to be offset by the forfeiture of any specific property).

53. The grand jury finds probable cause to believe that the property subject to forfeiture by PAUL J. MANAFORT, JR., includes, but is not limited to, the following listed assets:

    a. The real property and premises commonly known as 377 Union Street, Brooklyn, New York 11231 (Block 429, Lot 65), including all appurtenances, improvements, and attachments thereon, and any property traceable thereto;

b. The real property and premises commonly known as 29 Howard Street, #4D, New York, New York 10013 (Block 209, Lot 1104), including all appurtenances, improvements, and attachments thereon, and any property traceable thereto;

c. The real property and premises commonly known as 1046 N. Edgewood Street, Arlington, Virginia 22201, including all appurtenances, improvements, and attachments thereon, and any property traceable thereto;

d. The real property and premises commonly known as 174 Jobs Lane, Water Mill, New York 11976, including all appurtenances, improvements, and attachments thereon, and any property traceable thereto;

e. Northwestern Mutual Universal Life Insurance Policy 18268327, and any property traceable thereto;

f. All funds held in account number XXXX7988 at Charles A. Schwab & Co. Inc., and any property traceable thereto; and

g. All funds held in account number XXXXXX0969 at The Federal Savings Bank, and any property traceable thereto.

Substitute Assets

54. If any of the property described above as being subject to forfeiture, as a result of any act or omission of the defendants --

a. cannot be located upon the exercise of due diligence;

b. has been transferred or sold to, or deposited with, a third party;

c   has been placed beyond the jurisdiction of the court;

d. has been substantially diminished in value; or

e. has been commingled with other property that cannot be subdivided without difficulty;

-- it is the intent of the United States of America, pursuant to Title 18, United States Code, Section 982(6) and Title 28, United States Code, Section 246 l(c), incorporating Title 21, United States Code, Section 853, to seek forfeiture of any other property of said defendants.

Signed: Robert S. Mueller, III
Special Counsel

CHAPTER 10: PUBLIC REPORT ON RUSSIAN ACTIVITIES, JULY 3, 2018

Public Report on the Intelligence Community Assessment Review by the Senate Select Committee on Intelligence - July 3, 2018

The Intelligence Community Assessment: Assessing Russian Activities and Intentions in Recent U.S. Elections

I. *Summary*

1. The Senate Select Committee on Intelligence (SSCI) is conducting a bipartisan investigation into a wide range of Russian activities relating to the 2016 U.S. presidential election. While elements of the investigation are ongoing, the Committee is releasing initial, unclassified findings on a rolling basis as distinct pieces of the investigation conclude.

2. The Committee has concluded an in-depth review of the Intelligence Community Assessment (ICA) produced by CIA, NSA, and FBI in January of 2017 on Russian interference in the 2016 U.S. presidential election (*Assessing Russian Activities and Intentions in Recent U.S. Elections*; declassified version released January 6, 2017) and have initial findings to share with the American people.

   a. The ICA was a seminal intelligence product with significant policy implications. In line with its historical role, the Committee had a responsibility to conduct an in-depth review of the document.

   b. In conducting its examination, the Committee reviewed thousands of pages of source documents and conducted interviews with all the relevant parties - including agency heads, managers, and line analysts - who were involved in developing the analysis and drafting the assessment.

   c. The Committee is preparing a comprehensive, classified report detailing our conclusions regarding the ICA on Russian activities. That report, when complete, will be submitted for a classification review, and the unclassified version will be released to the public.

II. *Initial Findings*

3.   The Intelligence Community Assessment (ICA) released in January 2017 assessed that Russian activities in the run-up to the 2016 presidential election represented a significant escalation in a long history of Russian attempts to interfere in U.S. domestic politics. This escalation was made possible by cyber-espionage and cyber-driven covert influence operations, conducted as part of a broader "active measures" campaign that included overt messaging through Russian-controlled propaganda platforms. The ICA revealed key elements of a comprehensive and multifaceted Russian campaign against the United States as it was understood by the U.S. Intelligence Community at the end of 2016.

4.   President Obama in early December 2016 tasked the Intelligence Community with writing an assessment that would capture the existing intelligence on Russian interference in U.S. elections. By early January, the CIA, NSA, and FBI produced a joint assessment under the auspices of the ODNI, titled *Assessing Russian Activities and Intentions in Recent U.S. Elections,* which included both classified and unclassified versions. Only three agencies were represented in the drafting process because of the extreme sensitivity of the sources and methods involved.

5.   The Committee finds that the Intelligence Community met President Obama's tasking and that the ICA is a sound intelligence product. While the Committee had to rely on agencies that the sensitive information and accesses had been accurately reported, as part of our inquiry the Committee reviewed analytic procedures, interviewed senior intelligence officers well-versed with the information, and based our findings on the entire body of intelligence reporting included in the ICA.

6.   The Committee finds the difference in confidence levels between the NSA and the CIA and FBI on the assessment that "Putin and the Russian Government aspired to help President-elect Trump's election chances" appropriately represents analytic differences and was reached in a professional and transparent manner.

7.   In all the interviews of those who drafted and prepared the ICA, the Committee heard consistently that analysts were under no politically motivated pressure to reach any conclusions. All analysts expressed that they were free to debate, object to content, and assess confidence levels, as is normal and proper for the analytic process.

8.   As the inquiry has progressed since January 2017, the Committee has seen additional examples of Russia's attempts to sow discord, undermine democratic institutions, and interfere in U.S. elections and those of our allies.

III.   *Russian Efforts to Influence the 2016 Election*

9.   The ICA states that:*"Russian efforts to influence the 2016 U.S. presidential election represent the most recent expression of Moscow's long-standing desire*

to undermine the U.S.-led liberal democratic order, but these activities demonstrated a significant escalation in directness, level of activity, and scope of effort compared to previous operations." (Intelligence Community Assessment: Assessing Russian Activities and Intentions in Recent U.S. Elections, 6 January 2017. P.ii). [NOTE: all page numbers referenced are from the Unclassified ICA]

    a. The Committee found that this judgment was supported by the evidence presented in the ICA. Since its publication, further details have come to light that bolster the assessment.

    b. The ICA pointed to initial evidence of Russian activities against multiple U.S. state or local electoral boards. Since the ICA was published, the Committee has learned more about Russian attempts to infiltrate state election infrastructure, as outlined in the findings and recommendations the Committee issued in March 2018.

    c. While the ICA briefly discussed the activities of the Internet Research Agency, the Committee's investigation has exposed a far more extensive Russian effort to manipulate social media outlets to sow discord and to interfere in the 2016 election and American society.

IV.   *Russian Leadership Intentions*

    10.   The ICA states that: *"We assess Russian President Vladimir Putin ordered an influence campaign in 2016 aimed at the U.S. presidential election. Russia's goals were to undermine public faith in the U.S. democratic process, denigrate Secretary Clinton, and harm her electability and potential presidency. We further assess Putin and the Russian Government developed a clear preference for President-elect Trump."* (Intelligence Community Assessment: Assessing Russian Activities and Intentions in Recent U.S. Elections, 6 January 2017. P.ii.)

    a. The Committee found that the ICA provided a range of all-source reporting to support these assessments.

    b. The Committee concurs with intelligence and open-source assessments that this influence campaign was approved by President Putin.

    c. Further, a body of reporting, to include different intelligence disciplines, open source reporting on Russian leadership policy preferences, and Russian media content, showed that Moscow sought to denigrate Secretary Clinton.

    d. The ICA relies on public Russian leadership commentary, Russian state media reports, public examples of where Russian interests would have aligned with candidates' policy statements, and a body of intelligence reporting to support the assessment that Putin and the Russian Government developed a clear preference for Trump.

    11.   The ICA also states that: *"We also assess Putin and the Russian*

Government aspired to help President-elect Trump's election chances when possible by discrediting Secretary Clinton and publicly contrasting her unfavorably to him." (Intelligence Community Assessment: Assessing Russian Activities and Intentions in Recent U.S. Elections, 6 January 2017. P.ii.)

    a. The Committee found that the ICA provided intelligence and open source reporting to support this assessment, and information obtained subsequent to publication of the ICA provides further support.

    b. This is the only assessment in the ICA that had different confidence levels between the participating agencies -the CIA and FBI assessed with "high confidence" and the NSA assessed with "moderate confidence"-so the Committee gave this section additional attention.

    12. The Committee found that the analytical disagreement was reasonable, transparent, and openly debated among the agencies and analysts, with analysts, managers, and agency heads on both sides of the confidence level articulately justifying their positions.

V.   *Russian Cyber Operations*

    13. The ICA states that: *"Russia's intelligence services conducted cyber operations against targets associated with the 2016 U.S. presidential election, including targets associated with both major U.S. political parties. We assess Russian intelligence services collected against the U.S . primary campaigns, think tanks, and lobbying groups they viewed as likely to shape future U.S. policies. In July 2015, Russian intelligence gained access to Democratic National Committee (DNC) networks and maintained that access until at least June 2016."* (Intelligence Community Assessment:Assessing Russian Activities and Intention sin Recent U.S.Elections, 6 January 2017. P.2.)

    a. The Committee found this judgment supported by intelligence and further supported by our own investigation. Separate from the ICA, the Committee has conducted interviews of key individuals who have provided additional insights into these incidents.

VI.   *Russian Propaganda*

    14. The ICA states that: *"Russia's state-run propaganda machine-comprised of its domestic media apparatus, outlets targeting global audiences such as RT and Sputnik, and a network of quasi-governmental trolls-contributed to the influence campaign by serving as a platform for Kremlin messaging to Russian and international audiences."* (Intelligence Community Assessment: Assessing Russian Activities and Intentions in Recent U.S. Elections, 6 January 2017. P.3.)

    a. The ICA provides a summary of Russian state media operations in 2012 and notes that RT (formerly Russia Today) and Sputnik are coordinated Russian· state platforms. The ICA fails to provide an updated assessment of this capability in 2016, which the Committee finds to be a shortcoming in the ICA, as this information was available in open source.

      b.   The Committee notes that the ICA does not comment on the potential effectiveness of this propaganda campaign, because the U.S. Intelligence Community makes no assessments on U.S. domestic political processes.

      VII.   *Historical Context*

      15.   The ICA states that: *"During the Cold War, the Soviet Union used intelligence officers, influence agents, forgeries, and press placements to disparage candidates perceived as hostile to the Kremlin, according to a former KGB archivist...For decades, Russian and Soviet intelligence services have sought to collect insider information from U.S. political parties that could help Russian leaders understand a new U.S. administration's plans and priorities."* (Intelligence Community Assessment: Assessing Russian Activities and Intentions in Recent U.S. Elections, 6 January 2017. P.5.)

      a.   The Committee found the ICA's treatment of the historical context of Russian interference in U.S. domestic politics perfunctory.

      b.   The unclassified ICA cites efforts to collect on the 2008 election and the Soviet recruitment of an activist who reported on Jimmy Carter's campaign in the 1970s, demonstrating two examples of Russian interest in U.S. elections. The ICA failed entirely to summarize historic collection by U.S. agencies as well as extensive open-source reporting - significant elements of which are derived from Russian intelligence archives - to present a more relevant historical context.

      VIII.   *Counterintelligence Investigations*

      16.   The ICA did not attempt to address potential counterintelligence investigations - for example, whether Russian intelligence services attempted to recruit sources with access to any campaign. The FBI had a collection of reports a former foreign intelligence officer was hired to compile as opposition research for the U.S. election, referred to as the "dossier," when the ICA was drafted. However, those reports remained separate from the conclusions of the ICA. All individuals the Committee interviewed verified that the dossier did not in any way inform the analysis in the ICA- including the key findings - because it was unverified information and had not been disseminated as serialized intelligence reporting.

      a.   The Committee will address the contents of the reports and their handling by the United States Government in a separate part of its report.

      IX.   *Conclusion*

      17.   Finally, the Committee notes that, as is the case with all intelligence questions, information continues to be gathered and analyzed. The Committee believes the conclusions of the ICA are sound, and notes that collection and analysis subsequent to the ICA's publication continue to reinforce its

assessments. The Committee will remain vigilant in its oversight of the ongoing challenges presented by foreign nations attempting to secretly influence U.S. affairs.

Published by the U.S. Senate Select Committee on Intelligence - July 3, 2018

CHAPTER 11: DNC HACKERS, JULY 13, 2018

UNITED STATES v. BORISOVICH NETYKSHO, BORIS ALEKSEYEVICH ANTONOV, DMITRIY SERGEYEVICH BADIN, IVAN SERGEYEVICH YERMAKOV, ALEKSEY VIKTOROVICH LUKASHEV, SERGEY ALEKSANDROVICH MORGACHEV, NIKOLAY YURYEVICH KOZACHEK, PAVEL VYACHESLAVOVICH YERSHOV, ARTEM ANDREYEVICH MALYSHEV, ALEKSANDR VLADIMIROVICH OSADCHUK, ALEKSEY ALEKSANDROVICH POTEMKIN and ANATOLIY SERGEYEVICH KOVALEV.

FILED: July 13, 2018 in the United States District Court for the District of Columbia

Editor's Note: In this indictment, Special Counsel Mueller goes after the operatives in Russia who - at the behest of their government - hacked into the DNC's servers and email system and executed numerous spearphishing operations in an attempt to hack into people's email accounts that were hosted by companies such as Google and Yahoo. The most successful of these later ops came when this group was able to download thousands of, Clinton campaign chairman, John Podesta's personal emails. After obtaining the material, the group then published the 'dirt' via Wikileaks and their own Wikileaks clone site, DCLeaks.

Indictment

The Grand Jury for the District of Columbia charges:

COUNT ONE: Conspiracy to Commit an Offense Against the United States (18 U.S.C. §§ 371 & 3559 (g)(1))

1.   The In or around 2016, the Russian Federation ("Russia") operated a military intelligence agency called the Main Intelligence Directorate of the General Staff ("GRU"). The GRU had multiple units, including Units 26165 and 74455, engaged in cyber operations that involved the staged releases of documents stolen through computer intrusions. These units conducted large- scale cyber operations to interfere with the 2016 U.S. presidential election.

2.   Defendants VIKTOR BORISOVICH NETYKSHO, BORIS ALEKSEYEVICH ANTONOV, DMITRIY SERGEYEVICH BADIN, IVAN SERGEYEVICH YERMAKOV, ALEKSEY VIKTOROVICH LUKASHEV, SERGEY ALEKSANDROVICH

MORGACHEV, NIKOLAY YURYEVICH KOZACHEK, PAVEL VYACHESLAVOVICH YERSHOV, ARTEM ANDREYEVICH MALYSHEV, ALEKSANDR VLADIMIROVICH OSADCHUK, and ALEKSEY ALEKSANDROVICH POTEMKIN were GRU officers who knowingly and intentionally conspired with each other, and with persons known and unknown to the Grand Jury (collectively the "Conspirators"), to gain unauthorized access (to "hack") into the computers of U.S. persons and entities involved in the 2016 U.S. presidential election, steal documents from those computers, and stage releases of the stolen documents to interfere with the 2016 U.S. presidential election.

3. Starting in at least March 2016, the Conspirators used a variety of means to hack the email accounts of volunteers and employees of the U.S. presidential campaign of Hillary Clinton (the "Clinton Campaign"), including the email account of the Clinton Campaign's chairman.

4. By in or around April 2016, the Conspirators also hacked into the computer networks of the Democratic Congressional Campaign Committee ("DCCC") and the Democratic National Committee ("DNC"). The Conspirators covertly monitored the computers of dozens of DCCC and DNC employees, implanted hundreds of files containing malicious computer code ("malware"), and stole emails and other documents from the DCCC and DNC.

5. By in or around April 2016, the Conspirators began to plan the release of materials stolen from the Clinton Campaign, DCCC, and DNC.

6. Beginning in or around June 2016, the Conspirators staged and released tens of thousands of the stolen emails and documents. They did so using fictitious online personas, including "DCLeaks" and "Guccifer 2.0."

7. The Conspirators also used the Guccifer 2.0 persona to release additional stolen documents through a website maintained by an organization ("Organization 1"), that had previously posted documents stolen from U.S. persons, entities, and the U.S. government. The Conspirators continued their U.S. election-interference operations through in or around November 2016.

8. To hide their connections to Russia and the Russian government, the Conspirators used false identities and made false statements about their identities. To further avoid detection, the Conspirators used a network of computers located across the world, including in the United States, and paid for this infrastructure using cryptocurrency.

I. *Defendants*

9. Defendant VIKTOR BORISOVICH NETYKSHO (Нетыкшо Виктор Борисович) was the Russian military officer in command of Unit 26165, located at 20 Komsomolskiy Prospekt, Moscow, Russia. Unit 26165 had primary responsibility for hacking the DCCC and DNC, as well as the email accounts of individuals affiliated with the Clinton Campaign.

10. Defendant BORIS ALEKSEYEVICH ANTONOV (Антонов Борис Алексеевич) was a Major in the Russian military assigned to Unit 26165. ANTONOV oversaw a department within Unit 26165 dedicated to targeting military, political, governmental, and non-governmental organizations with spearphishing emails and other computer intrusion activity. ANTONOV held the title "Head of Department." In or around 2016, ANTONOV supervised other co-conspirators who targeted the DCCC, DNC, and individuals affiliated with the Clinton Campaign.

11. Defendant DMITRIY SERGEYEVICH BADIN (Бадин Дмитрий Сергеевич) was a Russian military officer assigned to Unit 26165 who held the title "Assistant Head of Department." In or around 2016, BADIN, along with ANTONOV, supervised other co-conspirators who targeted the DCCC, DNC, and individuals affiliated with the Clinton Campaign.

12. Defendant IVAN SERGEYEVICH YERMAKOV (Ермаков Иван Сергеевич) was a Russian military officer assigned to ANTONOV's department within Unit 26165. Since in or around 2010, YERMAKOV used various online personas, including "Kate S. Milton," "James McMorgans," and "Karen W. Millen," to conduct hacking operations on behalf of Unit 26165. In or around March 2016, YERMAKOV participated in hacking at least two email accounts from which campaign-related documents were released through DCLeaks. In or around May 2016, YERMAKOV also participated in hacking the DNC email server and stealing DNC emails that were later released through Organization 1.

13. Defendant ALEKSEY VIKTOROVICH LUKASHEV (Лукашев Алексей Викторович) was a Senior Lieutenant in the Russian military assigned to ANTONOV's department within Unit 26165. LUKASHEV used various online personas, including "Den Katenberg" and "Yuliana Martynova." In or around 2016, LUKASHEV sent spearphishing emails to members of the Clinton Campaign and affiliated individuals, including the chairman of the Clinton Campaign.

14. Defendant SERGEY ALEKSANDROVICH MORGACHEV (Моргачев Сергей Александрович) was a Lieutenant Colonel in the Russian military assigned to Unit 26165. MORGACHEV oversaw a department within Unit 26165 dedicated to developing and managing malware, including a hacking tool used by the GRU known as "X-Agent." During the hacking of the DCCC and DNC networks, MORGACHEV supervised the co-conspirators who developed and monitored the X-Agent malware implanted on those computers.

15. Defendant NIKOLAY YURYEVICH KOZACHEK (Козачек Николай Юрьевич) was a Lieutenant Captain in the Russian military assigned to MORGACHEV's department within Unit 26165. KOZACHEK used a variety of monikers, including "kazak" and "blablabla1234565." KOZACHEK developed, customized, and monitored X-Agent malware used to hack the DCCC and DNC networks beginning in or around April 2016.

16. Defendant PAVEL VYACHESLAVOVICH YERSHOV (Ершов Павел Вячеславович) was a Russian military officer assigned to MORGACHEV's department within Unit 26165. In or around 2016, YERSHOV assisted KOZACHEK and other co-conspirators in testing and customizing X-Agent malware before actual deployment and use.

17. Defendant ARTEM ANDREYEVICH MALYSHEV (Малышев Артём Андреевич) was a Second Lieutenant in the Russian military assigned to MORGACHEV's department within Unit 26165. MALYSHEV used a variety of monikers, including "djangomagicdev" and "realblatr." In or around 2016, MALYSHEV monitored X-Agent malware implanted on the DCCC and DNC networks.

18. Defendant ALEKSANDR VLADIMIROVICH OSADCHUK (Осадчук Александр Владимирович) was a Colonel in the Russian military and the commanding officer of Unit 74455. Unit 74455 was located at 22 Kirova Street, Khimki, Moscow, a building referred to within the GRU as the "Tower." Unit 74455 assisted in the release of stolen documents through the DCLeaks and Guccifer 2.0 personas, the promotion of those releases, and the publication of anti-Clinton content on social media accounts operated by the GRU.

19. Defendant ALEKSEY ALEKSANDROVICH POTEMKIN (Потемкин Алексей Александрович) was an officer in the Russian military assigned to Unit 74455. POTEMKIN was a supervisor in a department within Unit 74455 responsible for the administration of computer infrastructure used in cyber operations. Infrastructure and social media accounts administered by POTEMKIN's department were used, among other things, to assist in the release of stolen documents through the DCLeaks and Guccifer 2.0 personas.

II. Object of the Conspiracy

20. The object of the conspiracy was to hack into the computers of U.S. persons and entities involved in the 2016 U.S. presidential election, steal documents from those computers, and stage releases of the stolen documents to interfere with the 2016 U.S. presidential election.

III. Manner and Means of the Conspiracy

Spearfishing Operations

21. ANTONOV, BADIN, YERMAKOV, LUKASHEV, and their co-conspirators targeted victims using a technique known as spearphishing to steal victims' passwords or otherwise gain access to their computers. Beginning by at least March 2016, the Conspirators targeted over 300 individuals affiliated with the Clinton Campaign, DCCC, and DNC.

a. For example, on or about March 19, 2016, LUKASHEV and his co-conspirators created and sent a spearphishing email to the chairman of the Clinton Campaign. LUKASHEV used the account "john356gh" at an online service that abbreviated lengthy website addresses (referred to as a "URL-shortening service"). LUKASHEV used the account to mask a link contained in the spearphishing email, which directed the recipient to a GRU-created website. LUKASHEV altered the appearance of the sender email address in order to make it look like the email was a security notification from Google (a technique known as "spoofing"), instructing the user to change his password by clicking the embedded link. Those instructions were followed. On or about March 21, 2016, LUKASHEV, YERMAKOV, and their co-conspirators stole the contents of the chairman's email account, which consisted of over 50,000 emails.

  b. Starting on or about March 19, 2016, LUKASHEV and his co-conspirators sent spearphishing emails to the personal accounts of other individuals affiliated with the Clinton Campaign, including its campaign manager and a senior foreign policy advisor. On or about March 25, 2016, LUKASHEV used the same john356gh account to mask additional links included in spearphishing emails sent to numerous individuals affiliated with the Clinton Campaign, including Victims 1 and 2. LUKASHEV sent these emails from the Russia-based email account hi.mymail@yandex.com that he spoofed to appear to be from Google.

  c. On or about March 28, 2016, YERMAKOV researched the names of Victims 1 and 2 and their association with Clinton on various social media sites. Through their spearphishing operations, LUKASHEV, YERMAKOV, and their co-conspirators successfully stole email credentials and thousands of emails from numerous individuals affiliated with the Clinton Campaign. Many of these stolen emails, including those from Victims 1 and 2, were later released by the Conspirators through DCLeaks.

  d. On or about April 6, 2016, the Conspirators created an email account in the name (with a one-letter deviation from the actual spelling) of a known member of the Clinton Campaign. The Conspirators then used that account to send spearphishing emails to the work accounts of more than thirty different Clinton Campaign employees. In the spearphishing emails, LUKASHEV and his co-conspirators embedded a link purporting to direct the recipient to a document titled "hillary- clinton-favorable-rating.xlsx." In fact, this link directed the recipients' computers to a GRU-created website.

  22. The Conspirators spearphished individuals affiliated with the Clinton Campaign throughout the summer of 2016. For example, on or about July 27, 2016, the Conspirators attempted after hours to spearphish for the first time email accounts at a domain hosted by a third- party provider and used by Clinton's

personal office. At or around the same time, they also targeted seventy-six email addresses at the domain for the Clinton Campaign.

Hacking into the DCCC Network

23. Beginning in or around March 2016, the Conspirators, in addition to their spearphishing efforts, researched the DCCC and DNC computer networks to identify technical specifications and vulnerabilities.

a. For example, beginning on or about March 15, 2016, YERMAKOV ran a technical query for the DNC's internet protocol configurations to identify connected devices.

b. On or about the same day, YERMAKOV searched for open-source information about the DNC network, the Democratic Party, and Hillary Clinton.

c. On or about April 7, 2016, YERMAKOV ran a technical query for the DCCC's internet protocol configurations to identify connected devices.

24. By in or around April 2016, within days of YERMAKOV's searches regarding the DCCC, the Conspirators hacked into the DCCC computer network. Once they gained access, they installed and managed different types of malware to explore the DCCC network and steal data.

a. On or about April 12, 2016, the Conspirators used the stolen credentials of a DCCC Employee ("DCCC Employee 1") to access the DCCC network. DCCC Employee 1 had received a spearphishing email from the Conspirators on or about April 6, 2016, and entered her password after clicking on the link.

b. Between in or around April 2016 and June 2016, the Conspirators installed multiple versions of their X-Agent malware on at least ten DCCC computers, which allowed them to monitor individual employees' computer activity, steal passwords, and maintain access to the DCCC network.

c. X-Agent malware implanted on the DCCC network transmitted information from the victims' computers to a GRU-leased server located in Arizona. The Conspirators referred to this server as their "AMS" panel. KOZACHEK, MALYSHEV, and their co-conspirators logged into the AMS panel to use X-Agent's keylog and screenshot functions in the course of monitoring and surveillance activity on the DCCC computers. The keylog function allowed the Conspirators to capture keystrokes entered by DCCC employees. The screenshot function allowed the Conspirators to take pictures of the DCCC employees' computer screens.

d. For example, on or about April 14, 2016, the Conspirators repeatedly activated X-Agent's keylog and screenshot functions to surveil

DCCC Employee 1's computer activity over the course of eight hours. During that time, the Conspirators captured DCCC Employee 1's communications with co-workers and the passwords she entered while working on fundraising and voter outreach projects. Similarly, on or about April 22, 2016, the Conspirators activated X-Agent's keylog and screenshot functions to capture the discussions of another DCCC Employee ("DCCC Employee 2") about the DCCC's finances, as well as her individual banking information and other personal topics.

25. On or about April 19, 2016, KOZACHEK, YERSHOV, and their co-conspirators remotely configured an overseas computer to relay communications between X-Agent malware and the AMS panel and then tested X-Agent's ability to connect to this computer. The Conspirators referred to this computer as a "middle server." The middle server acted as a proxy to obscure the connection between malware at the DCCC and the Conspirators' AMS panel. On or about April 20, 2016, the Conspirators directed X-Agent malware on the DCCC computers to connect to this middle server and receive directions from the Conspirators.

Hacking into the DNC Network

26. On or about April 18, 2016, the Conspirators hacked into the DNC's computers through their access to the DCCC network. The Conspirators then installed and managed different types of malware (as they did in the DCCC network) to explore the DNC network and steal documents.

a.   On or about April 18, 2016, the Conspirators activated X-Agent's keylog and screenshot functions to steal credentials of a DCCC employee who was authorized to access the DNC network. The Conspirators hacked into the DNC network from the DCCC network using stolen credentials. By in or around June 2016, they gained access to approximately thirty-three DNC computers.

b.   In or around April 2016, the Conspirators installed X-Agent malware on the DNC network, including the same versions installed on the DCCC network. MALYSHEV and his co-conspirators monitored the X-Agent malware from the AMS panel and captured data from the victim computers. The AMS panel collected thousands of keylog and screenshot results from the DCCC and DNC computers, such as a screenshot and keystroke capture of DCCC Employee 2 viewing the DCCC's online banking information.

Theft of DCCC and DNC Documents

27. The Conspirators searched for and identified computers within the DCCC and DNC networks that stored information related to the 2016 U.S. presidential election. For example, on or about April 15, 2016, the Conspirators searched one

hacked DCCC computer for terms that included "hillary," "cruz," and "trump." The Conspirators also copied select DCCC folders, including "Benghazi Investigations." The Conspirators targeted computers containing information such as opposition research and field operation plans for the 2016 elections.

28. To enable them to steal a large number of documents at once without detection, the Conspirators used a publicly available tool to gather and compress multiple documents on the DCCC and DNC networks. The Conspirators then used other GRU malware, known as "X-Tunnel," to move the stolen documents outside the DCCC and DNC networks through encrypted channels.

a, For example, on or about April 22, 2016, the Conspirators compressed gigabytes of data from DNC computers, including opposition research. The Conspirators later moved the compressed DNC data using X-Tunnel to a GRU-leased computer located in Illinois.

b. On or about April 28, 2016, the Conspirators connected to and tested the same computer located in Illinois. Later that day, the Conspirators used X-Tunnel to connect to that computer to steal additional documents from the DCCC network.

29. Between on or about May 25, 2016 and June 1, 2016, the Conspirators hacked the DNC Microsoft Exchange Server and stole thousands of emails from the work accounts of DNC employees. During that time, YERMAKOV researched PowerShell commands related to accessing and managing the Microsoft Exchange Server.

30. On or about May 30, 2016, MALYSHEV accessed the AMS panel in order to upgrade custom AMS software on the server. That day, the AMS panel received updates from approximately thirteen different X-Agent malware implants on DCCC and DNC computers.

31. During the hacking of the DCCC and DNC networks, the Conspirators covered their tracks by intentionally deleting logs and computer files. For example, on or about May 13, 2016, the Conspirators cleared the event logs from a DNC computer. On or about June 20, 2016, the Conspirators deleted logs from the AMS panel that documented their activities on the panel, including the login history.

Efforts to Remain on the DCCC and DNC Networks

32. Despite the Conspirators' efforts to hide their activity, beginning in or around May 2016, both the DCCC and DNC became aware that they had been hacked and hired a security company ("Company 1") to identify the extent of the intrusions. By in or around June 2016, Company 1 took steps to exclude intruders from the networks. Despite these efforts, a Linux-based version of X-Agent, programmed to communicate with the GRU-registered domain linuxkrnl.net, remained on the DNC network until in or around October 2016.

33. In response to Company 1's efforts, the Conspirators took countermeasures to maintain access to the DCCC and DNC networks.

    a. On or about May 31, 2016, YERMAKOV searched for open-source information about Company 1 and its reporting on X-Agent and X-Tunnel. On or about June 1, 2016, the Conspirators attempted to delete traces of their presence on the DCCC network using the computer program CCleaner.

    b. On or about June 14, 2016, the Conspirators registered the domain actblues.com, which mimicked the domain of a political fundraising platform that included a DCCC donations page. Shortly thereafter, the Conspirators used stolen DCCC credentials to modify the DCCC website and redirect visitors to the actblues.com domain.

    c. On or about June 20, 2016, after Company 1 had disabled X-Agent on the DCCC network, the Conspirators spent over seven hours unsuccessfully trying to connect to X-Agent. The Conspirators also tried to access the DCCC network using previously stolen credentials.

34. In or around September 2016, the Conspirators also successfully gained access to DNC computers hosted on a third-party cloud-computing service. These computers contained test applications related to the DNC's analytics. After conducting reconnaissance, the Conspirators gathered data by creating backups, or "snapshots," of the DNC's cloud-based systems using the cloud provider's own technology. The Conspirators then moved the snapshots to cloud-based accounts they had registered with the same service, thereby stealing the data from the DNC.

Stolen Documents Released through DCLeaks

35. More than a month before the release of any documents, the Conspirators constructed the online persona DCLeaks to release and publicize stolen election-related documents. On or about April 19, 2016, after attempting to register the domain electionleaks.com, the Conspirators registered the domain dcleaks.com through a service that anonymized the registrant. The funds used to pay for the dcleaks.com domain originated from an account at an online cryptocurrency service that the Conspirators also used to fund the lease of a virtual private server registered with the operational email account dirbinsaabol@mail.com. The dirbinsaabol email account was also used to register the john356gh URL-shortening account used by LUKASHEV to spearphish the Clinton Campaign chairman and other campaign-related individuals.

36. On or about June 8, 2016, the Conspirators launched the public website dcleaks.com, which they used to release stolen emails. Before it shut down in or around March 2017, the site received over one million page views. The Conspirators falsely claimed on the site that DCLeaks was started by a group of

"American hacktivists," when in fact it was started by the Conspirators.

37.   Starting in or around June 2016 and continuing through the 2016 U.S. presidential election, the Conspirators used DCLeaks to release emails stolen from individuals affiliated with the Clinton Campaign. The Conspirators also released documents they had stolen in other spearphishing operations, including those they had conducted in 2015 that collected emails from individuals affiliated with the Republican Party.

38.   On or about June 8, 2016, and at approximately the same time that the dcleaks.com website was launched, the Conspirators created a DCLeaks Facebook page using a preexisting social media account under the fictitious name "Alice Donovan." In addition to the DCLeaks Facebook page, the Conspirators used other social media accounts in the names of fictitious U.S. persons such as "Jason Scott" and "Richard Gingrey" to promote the DCLeaks website. The Conspirators accessed these accounts from computers managed by POTEMKIN and his co-conspirators.

39.   On or about June 8, 2016, the Conspirators created the Twitter account @dcleaks_. The Conspirators operated the @dcleaks_ Twitter account from the same computer used for other efforts to interfere with the 2016 U.S. presidential election. For example, the Conspirators used the same computer to operate the Twitter account @BaltimoreIsWhr, through which they encouraged U.S. audiences to "[j]oin our flash mob" opposing Clinton and to post images with the hashtag #BlacksAgainstHillary.

Stolen Documents Released through Guccifer 2.0

40.   On or about June 14, 2016, the DNC—through Company 1—publicly announced that it had been hacked by Russian government actors. In response, the Conspirators created the online persona Guccifer 2.0 and falsely claimed to be a lone Romanian hacker to undermine the allegations of Russian responsibility for the intrusion.

41.   On or about June 15, 2016, the Conspirators logged into a Moscow-based server used and managed by Unit 74455 and, between 4:19 PM and 4:56 PM Moscow Standard Time, searched for certain words and phrases, including:

Search Term(s)
"some hundred sheets"
"some hundreds of sheets"
dcleaks
illuminati

широко известный перевод [widely known translation]
"worldwide known"
"think twice about"
"company's competence"

42. Later that day, at 7:02 PM Moscow Standard Time, the online persona Guccifer 2.0 published its first post on a blog site created through WordPress. Titled "DNC's servers hacked by a lone hacker," the post used numerous English words and phrases that the Conspirators had searched for earlier that day (bolded below):

> "**Worldwide known** cyber security company [Company 1] announced that the Democratic National Committee (DNC) servers had been hacked by "sophisticated" hacker groups.
>
> I'm very pleased the company appreciated my skills so highly))) [. . .]
>
> Here are just a few docs from many thousands I extracted when hacking into DNC's network. [. . .]
>
> **Some hundred sheets**! This's a serious case, isn't it? [. . .]
>
> I guess [Company 1] customers should **think twice about company's competence.**
>
> F[***] the **Illuminati** and their conspiracies!!!!!!!!! F[***] [Company 1]!!!!!!!!!"

43. Between in or around June 2016 and October 2016, the Conspirators used Guccifer 2.0 to release documents through WordPress that they had stolen from the DCCC and DNC. The Conspirators, posing as Guccifer 2.0, also shared stolen documents with certain individuals.

    a. On or about August 15, 2016, the Conspirators, posing as Guccifer 2.0, received a request for stolen documents from a candidate for the U.S. Congress. The Conspirators responded using the Guccifer 2.0 persona and sent the candidate stolen documents related to the candidate's opponent.

    b. On or about August 22, 2016, the Conspirators, posing as Guccifer 2.0, transferred approximately 2.5 gigabytes of data stolen from the DCCC to a then-registered state lobbyist and online source of political news. The stolen data included donor records and personal identifying information for more than 2,000 Democratic donors.

c.   On or about August 22, 2016, the Conspirators, posing as Guccifer 2.0, sent a reporter stolen documents pertaining to the Black Lives Matter movement. The reporter responded by discussing when to release the documents and offering to write an article about their release.

44.   The Conspirators, posing as Guccifer 2.0, also communicated with U.S. persons about the release of stolen documents. On or about August 15, 2016, the Conspirators, posing as Guccifer 2.0, wrote to a person who was in regular contact with senior members of the presidential campaign of Donald J. Trump, "thank u for writing back . . . do u find anyt[h]ing interesting in the docs i posted?" On or about August 17, 2016, the Conspirators added, "please tell me if i can help u anyhow . . . it would be a great pleasure to me." On or about September 9, 2016, the Conspirators, again posing as Guccifer 2.0, referred to a stolen DCCC document posted online and asked the person, "what do u think of the info on the turnout model for the democrats entire presidential campaign." The person responded, "[p]retty standard."

45.   The Conspirators conducted operations as Guccifer 2.0 and DCLeaks using overlapping computer infrastructure and financing.

a.   For example, between on or about March 14, 2016 and April 28, 2016, the Conspirators used the same pool of bitcoin funds to purchase a virtual private network ("VPN") account and to lease a server in Malaysia. In or around June 2016, the Conspirators used the Malaysian server to host the dcleaks.com website. On or about July 6, 2016, the Conspirators used the VPN to log into the @Guccifer_2 Twitter account. The Conspirators opened that VPN account from the same server that was also used to register malicious domains for the hacking of the DCCC and DNC networks.

b.   On or about June 27, 2016, the Conspirators, posing as Guccifer 2.0, contacted a U.S. reporter with an offer to provide stolen emails from "Hillary Clinton's staff." The Conspirators then sent the reporter the password to access a nonpublic, password-protected portion of dcleaks.com containing emails stolen from Victim 1 by LUKASHEV, YERMAKOV, and their co-conspirators in or around March 2016.

46.   On or about January 12, 2017, the Conspirators published a statement on the Guccifer 2.0 WordPress blog, falsely claiming that the intrusions and release of stolen documents had "totally no relation to the Russian government."

Use of Organization 1

47.   In order to expand their interference in the 2016 U.S. presidential election, the Conspirators transferred many of the documents they stole from the DNC and the chairman of the Clinton Campaign to Organization 1. The Conspirators, posing as Guccifer 2.0, discussed the release of the stolen documents and the timing of those releases with Organization 1 to heighten their impact on the 2016 U.S. presidential election.

      a.   On or about June 22, 2016, Organization 1 sent a private message to Guccifer 2.0 to "[s]end any new material [stolen from the DNC] here for us to review and it will have a much higher impact than what you are doing." On or about July 6, 2016, Organization 1 added, "if you have anything hillary related we want it in the next tweo [sic] days prefable [sic] because the DNC [Democratic National Convention] is approaching and she will solidify bernie supporters behind her after." The Conspirators responded, "ok . . . i see." Organization 1 explained, "we think trump has only a 25% chance of winning against hillary . . . so conflict between bernie and hillary is interesting."

      b.   After failed attempts to transfer the stolen documents starting in late June 2016, on or about July 14, 2016, the Conspirators, posing as Guccifer 2.0, sent Organization 1 an email with an attachment titled "wk dnc link1.txt.gpg." The Conspirators explained to Organization 1 that the encrypted file contained instructions on how to access an online archive of stolen DNC documents. On or about July 18, 2016, Organization 1 confirmed it had "the 1Gb or so archive" and would make a release of the stolen documents "this week."

48.   On or about July 22, 2016, Organization 1 released over 20,000 emails and other documents stolen from the DNC network by the Conspirators. This release occurred approximately three days before the start of the Democratic National Convention. Organization 1 did not disclose Guccifer 2.0's role in providing them. The latest-in-time email released through Organization 1 was dated on or about May 25, 2016, approximately the same day the Conspirators hacked the DNC Microsoft Exchange Server.

49.   On or about October 7, 2016, Organization 1 released the first set of emails from the chairman of the Clinton Campaign that had been stolen by LUKASHEV and his co-conspirators. Between on or about October 7, 2016 and November 7, 2016, Organization 1 released approximately thirty-three tranches of documents that had been stolen from the chairman of the Clinton Campaign. In total, over 50,000 stolen documents were released.

IV.   Statutory Allegations

50.   Paragraphs 1 through 49 of this Indictment are re-alleged and incorporated by reference as if fully set forth herein.

51.   From at least in or around March 2016 through November 2016, in the District of Columbia and elsewhere, Defendants NETYKSHO, ANTONOV, BADIN, YERMAKOV, LUKASHEV, MORGACHEV, KOZACHEK, YERSHOV, MALYSHEV, OSADCHUK, and POTEMKIN, together with others known and unknown to the Grand Jury, knowingly and intentionally conspired to commit offenses against the United States, namely:

a.   To knowingly access a computer without authorization and exceed authorized access to a computer, and to obtain thereby information from a protected computer, where the value of the information obtained exceeded $5,000, in violation of Title 18, United States Code, Sections 1030(a)(2)(C) and 1030(c)(2)(B); and

b.   To knowingly cause the transmission of a program, information, code, and command, and as a result of such conduct, to intentionally cause damage without authorization to a protected computer, and where the offense did cause and, if completed, would have caused, loss aggregating $5,000 in value to at least one person during a one-year period from a related course of conduct affecting a protected computer, and damage affecting at least ten protected computers during a one-year period, in violation of Title 18, United States Code, Sections 1030(a)(5)(A) and 1030(c)(4)(B).

52.   In furtherance of the Conspiracy and to effect its illegal objects, the Conspirators committed the overt acts set forth in paragraphs 1 through 19, 21 through 49, 55, and 57 through 64, which are re-alleged and incorporated by reference as if fully set forth herein.

53.   In furtherance of the Conspiracy, and as set forth in paragraphs 1 through 19, 21 through 49, 55, and 57 through 64, the Conspirators knowingly falsely registered a domain name and knowingly used that domain name in the course of committing an offense, namely, the Conspirators registered domains, including dcleaks.com and actblues.com, with false names and addresses, and used those domains in the course of committing the felony offense charged in Count One.

(All in violation of Title 18, United States Code, Sections 371 and 3559(g)(1))

COUNTS TWO THROUGH NINE: Aggravated Identity Theft (18 U.S.C. §§ 1028(a)(1) & (2))

54.   Paragraphs 1 through 19, 21 through 49, and 57 through 64 of this Indictment are re-alleged and incorporated by reference as if fully set forth herein.

55.   On or about the dates specified below, in the District of Columbia

and elsewhere, Defendants VIKTOR BORISOVICH NETYKSHO, BORIS ALEKSEYEVICH ANTONOV, DMITRIY SERGEYEVICH BADIN, IVAN SERGEYEVICH YERMAKOV, ALEKSEY VIKTOROVICH LUKASHEV, SERGEY ALEKSANDROVICH MORGACHEV, NIKOLAY YURYEVICH KOZACHEK, PAVEL VYACHESLAVOVICH YERSHOV, ARTEM ANDREYEVICH MALYSHEV, ALEKSANDR VLADIMIROVICH OSADCHUK, and ALEKSEY ALEKSANDROVICH POTEMKIN did knowingly transfer, possess, and use, without lawful authority, a means of identification of another person during and in relation to a felony violation enumerated in Title 18, United States Code, Section 1028A(c), namely, computer fraud in violation of Title 18, United States Code, Sections 1030(a)(2)(C) and 1030(c)(2)(B), knowing that the means of identification belonged to another real person:

Count	Approximate Date	Victim	Means of Identification
2	March 21, 2016	Victim 3	Username and password for personal email account
3	March 25, 2016	Victim 1	Username and password for personal email account
4	April 12, 2016	Victim 4	Username and password for DCCC computer network
5	April 15, 2016	Victim 5	Username and password for DCCC computer network
6	April 18, 2016	Victim 6	Username and password for DCCC computer network
7	May 10, 2016	Victim 7	Username and password for DNC computer network
8	June 2, 2016	Victim 2	Username and password for personal email account
9	July 6, 2016	Victim 8	Username and password for personal email account

(All in violation of Title 18, United States Code, Sections 1028A(a)(1) and 2.)

COUNT TEN: Conspiracy to Launder Money (18 U.S.C. § 1956(h))

56.   Paragraphs 1 through 19, 21 through 49, and 55 are re-alleged and incorporated by reference as if fully set forth herein.

57. To facilitate the purchase of infrastructure used in their hacking activity—including hacking into the computers of U.S. persons and entities involved in the 2016 U.S. presidential election and releasing the stolen documents—the Defendants conspired to launder the equivalent of more than $95,000 through a web of transactions structured to capitalize on the perceived anonymity of cryptocurrencies such as bitcoin.

58. Although the Conspirators caused transactions to be conducted in a variety of currencies, including U.S. dollars, they principally used bitcoin when purchasing servers, registering domains, and otherwise making payments in furtherance of hacking activity. Many of these payments were processed by companies located in the United States that provided payment processing services to hosting companies, domain registrars, and other vendors both international and domestic. The use of bitcoin allowed the Conspirators to avoid direct relationships with traditional financial institutions, allowing them to evade greater scrutiny of their identities and sources of funds.

59. All bitcoin transactions are added to a public ledger called the Blockchain, but the Blockchain identifies the parties to each transaction only by alphanumeric identifiers known as bitcoin addresses. To further avoid creating a centralized paper trail of all of their purchases, the Conspirators purchased infrastructure using hundreds of different email accounts, in some cases using a new account for each purchase. The Conspirators used fictitious names and addresses in order to obscure their identities and their links to Russia and the Russian government. For example, the dcleaks.com domain was registered and paid for using the fictitious name "Carrie Feehan" and an address in New York. In some cases, as part of the payment process, the Conspirators provided vendors with nonsensical addresses such as "usa Denver AZ," "gfhgh ghfhgfh fdgfdg WA," and "1 2 dwd District of Columbia."

60. The Conspirators used several dedicated email accounts to track basic bitcoin transaction information and to facilitate bitcoin payments to vendors. One of these dedicated accounts, registered with the username "gfadel47," received hundreds of bitcoin payment requests from approximately 100 different email accounts. For example, on or about February 1, 2016, the gfadel47 account received the instruction to "[p]lease send exactly 0.026043 bitcoin to" a certain thirty-four character bitcoin address. Shortly thereafter, a transaction matching those exact instructions was added to the Blockchain.

61. On occasion, the Conspirators facilitated bitcoin payments using the same computers that they used to conduct their hacking activity, including to create and send test spearphishing emails. Additionally, one of these dedicated accounts was used by the Conspirators in or around 2015 to renew the registration of a domain (linuxkrnl.net) encoded in certain X-Agent malware installed on the DNC

network.

62. The Conspirators funded the purchase of computer infrastructure for their hacking activity in part by "mining" bitcoin. Individuals and entities can mine bitcoin by allowing their computing power to be used to verify and record payments on the bitcoin public ledger, a service for which they are rewarded with freshly-minted bitcoin. The pool of bitcoin generated from the GRU's mining activity was used, for example, to pay a Romanian company to register the domain dcleaks.com through a payment processing company located in the United States.

63. In addition to mining bitcoin, the Conspirators acquired bitcoin through a variety of means designed to obscure the origin of the funds. This included purchasing bitcoin through peer-to-peer exchanges, moving funds through other digital currencies, and using prepaid cards. They also enlisted the assistance of one or more third-party exchangers who facilitated layered transactions through digital currency exchange platforms providing heightened anonymity.

64. The Conspirators used the same funding structure—and in some cases, the very same pool of funds—to purchase key accounts, servers, and domains used in their election-related hacking activity.

    a. The bitcoin mining operation that funded the registration payment for dcleaks.com also sent newly-minted bitcoin to a bitcoin address controlled by "Daniel Farell," the persona that was used to renew the domain linuxkrnl.net. The bitcoin mining operation also funded, through the same bitcoin address, the purchase of servers and domains used in the GRU's spearphishing operations, including accounts-qooqle.com and account-gooogle.com.

    b. On or about March 14, 2016, using funds in a bitcoin address, the Conspirators purchased a VPN account, which they later used to log into the @Guccifer_2 Twitter account. The remaining funds from that bitcoin address were then used on or about April 28, 2016, to lease a Malaysian server that hosted the dcleaks.com website.

    c. The Conspirators used a different set of fictitious names (including "Ward DeClaur" and "Mike Long") to send bitcoin to a U.S. company in order to lease a server used to administer X-Tunnel malware implanted on the DCCC and DNC networks, and to lease two servers used to hack the DNC's cloud network.

65. From at least in or around 2015 through 2016, within the District of Columbia and elsewhere, Defendants VIKTOR BORISOVICH NETYKSHO, BORIS ALEKSEYEVICH ANTONOV, DMITRIY SERGEYEVICH BADIN, IVAN SERGEYEVICH YERMAKOV, ALEKSEY VIKTOROVICH LUKASHEV, SERGEY ALEKSANDROVICH MORGACHEV, NIKOLAY YURYEVICH KOZACHEK, PAVEL VYACHESLAVOVICH YERSHOV, ARTEM ANDREYEVICH MALYSHEV, ALEKSANDR VLADIMIROVICH

OSADCHUK, and ALEKSEY ALEKSANDROVICH POTEMKIN, together with others, known and unknown to the Grand Jury, did knowingly and intentionally conspire to transport, transmit, and transfer monetary instruments and funds to a place in the United States from and through a place outside the United States and from a place in the United States to and through a place outside the United States, with the intent to promote the carrying on of specified unlawful activity, namely, a violation of Title 18, United States Code, Section 1030, contrary to Title 18, United States Code, Section 1956(a)(2)(A).

(All in violation of Title 18, United States Code, Section 1956(h).)

COUNT ELEVEN: Conspiracy to Commit an Offense Against the United States (18 U.S.C. § 371)

66. Paragraphs 1 through 8 of this Indictment are re-alleged and incorporated by reference as if fully set forth herein.

I. Defendants

67. Paragraph 18 of this Indictment relating to ALEKSANDR VLADIMIROVICH OSADCHUK is re-alleged and incorporated by reference as if fully set forth herein.

68. Defendant ANATOLIY SERGEYEVICH KOVALEV (Ковалев Анатолий Сергеевич) was an officer in the Russian military assigned to Unit 74455 who worked in the GRU's 22 Kirova Street building (the Tower).

69. Defendants OSADCHUK and KOVALEV were GRU officers who knowingly and intentionally conspired with each other and with persons, known and unknown to the Grand Jury, to hack into the computers of U.S. persons and entities responsible for the administration of 2016 U.S. elections, such as state boards of elections, secretaries of state, and U.S. companies that supplied software and other technology related to the administration of U.S. elections.

II. Object of the Conspiracy

70. The object of the conspiracy was to hack into protected computers of persons and entities charged with the administration of the 2016 U.S. elections in order to access those computers and steal voter data and other information stored on those computers.

III. Manner and Means of the Conspiracy

71. In or around June 2016, KOVALEV and his co-conspirators researched domains used by U.S. state boards of elections, secretaries of state, and other election-related entities for website vulnerabilities. KOVALEV and his co-conspirators also searched for state political party email addresses, including filtered queries for email addresses listed on state Republican Party websites.

72.   In or around July 2016, KOVALEV and his co-conspirators hacked the website of a state board of elections ("SBOE 1") and stole information related to approximately 500,000 voters, including names, addresses, partial social security numbers, dates of birth, and driver's license numbers.

73.   In or around August 2016, KOVALEV and his co-conspirators hacked into the computers of a U.S. vendor ("Vendor 1") that supplied software used to verify voter registration information for the 2016 U.S. elections. KOVALEV and his co-conspirators used some of the same infrastructure to hack into Vendor 1 that they had used to hack into SBOE 1.

74.   In or around August 2016, the Federal Bureau of Investigation issued an alert about the hacking of SBOE 1 and identified some of the infrastructure that was used to conduct the hacking. In response, KOVALEV deleted his search history. KOVALEV and his co-conspirators also deleted records from accounts used in their operations targeting state boards of elections and similar election-related entities.

75.   In or around October 2016, KOVALEV and his co-conspirators further targeted state and county offices responsible for administering the 2016 U.S. elections. For example, on or about October 28, 2016, KOVALEV and his co-conspirators visited the websites of certain counties in Georgia, Iowa, and Florida to identify vulnerabilities.

76.   In or around November 2016 and prior to the 2016 U.S. presidential election, KOVALEV and his co-conspirators used an email account designed to look like a Vendor 1 email address to send over 100 spearphishing emails to organizations and personnel involved in administering elections in numerous Florida counties. The spearphishing emails contained malware that the Conspirators embedded into Word documents bearing Vendor 1's logo.

IV.   *Statutory Allegations*

77.   Between in or around June 2016 and November 2016, in the District of Columbia and elsewhere, Defendants OSADCHUK and KOVALEV, together with others known and unknown to the Grand Jury, knowingly and intentionally conspired to commit offenses against the United States, namely:

a.   To knowingly access a computer without authorization and exceed authorized access to a computer, and to obtain thereby information from a protected computer, where the value of the information obtained exceeded $5,000, in violation of Title 18, United States Code, Sections 1030(a)(2)(C) and 1030(c)(2)(B); and

b.   To knowingly cause the transmission of a program, information, code, and command, and as a result of such conduct, to intentionally cause damage without authorization to a protected computer, and where the offense did cause and, if completed, would have caused, loss aggregating $5,000 in value to at least one person during a one-year period from a related course of conduct affecting a protected computer, and damage affecting at least ten protected computers during a one-year period, in violation of Title 18, United States Code, Sections 1030(a)(5)(A) and 1030(c)(4)(B).

78.   In furtherance of the Conspiracy and to effect its illegal objects, OSADCHUK, KOVALEV, and their co-conspirators committed the overt acts set forth in paragraphs 67 through 69 and 71 through 76, which are re-alleged and incorporated by reference as if fully set forth herein.

(All in violation of Title 18, United States Code, Section 371.)

FORFEITURE ALLEGATION

79.   Pursuant to Federal Rule of Criminal Procedure 32.2, notice is hereby given to Defendants that the United States will seek forfeiture as part of any sentence in the event of Defendants' convictions under Counts One, Ten, and Eleven of this Indictment. Pursuant to Title 18, United States Code, Sections 982(a)(2) and 1030(i), upon conviction of the offenses charged in Counts One and Eleven, Defendants NETYKSHO, ANTONOV, BADIN, YERMAKOV, LUKASHEV, MORGACHEV, KOZACHEK, YERSHOV, MALYSHEV, OSADCHUK, POTEMKIN, and KOVALEV shall forfeit to the United States any property, real or personal, which constitutes or is derived from proceeds obtained directly or indirectly as a result of such violation, and any personal property that was used or intended to be used to commit or to facilitate the commission of such offense. Pursuant to Title 18, United States Code, Section 982(a)(1), upon conviction of the offense charged in Count Ten, Defendants NETYKSHO, ANTONOV, BADIN, YERMAKOV, LUKASHEV, MORGACHEV, KOZACHEK, YERSHOV,   MALYSHEV, OSADCHUK, and POTEMKIN shall forfeit to the United States any property, real or personal, involved in such offense, and any property traceable to such property. Notice is further given that, upon conviction, the United States intends to seek a judgment against each Defendant for a sum of money representing the property described in this paragraph, as applicable to each Defendant (to be offset by the forfeiture of any specific property).

SUBSTITUTE ASSETS

80.   If any of the property described above as being subject to forfeiture, as a result of any act or omission of any Defendant --

    a.   cannot be located upon the exercise of due diligence;

    b.   has been transferred or sold to, or deposited with, a third party;

    c.   has been placed beyond the jurisdiction of the court;

  d. has been substantially diminished in value; or

  e. has been commingled with other property that cannot be subdivided without difficulty;

-- it is the intent of the United States of America, pursuant to Title 18, United States Code, Section 982(b) and Title 28, United States Code, Section 2461(c), incorporating Title 21, United States Code, Section 853, to seek forfeiture of any other property of said Defendant.

 (Pursuant to 18 U.S.C. §§ 982 and 1030(i); 28 U.S.C. § 2461(c).)

       Signed: Robert S. Mueller, III
        Special Counsel

CHAPTER 12: PAUL MANAFORT, DEC. 7, 2018

UNITED STATES v. PAUL J. MANAFORT

FILED: December 7, 2018 in the United States District Court for the District of Columbia

Editor's Note: In this filing from the Special Counsel, the government details the myriad ways that Paul Manafort broke the plea agreement he reached with Mueller less than six months before. The prosecutors argue that they are well within their rights to throw out the terms of the deal while not releasing Manafort from the guilty pleas he made earlier because he acted in bad faith by continuing to lie to federal investigators.

GOVERNMENT'S SUBMISSION IN SUPPORT
OF ITS BREACH DETERMINATION

1. The United States of America, by and through Special Counsel Robert S. Mueller, III, respectfully makes this submission to summarize the basis for its determination that defendant Paul J. Manafort, Jr., has breached his plea agreement by making false statements. The government intends to rely on the defendant's false statements as a sentencing issue under 18 U.S.C. § 3553. We are prepared to prove the basis for the defendant's breach at a hearing that will establish each false statement through independent documentary and testimonial evidence, including Manafort's subsequent admissions. We separately submit a motion to permit filing under seal the factual material that relates to pending investigations or uncharged individuals.

I. Factual Background

2. On September 14, 2018, Manafort pleaded guilty to a superseding information, charging him with two conspiracy counts that together encompassed all the criminal conduct alleged in the superseding indictment in this district. As the Court is aware, that criminal conduct occurred for more than a decade and up through April 2018.

3. Manafort's plea agreement required that he cooperate "fully, truthfully, completely, and forthrightly" with the government. Plea Agreement, Doc. 422 ¶ 8; Plea Hr'g Tr. 39:10-17, 48:11-16, Sept. 14, 2018. The plea agreement further

provides that if the defendant fails "specifically to perform or to fulfill completely each and every one" of his obligations under the agreement, or "engages in any criminal activity prior to sentencing or during his cooperation," the defendant will be in breach of the agreement. Plea Agreement, Doc. 422 ¶ 13; The agreement further provides:

> "[s]hould it be judged by the Government in its sole discretion that the defendant has failed to cooperate fully, has intentionally given false, misleading or incomplete information or testimony, has committed or attempted to commit any further crimes, or has otherwise violated any provision of this agreement, the defendant will not be released from his pleas of guilty, but the Government will be released from its obligations under this agreement, including (a) not to oppose a downward adjustment of two levels for acceptance of responsibility described above... and (b) to file the motion for a downward departure for cooperation described above. Id. ¶ 13. A breach leaves intact all the obligations of the defendant as well as his guilty plea, but relieves the government of its promises under the agreement. Id. illf 4B, 8, & 13. Finally, the agreement provides that the government "shall be required to prove a breach of the Agreement only by good faith." Id. ¶ 13.

4.   Manafort met with the Special Counsel's Office and the Federal Bureau of Investigation (FBI) on twelve occasions; three of these meetings occurred prior to the defendant entering into his plea agreement. At four of the post-plea meetings, prosecutors from other Department of Justice components attended. Manafort was represented by defense counsel at every meeting with the government. Manafort also was called to testify before the grand jury on two occasions, October 26 and November 2, 2018.

5.   On November 8, 2018, the government informed defense counsel that it believed that Manafort had lied in multiple ways and on multiple occasions. It offered to provide further details and requested the defense to make any responsive submissions, orally or in writing, before the government made any final determination. The defense then met or spoke with the government on several occasions, where the government enumerated the basis for its views. These

communications occurred on November 13 -- 16 and 26. At the defense's request, the government agreed to seek an extension from the Court of the deadline for a joint status report, from November 16 to the 26. The government would not agree to an additional extension. In none of the communications with Manafort's counsel was any factual or legal argument made as to why the government's assessment of Manafort's credibility was erroneous or made without good faith.

II.   Legal Standard

6.   The principal question before this Court, should Manafort contest the government's determination, is whether the government has acted in good faith in determining that Manafort breached his obligations under the plea agreement by intentionally providing false, misleading, or incomplete information. In assessing the breach of a plea agreement, courts "look to principles of contract law," because 'a plea agreement is a contract."' United States v. Henry, 758 F.3d 427, 431 (D.C. Cir. 2014) (quoting United States v. Jones, 58 F.3d 688, 691 (D.C. Cir. 1995)). Where, as here, the plea agreement sets forth a standard for the government to prove a defendant's breach, courts rely on basic contract principles and apply the contractual standard—namely, that the government must prove it determined the defendant's breach "by good faith." Plea Agreement ¶ 13; see United States u. Shah, 263 F. Supp. 2d 10, 32-33 (D.D.C. 2003) (applying preponderance-of-the-evidence standard where the plea agreement provided for it).

7.   In describing the relevant facts, the government may proceed by proffer, cf. United States v. Smith, 79 F.3d 1208, 1210 (D.C. Cir. 1996) (government may proceed by proffer at detention stage), but is prepared to prove the following facts through documentary evidence and witness testimony at a hearing.

III.   Factual Basis for Breach

8.   The defendant breached his plea agreement in numerous ways by lying to the FBI and Special Counsel's Office. The principal lies relate to, among other things: Manafort's interactions with Konstantin Kilimnik; Kilimnik's participation in count two of the superseding information; a wire-transfer to a firm that was working for Manafort; information pertinent to another Department of Justice investigation; and (E) Manafort's contact with Administration officials. We briefly set forth each in turn.

A.   Interactions With Kilimnik

9.   Over the course of several interviews, Manafort lied about the fact [REDACTED] and Manafort falsely told investigators that after [REDACTED]. In fact, Manafort [REDACTED]. The evidence of the above includes electronic communications (including detailed descriptions, [REDACTED], draft [REDACTED],

and travel records. After being told of such evidence, Manafort conceded that he and Kilimnik discussed or may have discussed at each meeting. [REDACTED]

B.   Meeting With Kilimnik

10.   Manafort lied repeatedly about [REDACTED], first denying that he [REDACTED]. During the course of his debriefings, Manafort provided different explanations for [REDACTED]. Manafort first denied that he had [REDACTED], claiming that he (Manafort) [REDACTED]. At his next interview, Manafort was informed of evidence that Manafort then acknowledged. However, evidence (including email communications and testimonial evidence) demonstrates that [REDACTED]. [REDACTED]

C.   Kilimnik's Role In The Obstruction Conspiracy

11.   After signing the plea agreement, Manafort denied that Kilimnik was part of a criminal conspiracy to obstruct justice by reaching out to two witnesses to tailor their testimony to a false narrative that would exculpate them of a Foreign Agents Registration Act violation. Yet on September 14, 2018, Manafort pleaded guilty to count two of the superseding information, charging him with conspiring with Kilimnik to obstruct justice between February and April 2018 by trying to influence the testimony of the two witnesses. Superseding Criminal Information, Doc. 419 at 33-36; Statement of the Offenses and Other Acts, Doc. 423 TT 44-46; Plea Hr'g Tr.32:15 — 33:16, 34:17-20. When asked whether his prior plea and sworn admissions were truthful, Manafort conceded that Kilimnik had conspired with him.

D.   Payment To A Firm Working For Manafort

12.   After signing the plea agreement, Manafort lied about a $125,000 payment made toward a debt incurred by Manafort to a firm working for Manafort in 2017. Records establish that the payment came from another firm (Firm A), which performed work for an entity (Entity B). Manafort has a long relationship with the heads of Firm A and Entity B. Entity B had engaged Firm A at Manafort's suggestion to perform certain work. Under the terms of the contract, Firm A was to receive a 6% commission on expenditures made to it from Entity B.Manafort made several inconsistent statements to the government about the payment: that it was repayment of a debt owed to Manafort by the head of Entity B (whereas the banking records showed the payment came from Firm A); that it was income to Manafort for work performed for Firm A in the past; and that it was a loan from Firm A to Manafort.

13.   Other documentary and/or testimonial evidence establishes that: [REDACTED]; and the contract between Firm A and Entity B contains a provision that the full 6% commission will go to Firm A.

E.   Another DOJ Investigation

14.   During meetings with the government prior to pleading guilty and signing his plea agreement, Manafort provided information about [REDACTED] that

was pertinent to an investigation in another district. However, after signing the plea agreement, Manafort told the government (including Department of Justice personnel handling this investigation) a different and exculpatory version of the events. He then subsequently changed that version in order to more closely conform to his earlier statements, after defense counsel in the government's presence showed him notes that defense counsel represented had been taken of the earlier proffer session.

F.   *Contact With The Administration*

15.   After signing the plea agreement, Manafort stated he had no direct or indirect communications with anyone in the Administration while they were in the Administration and that he never asked anyone to try to communicate a message to anyone in the Administration on any subject matter. Manafort stated that he spoke with certain individuals before they worked for the Administration or after they left the Administration.

16.   The evidence demonstrates that Manafort lied about his contacts. The evidence demonstrates that Manafort had contacts with Administration officials. For instance, in a text exchange from May 26, 2018, Manafort authorized a person to speak with an Administration official on Manafort's behalf. Separately, according to another Manafort colleague, Manafort said in February 2018 that Manafort had been in communication with a senior Administration official up through February 2018. A review of documents recovered from a search of Manafort's electronic documents demonstrates additional contacts with Administration officials.

17.   As summarized above, in his interviews with the Special Counsel's Office and the FBI, Manafort told multiple discernible lies — these were not instances of mere memory lapses. If the defendant contends the government has not acted in good faith, the government is available to prove the false statements at a hearing. Further, to the extent that the defendant contests specific false statements that implicate ongoing investigations, the government is available to provide relevant evidence to the Court ex parte.

Respectfully Submitted,

Signed: Robert S. Mueller, III
Special Counsel

Prepared By: Andrew Weissmann, Jeannie S. Rhee & Greg D. Andres
Senior/Assistant Special Counsels

CHAPTER 13: ROGER STONE, JAN. 24, 2019

UNITED STATES v. ROGER JASON STONE, JR.

FILED: January 24, 2019 in the U.S. District Court for the District of Columbia

Editor's Note: Roger Stone has been an associate of Trump's for decades, and has been encouraging him to run for president since the 1980s. He describes himself as a political "dirty-trickster" and is the subject of the documentary "Get Me Roger Stone."

Indictment

The Grand Jury for the District of Columbia charges:

I.   *Introduction*

1.   By in or around May 2016, the Democratic National Committee ("DNC") and the Democratic Congressional Campaign Committee ("DCCC") became aware that their computer systems had been compromised by unauthorized intrusions and hired a security company ("Company 1") to identify the extent of the intrusions.

2.   On or about June 14, 2016, the DNC—through Company 1—publicly announced that it had been hacked by Russian government actors.

3.   From in or around July 2016 through in or around November 2016, an organization ("Organization 1"), which had previously posted documents stolen by others from U.S. persons, entities, and the U.S. government, released tens of thousands of documents stolen from the DNC and the personal email account of the chairman of the U.S. presidential campaign of Hillary Clinton ("Clinton Campaign").

   a.   On or about July 22, 2016, Organization 1 released documents stolen from the DNC.

   b.   Between on or about October 7, 2016 and on or about November 7, 2016, Organization 1 released approximately 33 tranches of documents that had been stolen from the personal email account of the Clinton Campaign chairman, totaling over 50,000 stolen documents.

4.   ROGER JASON STONE, JR. was a political consultant who worked for decades in U.S. politics and on U.S. political campaigns. STONE was an official on the U.S. presidential campaign of Donald J. Trump ("Trump Campaign") until in or

around August 2015, and maintained regular contact with and publicly supported the Trump Campaign through the 2016 election.

5.   During the summer of 2016, STONE spoke to senior Trump Campaign officials about Organization 1 and information it might have had that would be damaging to the Clinton Campaign. STONE was contacted by senior Trump Campaign officials to inquire about future releases by Organization 1.

6.   By in or around early August 2016, STONE was claiming both publicly and privately to have communicated with Organization 1. By in or around mid-August 2016, Organization 1 made a public statement denying direct communication with STONE. Thereafter, STONE said that his communication with Organization 1 had occurred through a person STONE described as a "mutual friend," "go-between," and "intermediary." STONE also continued to communicate with members of the Trump Campaign about Organization 1 and its intended future releases.

7.   After the 2016 U.S. presidential election, the U.S. House of Representatives Permanent Select Committee on Intelligence ("HPSCI"), the U.S. Senate Select Committee on Intelligence ("SSCI"), and the Federal Bureau of Investigation ("FBI") opened or announced their respective investigations into Russian interference in the 2016 U.S. presidential election, which included investigating STONE's claims of contact with Organization 1.

8.   In response, STONE took steps to obstruct these investigations. Among other steps to obstruct the investigations, STONE:

   a.   Made multiple false statements to HPSCI about his interactions regarding Organization 1, and falsely denied possessing records that contained evidence of these interactions; and

   b.   Attempted to persuade a witness to provide false testimony to and withhold pertinent information from the investigations.

II.   Other Relevant Individuals

9.   Person 1 was a political commentator who worked with an online media publication during the 2016 U.S. presidential campaign. Person 1 spoke regularly with STONE throughout the campaign, including about the release of stolen documents by Organization 1.

10.   Person 2 was a radio host who had known STONE for more than a decade. In testimony before HPSCI on or about September 26, 2017, STONE described Person 2 (without naming him) as an "intermediary," "go-between," and "mutual friend" to the head of Organization 1. In a follow-up letter to HPSCI dated October 13, 2017, STONE identified Person 2 by name and claimed Person 2 was the "gentleman who confirmed for Mr. Stone" that the head of Organization 1 had "'[e]mails related to Hillary Clinton which are pending publication.'"

III. Background

STONE's Communications About Organization 1 During the Campaign

11.   By in or around June and July 2016, STONE informed senior Trump Campaign officials that he had information indicating Organization 1 had documents whose release would be damaging to the Clinton Campaign. The head of Organization 1 was located at all relevant times at the Ecuadorian Embassy in London, United Kingdom.

12.   After the July 22, 2016 release of stolen DNC emails by Organization 1, a senior Trump Campaign official was directed to contact STONE about any additional releases and what other damaging information Organization 1 had regarding the Clinton Campaign. STONE thereafter told the Trump Campaign about potential future releases of damaging material by Organization 1.

13.   STONE also corresponded with associates about contacting Organization 1 in order to obtain additional emails damaging to the Clinton Campaign.

a.   On or about July 25, 2016, STONE sent an email to Person 1 with the subject line, "Get to [the head of Organization 1]." The body of the message read, "Get to [the head of Organization 1] [a]t Ecuadorian Embassy in London and get the pending [Organization 1] emails . . . they deal with Foundation, allegedly." On or about the same day, Person 1 forwarded STONE's email to an associate who lived in the United Kingdom and was a supporter of the Trump Campaign.

b.   On or about July 31, 2016, STONE emailed Person 1 with the subject line, "Call me MON." The body of the email read in part that Person 1's associate in the United Kingdom "should see [the head of Organization 1]."

c.   On or about August 2, 2016, Person 1 emailed STONE. Person 1 wrote that he was currently in Europe and planned to return in or around mid-August. Person 1 stated in part, "Word is friend in embassy plans 2 more dumps. One shortly after I'm back. 2nd in Oct. Impact planned to be very damaging." The phrase "friend in embassy" referred to the head of Organization 1. Person 1 added in the same email, "Time to let more than [the Clinton Campaign chairman] to be exposed as in bed w enemy if they are not ready to drop HRC. That appears to be the game hackers are now about. Would not hurt to start suggesting HRC old, memory bad, has stroke – neither he nor she well. I expect that much of next dump focus, setting stage for Foundation debacle."

14. Starting in early August 2016, after receiving the August 2, 2016 email from Person 1, STONE made repeated statements about information he claimed to have learned from the head of Organization 1.

a. On or about August 8, 2016, STONE attended a public event at which he stated, "I actually have communicated with [the head of Organization 1]. I believe the next tranche of his documents pertain to the Clinton Foundation, but there's no telling what the October surprise may be."

b. On or about August 12, 2016, STONE stated during an interview that he was "in communication with [the head of Organization 1]" but was "not at liberty to discuss what I have."

c. On or about August 16, 2016, STONE stated during an interview that "it became known on this program that I have had some back-channel communication with [Organization 1] and [the head of Organization 1]." In a second interview on or about the same day, STONE stated that he "communicated with [the head of Organization 1]" and that they had a "mutual acquaintance who is a fine gentleman."

d. On or about August 18, 2016, STONE stated during a television interview that he had communicated with the head of Organization 1 through an "intermediary, somebody who is a mutual friend."

e. On or about August 23, 2016, Person 2 asked STONE during a radio interview, "You've been in touch indirectly with [the head of Organization 1]. . . . Can you give us any kind of insight? Is there an October surprise happening?" STONE responded, "Well, first of all, I don't want to intimate in any way that I control or have influence with [the head of Organization 1] because I do not. . . . We have a mutual friend, somebody we both trust and therefore I am a recipient of pretty good information."

15. Beginning on or about August 19, 2016, STONE exchanged written communications, including by text message and email, with Person 2 about Organization 1 and what the head of Organization 1 planned to do.

a. On or about August 19, 2016, Person 2 sent a text message to STONE that read in part, "I'm going to have [the head of Organization 1] on my show next Thursday." On or about August 21, 2016, Person 2 sent another text message to STONE, writing in part, "I have [the head of Organization 1] on Thursday so I'm completely tied up on that day."

b. On or about August 25, 2016, the head of Organization 1 was a guest on Person 2's radio show for the first time. On or about August 26, 2016, Person 2 sent a text message to STONE that stated, "[the head of Organization 1] talk[ed] about you last night." STONE asked what the head of Organization 1 said, to which Person 2 responded, "He didn't say anything bad we were talking about how the Press is trying to make it look like you and he are in cahoots."

    c. On or about August 27, 2016, Person 2 sent text messages to STONE that said, "We are working on a [head of Organization 1] radio show," and that he (Person 2) was "in charge" of the project. In a text message sent later that day, Person 2 added, "[The head of Organization 1] has kryptonite on Hillary."

    d. On or about September 18, 2016, STONE sent a text message to Person 2 that said, "I am emailing u a request to pass on to [the head of Organization 1]." Person 2 responded "Ok," and added in a later text message, "[j]ust remember do not name me as your connection to [the head of Organization 1] you had one before that you referred to."

    i. On or about the same day, September 18, 2016, STONE emailed Person 2 an article with allegations against then-candidate Clinton related to her service as Secretary of State. STONE stated, "Please ask [the head of Organization 1] for any State or HRC email from August 10 to August 30—particularly on August 20, 2011 that mention [the subject of the article] or confirm this narrative."

    ii. On or about September 19, 2016, STONE texted Person 2 again, writing, "Pass my message . . . to [the head of Organization 1]." Person 2 responded, "I did." On or about September 20, 2016, Person 2 forwarded the request to a friend who was an attorney with the ability to contact the head of Organization 1. Person 2 blind- copied STONE on the forwarded email.

    e. On or about September 30, 2016, Person 2 sent STONE via text message a photograph of Person 2 standing outside the Ecuadorian Embassy in London where the head of Organization 1 was located.

    f. On or about October 1, 2016, which was a Saturday, Person 2 sent STONE text messages that stated, "big news Wednesday . . . now pretend u don't know me . . . Hillary's campaign will die this week." In the days preceding these messages, the press had reported that the head of Organization 1 planned to make a public announcement on or about Tuesday, October 4, 2016, which was reported to be the ten-year anniversary of the founding of Organization 1.

    g. On or about October 2, 2016, STONE emailed Person 2, with the subject line "WTF?," a link to an article reporting that Organization 1 was canceling its "highly anticipated Tuesday announcement due to security concerns." Person 2 responded to STONE, "head fake."

    h. On or about the same day, October 2, 2016, STONE texted Person 2 and asked, "Did [the head of Organization 1] back off." On or about October 3, 2016, Person 2 initially responded, "I can't tal[k] about it." After further exchanges with STONE, Person 2 said, "I think it[']s on for tomorrow." Person 2 added later that day, "Off the Record Hillary and her people are doing a full-court press they [sic] keep [the head of Organization 1] from making the next dump . . . That's all I can tell you on this line . . . Please leave my name out of it."

16.   In or around October 2016, STONE made statements about Organization 1's future releases, including statements similar to those that Person 2 made to him. For example:

a.   On or about October 3, 2016, STONE wrote to a supporter involved with the Trump Campaign, "Spoke to my friend in London last night. The payload is still coming."

b.   Also on or about October 3, 2016, STONE received an email from a reporter who had connections to a high-ranking Trump Campaign official that asked, "[the head of Organization 1] – what's he got? Hope it's good." STONE responded in part, "It is. I'd tell [the high-ranking Trump Campaign official] but he doesn't call me back."

c.   On or about October 4, 2016, the head of Organization 1 held a press conference but did not release any new materials pertaining to the Clinton Campaign. Shortly afterwards, STONE received an email from the high-ranking Trump Campaign official asking about the status of future releases by Organization 1. STONE answered that the head of Organization 1 had a "[s]erious security concern" but that Organization 1 would release "a load every week going forward."

d.   Later that day, on or about October 4, 2016, the supporter involved with the Trump Campaign asked STONE via text message if he had "hear[d] anymore from London." STONE replied, "Yes - want to talk on a secure line - got Whatsapp?" STONE subsequently told the supporter that more material would be released and that it would be damaging to the Clinton Campaign.

17.   On or about October 7, 2016, Organization 1 released the first set of emails stolen from the Clinton Campaign chairman. Shortly after Organization 1's release, an associate of the high- ranking Trump Campaign official sent a text message to STONE that read "well done." In subsequent conversations with senior Trump Campaign officials, STONE claimed credit for having correctly predicted the October 7, 2016 release.

IV.   The Investigations

18.   In or around 2017, government officials publicly disclosed investigations into Russian interference in the 2016 U.S. presidential election and possible links to individuals associated with the campaigns.

a.   On or about January 13, 2017, the chairman and vice chairman of SSCI announced the committee would conduct an inquiry that would investigate, among other things, any intelligence regarding links between Russia and individuals associated with political campaigns, as well as Russian cyber activity and other "active measures" directed against the United States in connection with the 2016 election.

b.   On or about January 25, 2017, the chairman and ranking member of HPSCI announced that HPSCI had been conducting an inquiry similar to SSCI's.

c.   On or about March 20, 2017, the then-director of the FBI testified at a HPSCI hearing and publicly disclosed that the FBI was investigating Russian interference in the 2016 election and possible links and coordination between the Trump Campaign and the Russian government.

d.   By in or around August 2017, news reports stated that a federal grand jury had opened an investigation into matters relating to Russian government efforts to interfere in the 2016 election, including possible links and coordination between the Trump Campaign and the Russian government.

STONE's False Testimony to HPSCI

19.   In or around May 2017, HPSCI sent a letter requesting that STONE voluntarily appear before the committee and produce any documents, records, electronically stored information including e-mail, communication, recordings, data and tangible things (including, but not limited to, graphs, charts, photographs, images and other documents) regardless of form, other than those widely available (e.g., newspaper articles) that reasonably could lead to the discovery of any facts within the investigation's publicly- announced parameters. On or about May 22, 2017, STONE caused a letter to be submitted to HPSCI stating that "Mr. Stone has no documents, records, or electronically stored information, regardless of form, other than those widely available that reasonably could lead to the discovery of any facts within the investigation's publicly-announced parameters."

20.   On or about September 26, 2017, STONE testified before HPSCI in Washington, D.C. as part of the committee's ongoing investigation. In his opening statement, STONE stated, "These hearings are largely based on a yet unproven allegation that the Russian state is responsible for the hacking of the DNC and [the Clinton Campaign chairman] and the transfer of that information to [Organization 1]." STONE further stated that "[m]embers of this Committee" had made certain "assertions against me which must be rebutted here today," which included "[t]he charge that I knew in advance about, and predicted, the hacking of Clinton campaign

chairman['s] email, [and] that I had advanced knowledge of the source or actual content of the [Organization 1] disclosures regarding Hillary Clinton."

21. In the course of his HPSCI testimony, STONE made deliberately false and misleading statements to the committee concerning, among other things, his possession of documents pertinent to HPSCI's investigation; the source for his early August 2016 statements about Organization 1; requests he made for information from the head of Organization 1; his communications with his identified intermediary; and his communications with the Trump Campaign about Organization 1.

STONE's False & Misleading Testimony RE Possession of Pertinent Documents

22. During his HPSCI testimony, STONE was asked, "So you have no emails to anyone concerning the allegations of hacked documents . . . or any discussions you have had with third parties about [the head of Organization 1]? You have no emails, no texts, no documents whatsoever, any kind of that nature?" STONE falsely and misleadingly answered, "That is correct.Not to my knowledge."

23. In truth and in fact, STONE had sent and received numerous emails and text messages during the 2016 campaign in which he discussed Organization 1, its head, and its possession of hacked emails. At the time of his false testimony, STONE was still in possession of many of these emails and text messages, including:

a. The email from STONE to Person 1 on or about July 25, 2016 that read in part, "Get to [the head of Organization 1] [a]t Ecuadorian Embassy in London and get the pending [Organization 1] emails . . . they deal with Foundation, allegedly.";

b. The email from STONE to Person 1 on or about July 31, 2016 that said an associate of Person 1 "should see [the head of Organization 1].";

c. The email from Person 1 to STONE on or about August 2, 2016 that stated in part, "Word is friend in embassy plans 2 more dumps. One shortly after I'm back. 2nd in Oct. Impact planned to be very damaging.";

d. Dozens of text messages and emails, beginning on or about August 19, 2016 and continuing through the election, between STONE and Person 2 in which they discussed Organization 1 and the head of Organization 1;

e. The email from STONE on or about October 3, 2016 to the supporter involved with the Trump Campaign, which read in part, "Spoke to my friend in London last night. The payload is still coming."; and

f. The emails on or about October 4, 2016 between STONE and the high-ranking member of the Trump Campaign, including STONE's statement that Organization 1 would release "a load every week going forward."

24. By falsely claiming that he had no emails or text messages in his possession that referred to the head of Organization 1, STONE avoided providing a basis for HPSCI to subpoena records in his possession that could have shown that other aspects of his testimony were false and misleading.

STONE's False and Misleading Testimony About His Early August 2016 Statements

25. During his HPSCI testimony on or about September 26, 2017, STONE was asked to explain his statements in early August 2016 about being in contact with the head of Organization 1. STONE was specifically asked about his statement on or about August 8, 2016 that "I've actually communicated with [the head of Organization 1]," as well as his statement on or about August 12, 2016 that he was "in communication with [the head of Organization 1]" but was "not at liberty to discuss what I have."

26. STONE responded that his public references to having a means of contacting Organization 1 referred exclusively to his contact with a journalist, who STONE described as a "go-between, as an intermediary, as a mutual friend" of the head of Organization 1. STONE stated that he asked this individual, his intermediary, "to confirm what [the head of Organization 1] ha[d] tweeted, himself, on July 21st, that he ha[d] the Clinton emails and that he [would] publish them." STONE further stated that the intermediary "was someone I knew had interviewed [the head of Organization 1]. And I merely wanted confirmation of what he had tweeted on the 21st." STONE declined to tell HPSCI the name of this "intermediary" but provided a description in his testimony that was consistent with Person 2.

27. On or about October 13, 2017, STONE caused a letter to be submitted to HPSCI that identified Person 2 by name as the "gentleman who confirmed for Mr. Stone" that the head of Organization 1 had "'[e]mails related to Hillary Clinton which are pending publication.'"

28. STONE's explanation of his August 2016 statements about communicating with the head of Organization 1 was false and misleading. In truth and in fact, the first time Person 2 interviewed the head of Organization 1 was on or about August 25, 2016, after STONE made his August 8 and August 12, 2016 public statements. Similarly, at the time STONE made his August 2016 statements, STONE had directed Person 1—not Person 2—to contact the head of Organization 1. And Person 1—not Person 2—had told STONE in advance of STONE's August 8 and August 12, 2016 public statements that "[w]ord is friend in embassy plans 2 more dumps," including one in October. At no time did STONE identify Person 1 to HPSCI as another individual STONE contacted to serve as a "go-between," "intermediary," or other source of information from Organization 1. STONE also never disclosed his

exchanges with Person 1 when answering HPSCI's questioning about STONE's August 8 and August 12, 2016 statements.

STONE's False & Misleading Testimony RE Requests for Information from Organization 1

29. During his HPSCI testimony, STONE was asked, "[W]hat was the extent of the communication with [the intermediary]?" STONE replied, "I asked him to confirm . . . that the tweet of [the head of Organization 1] of the 21st was accurate, that they did in fact have . . . Hillary Clinton emails and that they would release them." STONE was then asked, "Did you ask [the intermediary] to communicate anything else to [the head of Organization 1]?" STONE falsely and misleadingly responded, "I did not." STONE was then asked, "Did you ask [the intermediary] to do anything on your own behalf?" STONE falsely and misleadingly responded, "I did not."

30. In truth and in fact, STONE directed both Person 1 and Person 2 to pass on requests to the head of Organization 1 for documents that STONE believed would be damaging to the Clinton Campaign. For example:

a. As described above, on or about July 25, 2016, STONE sent Person 1 an email that read, "Get to [the head of Organization 1] [a]t Ecuadorian Embassy in London and get the pending [Organization 1] emails . . . they deal with Foundation, allegedly."

b. On or about September 18, 2016, STONE sent a text message to Person 2 that said, "I am emailing u a request to pass on to [the head of Organization 1]," and then emailed Person 2 an article with allegations against then-candidate Clinton related to her service as Secretary of State. STONE added, "Please ask [the head of Organization 1] for any State or HRC email from August 10 to August 30— particularly on August 20, 2011 that mention [the subject of the article] or confirm this narrative."

c. On or about September 19, 2016, STONE texted Person 2 again, writing "Pass my message . . . to [the head of Organization 1]." Person 2 responded, "I did," and the next day Person 2, on an email blind-copied to STONE, forwarded the request to an attorney who had the ability to contact the head of Organization 1. STONE's False and Misleading Testimony About Communications with His Identified Intermediary

31. During his HPSCI testimony, STONE was asked repeatedly about his communications with the person he identified as his intermediary. STONE falsely and misleadingly stated that he had never communicated with his intermediary in writing in any way. During one exchange, STONE falsely and misleadingly claimed only to have spoken with the intermediary telephonically:

i. Q: [H]ow did you communicate with the intermediary? A: Over the phone.

ii. Q: And did you have any other means of communicating with the intermediary? A: No.

iii. Q: No text messages, no – none of the list, right? A: No.

Later during his testimony, STONE again denied communicating with his intermediary in writing:

i. Q: So you never communicated with your intermediary in writing in any way? A: No.

ii. Q: Never emailed him or texted him? A: He's not an email guy.

iii. Q: So all your conversations with him were in person or over the phone? A: Correct.

32. In truth and in fact, as described above, STONE and Person 2 (who STONE identified to HPSCI as his intermediary) engaged in frequent written communication by email and text message. STONE also engaged in frequent written communication by email and text message with Person 1, who also provided STONE with information regarding Organization 1.

33. Written communications between STONE and Person 1 and between STONE and Person 2 continued through STONE's HPSCI testimony. Indeed, on or about September 26, 2017—the day that STONE testified before HPSCI and denied having ever sent or received emails or text messages from Person 2—STONE and Person 2 exchanged over thirty text messages.

34. Certain electronic messages between STONE and Person 1 and between STONE and Person 2 would have been material to HPSCI. For example:

a. In or around July 2016, STONE emailed Person 1 to "get to" the head of Organization 1 and obtain the pending emails.

b. In or around September 2016, STONE sent messages directing Person 2 to pass a request to the head of Organization 1.

c. On or about January 6, 2017, Person 2 sent STONE an email that had the subject line "Back channel bs." In the email, Person 2 wrote, "Well I have put together timelines[] and you [] said you have a back-channel way back a month before I had [the head of Organization 1] on my show . . . I have never had a conversation with [the head of Organization 1] other than my radio show . . . I have pieced it all together . . . so you may as well tell the truth that you had no back-channel or there's the guy you were talking about early August."

STONE's False and Misleading Testimony About Communications with the Trump Campaign

35. During his HPSCI testimony, STONE was asked, "did you discuss your conversations with the intermediary with anyone involved in the Trump

campaign?" STONE falsely and misleadingly answered, "I did not." In truth and in fact, and as described above, STONE spoke to multiple individuals involved in the Trump Campaign about what he claimed to have learned from his intermediary to Organization 1, including the following:

    a.   On multiple occasions, STONE told senior Trump Campaign officials about materials possessed by Organization 1 and the timing of future releases.

    b.   On or about October 3, 2016, STONE wrote to a supporter involved with the Trump Campaign, "Spoke to my friend in London last night. The payload is still coming."

    c.   On or about October 4, 2016, STONE told a high-ranking Trump Campaign official that the head of Organization 1 had a "[s]erious security concern" but would release "a load every week going forward."

Attempts to Prevent Person 2 from Contradicting STONE's False Statements to HPSCI

36.   On or about October 19, 2017, STONE sent Person 2 an excerpt of his letter to HPSCI that identified Person 2 as his "intermediary" to Organization 1. STONE urged Person 2, if asked by HPSCI, to falsely confirm what STONE had previously testified to, including that it was Person 2 who provided STONE with the basis for STONE's early August 2016 statements about contact with Organization 1. Person 2 repeatedly told STONE that his testimony was false and told him to correct his testimony to HPSCI. STONE did not do so. STONE then engaged in a prolonged effort to prevent Person 2 from contradicting STONE's false statements to HPSCI.

37.   In or around November 2017, Person 2 received a request from HPSCI to testify voluntarily before the committee. After being contacted by HPSCI, Person 2 spoke and texted repeatedly with STONE. In these discussions, STONE sought to have Person 2 testify falsely either that Person 2 was the identified intermediary or that Person 2 could not remember what he had told STONE. Alternatively, STONE sought to have Person 2 invoke his Fifth Amendment right against self- incrimination. For example:

    a.   On or about November 19, 2017, in a text message to STONE, Person 2 said that his lawyer wanted to see him (Person 2). STONE responded, "'Stonewall it. Plead the fifth. Anything to save the plan' . . . Richard Nixon." On or about November 20, 2017, Person 2 informed HPSCI that he declined HPSCI's request for a voluntary interview.

    b.   On or about November 21, 2017, Person 2 texted STONE, "I was told that the house committee lawyer told my lawyer that I will be getting a subpoena." STONE responded, "That was the point at which your lawyers should have told them you would assert your 5th Amendment rights if compelled to appear."

    c.   On or about November 28, 2017, Person 2 received a subpoena compelling his testimony before HPSCI. Person 2 informed STONE of the subpoena.

    d.   On or about November 30, 2017, STONE asked Person 1 to write publicly about Person 2. Person 1 responded, "Are you sure you want to make something out of this now? Why not wait to see what [Person 2] does. You may be defending yourself too much—raising new questions that will fuel new inquiries. This may be a time to say less, not more." STONE responded by telling Person 1 that Person 2 "will take the 5th—but let's hold a day."

    e.   On multiple occasions, including on or about December 1, 2017, STONE told Person 2 that Person 2 should do a "Frank Pentangeli" before HPSCI in order to avoid contradicting STONE's testimony. Frank Pentangeli is a character in the film The Godfather: Part II, which both STONE and Person 2 had discussed, who testifies before a congressional committee and in that testimony claims not to know critical information that he does in fact know.

    f.   On or about December 1, 2017, STONE texted Person 2, "And if you turned over anything to the FBI you're a fool." Later that day, Person 2 texted STONE, "You need to amend your testimony before I testify on the 15th." STONE responded, "If you testify you're a fool. Because of trump I could never get away with a certain [sic] my Fifth Amendment rights but you can. I guarantee you you are the one who gets indicted for perjury if you're stupid enough to testify."

    38.   On or about December 12, 2017, Person 2 informed HPSCI that he intended to assert his Fifth Amendment privilege against self-incrimination if required to appear by subpoena. Person 2 invoked his Fifth Amendment privilege in part to avoid providing evidence that would show STONE's previous testimony to Congress was false.

    39.   Following Person 2's invocation of his Fifth Amendment privilege not to testify before HPSCI, STONE and Person 2 continued to have discussions about the various investigations into Russian interference in the 2016 election and what information Person 2 would provide to investigators. During these conversations, STONE repeatedly made statements intended to prevent Person 2 from cooperating with the investigations. For example:

    a.   On or about December 24, 2017, Person 2 texted STONE, "I met [the head of Organization 1] for f[i]rst time this yea[r] sept 7 . . . docs prove that. . . . You should be honest w fbi . . . there was no back channel . . .

be honest." STONE replied approximately two minutes later, "I'm not talking to the FBI and if your smart you won't either."

b. On or about April 9, 2018, STONE wrote in an email to Person 2, "You are a rat. A stoolie. You backstab your friends-run your mouth my lawyers are dying Rip you to shreds." STONE also said he would "take that dog away from you," referring to Person 2's dog. On or about the same day, STONE wrote to Person 2, "I am so ready. Let's get it on. Prepare to die [expletive]."

c. On or about May 21, 2018, Person 2 wrote in an email to STONE, "You should have just been honest with the house Intel committee . . . you've opened yourself up to perjury charges like an idiot." STONE responded, "You are so full of [expletive]. You got nothing. Keep running your mouth and I'll file a bar complaint against your friend [the attorney who had the ability to contact the head of Organization 1]."

COUNT ONE: Obstruction of Proceeding (18 U.S.C. § 1505 & 2)

40. Paragraphs 1 through 39 of this Indictment are re-alleged and incorporated by reference as if fully set forth herein.

41. From in or around May 2017 through at least December 2017, within the District of Columbia and elsewhere, the defendant ROGER JASON STONE, JR., corruptly influenced, obstructed, impeded, and endeavored to influence, obstruct, and impede the due and proper exercise of the power of inquiry under which any inquiry and investigation is being had by either House, and any committee of either House and any joint committee of the Congress, to wit: STONE testified falsely and misleadingly at a HPSCI hearing in or around September 2017; STONE failed to turn over and lied about the existence of responsive records to HPSCI's requests about documents; STONE submitted and caused to be submitted a letter to HPSCI falsely and misleadingly describing communications with Person 2; and STONE attempted to have Person 2 testify falsely before HPSCI or prevent him from testifying.

(All in violation of Title 18, United States Code, Sections 1505 & 2)

COUNTS 2-6: Making False Statements (18 U.S.C. § 1001(a)(2) & 2)

42. Paragraphs 1 through 39 of this Indictment are re-alleged and incorporated by reference as if fully set forth herein.

43. On or about September 26, 2017, within the District of Columbia and elsewhere, in a matter within the jurisdiction of the legislative branch of the Government of the United States, the defendant ROGER JASON STONE, JR., knowingly and willfully made and caused to be made materially false, fictitious, and fraudulent statements and representations, to wit:

False Statements by Indictment Count:

2) STONE testified falsely that he did not have emails with third parties about the head of Organization 1, and that he did not have any documents, emails, or text messages that refer to the head of Organization 1.

3) STONE testified falsely that his August 2016 references to being in contact with the head of Organization 1 were references to communications with a single "go-between," "mutual friend," and "intermediary," who STONE identified as Person 2.

4) STONE testified falsely that he did not ask the person he referred to as his "go-between," "mutual friend," and "intermediary," to communicate anything to the head of Organization 1 and did not ask the intermediary to do anything on STONE's behalf.

5) STONE testified falsely that he and the person he referred to as his "go-between," "mutual friend," and "intermediary" did not communicate via text message or email about Organization 1.

6) STONE testified falsely that he had never discussed his conversations with the person he referred to as his "go-between," "mutual friend," and "intermediary" with anyone involved in the Trump Campaign.

(All in violation of Title 18, United States Code, Sections 1001(a)(2) & 2)

COUNT 7: Witness Tampering (18 U.S.C. § 1512(b)(1))

44. Paragraphs 1 through 39 of this Indictment are re-alleged and incorporated by reference as if fully set forth herein.

45. Between in or around September 2017 and present, within the District of Columbia and elsewhere, the defendant ROGER JASON STONE, JR., knowingly and intentionally corruptly persuaded and attempted to corruptly persuade another person, to wit: Person 2, with intent to influence, delay, and prevent the testimony of any person in an official proceeding.

(All in violation of Title 18, United States Code, Section 1512(b)(1))

Signed: Robert S. Mueller, III
Special Counsel

CHAPTER 14: PAUL MANAFORT, FEB. 23, 2019

UNITED STATES v. PAUL J. MANAFORT, JR.

FILED: February 23, 2019 in the U.S. District Court for the District of Columbia

Editor's Note: This is the sentencing memo for Paul Manafort, submitted by the special counsel on February 23, 2019. Manafort's dual sentencings (the first in U.S. District Court for the Eastern District of Virginia; the second in U.S. District Court for the District of Columbia.) are scheduled for March 8th and March 13th, 2019.

GOVERNMENT'S SENTENCING MEMORANDUM

1.   The government submits this memorandum in connection with the sentencing of Paul J. Manafort, Jr., scheduled for March 13, 2019, in connection with his guilty plea to two counts of conspiracy in violation of 18 U.S.C. § 371. Consistent with the practice the Special Counsel's Office has followed, the government does not take a position with respect to a particular sentence to be imposed. Instead, the government sets forth its assessment of the nature of the offenses and offender and the applicable advisory sentencing guidelines and sentencing factors.

2.   Based on his relevant sentencing conduct, Manafort presents many aggravating sentencing factors and no warranted mitigating factors. Manafort committed an array of felonies for over a decade, up through the fall of 2018. Manafort chose repeatedly and knowingly to violate the law—whether the laws proscribed garden-variety crimes such as tax fraud, money laundering, obstruction of justice, and bank fraud, or more esoteric laws that he nevertheless was intimately familiar with, such as the Foreign Agents Registration Act (FARA). His criminal actions were bold, some of which were committed while under a spotlight due to his work as the campaign chairman and, later, while he was on bail from this Court. And the crimes he engaged in while on bail were not minor; they went to the heart of the criminal justice system, namely, tampering with witnesses so he would not be held accountable for his crimes. Even after he purportedly agreed to cooperate with the government in September 2018, Manafort, as this court found, lied to the Federal Bureau of Investigation (FBI), this office, and the grand jury. His deceit, which is a fundamental component of the crimes of conviction and relevant conduct, extended

to tax preparers, bookkeepers, banks, the Treasury Department, the Department of Justice National Security Division, the FBI, the Special Counsel's Office, the grand jury, his own legal counsel, Members of Congress, and members of the executive branch of the United States government. In sum, upon release from jail, Manafort presents a grave risk of recidivism. Specific deterrence is thus at its height, as is general deterrence of those who would engage in comparable concerted criminal conduct. See United States v. Fry, 851 F.3d 1329, 1332 (D.C. Cir. 2017) (district court correctly considered pertinent sentencing factors when it, among other things, "explained that the sentence would deter Fry and others who may be inclined in doing similar kinds of things" (internal quotations omitted)); United States v. Jackson, 848 F.3d 460, 466-67 (D.C. Cir. 2017) (citing 18 U.S.C. § 3553(a)(2)(B) & (C), the question for the sentencing court is whether the sentence is "sufficiently stiff to deter [the defendant] and others from committing similar crimes in the future."); United States v. Foy, 617 F.3d 1029, 1037 (8th Cir. 2010) (general deterrence interest in deterring "similarly situated persons.")

   3. Nothing about Manafort's upbringing, schooling, legal education, or family and financial circumstances mitigates his criminality. Indeed, as part of his plea agreement, Manafort agreed that, although he could dispute for instance the guideline calculation as to role in the offense, a downward departure from the government's estimated sentencing guideline range of 210 to 262 months is not warranted and he would not seek or suggest a departure or adjustment.

   The government has organized this submission as follows:

I. Procedural History

II. The Presentence Investigative Report ("PSR")

III. Manafort's Relevant Criminal Conduct And The Statutory Sentencing Factors Under 18 U.S.C. 3553(a):

  (A) Count One Conduct

  (B) Count Two Conduct

  (C) Post-Plea Conduct

IV. Conclusion

I. *Procedural History*

   4. The government details below the charges filed against Manafort in this Court and the United States District Court for the EDVA, and his subsequent convictions, guilty pleas, and failed cooperation.

The District Of Columbia Indictment and Arrest

   5. A grand jury sitting in the District of Columbia indicted Manafort and his employee Richard Gates on October 27, 2017, on eight counts. The charged conduct related to Manafort's work as an agent of the Government of Ukraine, the

Party of Regions and Opposition Bloc, and Ukrainian President Victor Yanukovych (collectively, "Ukraine"). For years, Manafort failed to register under FARA and caused others to fail to register. Manafort also conspired to fail to report both the income earned from his Ukraine engagement and the overseas accounts in which his funds were maintained. He later concealed that work by making false statements to the United States Department of Justice, specifically the FARA Unit of the National Security Division. Manafort also engaged from 2006 to 2016 in a money laundering conspiracy, with multiple objects. Among other things, his money laundering promoted his FARA crimes. The money laundering and tax conspiracies related to the tens of millions from Ukraine, maintained in myriad overseas accounts in Cyprus, St. Vincent and the Grenadines, and the United Kingdom, and transferred to the United States to pay fees to companies that engaged in the FARA scheme, as well as to purchase personal services, luxury items, real estate, and improvements to Manafort's homes in Bridgehampton, New York, and Palm Beach, Florida, among others.

6.   Manafort was allowed to surrender to the FBI on these charges on Monday, October 30, 2017, and was released on bail subject to a series of conditions, including home confinement and OPS monitoring.

Superseding Indictments In The District Of Columbia And Manafort's Remand

7.   On February 23, 2018, the grand jury charged Manafort in a superseding indictment that made several new allegations. Of note, it included an additional component of the FARA. scheme concerning the Hapsburg Group's lobbying in the United States. As the Court is aware, those new allegations led to Manafort and Konstantin Kilimnik promptly and repeatedly reaching out to two witnesses in order to coach them to lie about the work that the Hapsburg Group performed in the United States. On June 8, 2018, Manafort was charged with two additional crimes, along with Kilimnik: attempt and conspiracy to obstruct justice based on their efforts to tamper with these witnesses with respect to the FARA scheme. On June 15, 2018, after hearing from the parties, this Court remanded Manafort based on his criminal conduct while on pretrial release. That decision was affirmed on appeal.

The EDVA Indictment And Trial

8.   On February 22, 2018, a grand jury sitting in the EDVA returned a 32-count indictment against Manafort. Manafort was charged in connection with two types of schemes: one involved tax and FBAR violations; a second involved multiple bank fraud and bank fraud conspiracies. Specifically, Manafort was charged with:

(a) filing false tax returns as to his income and the existence of overseas accounts from 2010 to 2014 (Counts One through Five);

(b) failing to file FBARs in the years 2011 to 2014 (Counts Eleven through Fourteen); and

(c) bank fraud and bank fraud conspiracy (Counts Twenty'-Four to Thirty-Two).'

9.   As with the facts supporting the tax conspiracy charge in the District of Columbia, the substantive tax and FBAR charges related to millions in income earned in Ukraine. Additionally, the indictment contained new allegations, charging Manafort in nine bank fraud and bank fraud conspiracies, involving five loan applications to three separate financial institutions, seeking more than $25 million,. Four of these loan applications related to properties that Manafort purchased or improved with funds from his overseas accounts.

10.   Manafort elected to go to trial and on August 21, 2018, a jury convicted Manafort on eight counts: tax (5), FBAR (1), and bank fraud (2). The jury was hung on the remaining ten counts.'

Manafort's Guilty Pleas In The District of Columbia

11.   On September 14, 2018, on the eve of his second trial and after the jury selection process had commenced, Manafort pled guilty to a two-count superseding information pursuant to a plea agreement requiring his cooperation. Attachment A. The charges encompassed all of the factual allegations in the charges brought in this district. Count One charged Manafort with conspiracy against the United States, pursuant to 18 U.S.C. § 371. The conspiracy has as its objects: tax fraud (in violation of 26 U.S.C. § 7206(1)), FEAR crimes (in violation of 31 U.S.C. §§ 5312 and 5322(b)), a substantive FARA violation and making false statements to the Justice Department (in violation of both FARA 22 U.S.C. §§ 612, 618(a)(1) and 618(a)(2) and 18 U.S.C. § 1001(a)), and money laundering (in violation of 18 U.S.C. § 1956). Manafort's conduct underlying this charge was summarized in the Statement of the Offenses and Other Acts. During Manafort's allocution, he admitted that: he was part of a conspiracy that involved money laundering involving millions of dollars of his income being wired from offshore accounts for goods, services, and real estate; he concealed that income and the related purchases, and the offshore accounts themselves; he hid millions of dollars of other income by falsely characterizing it as "loans"; he lied to his bookkeeper and tax preparers both about the payments from overseas and the existence of the bank accounts from which the money was transferred; he engaged in extensive lobbying activities in the United States on behalf of Ukraine without registering for this work as required; he funneled over $11 million from overseas accounts to pay for lobbyists working for Ukraine to engage in unregistered lobbying in the United States; and in submissions

to the Department of Justice in November 2016 and February 2017, he caused false and misleading statements to be made relating to the lobbying work for Ukraine.

12.   Count Two charged a separate conspiracy to obstruct justice, concerning the tampering with two witnesses who had pertinent evidence about the work of the Hapsburg Group and its United States lobbying. Manafort pleaded guilty to conspiring with Kilimnik between February 23, 2018 and April 2018 to obstruct justice by reaching out to two witnesses to have them conform their testimony to a false set of facts.

II.   The PSR

13.   The government provided its objections to the PSR on February 14, 2018. A copy of that submission is attached hereto in Attachment F, and is incorporated herein. (Because it relates to the PSR, it is being filed under seal.) Because the government has not had the opportunity to respond to Manafort's submission to Probation, we note the following with respect to Manafort's objection, Manafort contends that [REDACTED].

III.   Manafort's Relevant Criminal Conduct And The Statutory Sentencing Factors

14.   Sentencing courts must consider the relevant section 3553(a) factors, which include: the nature and circumstances of the offense; the history and characteristics of the defendant; the need to promote respect for the law, provide a just punishment for the offense, and afford adequate deterrence to criminal conduct; and the need to avoid unwarranted sentencing disparities. 18 U.S.C. § 3553(a). Below, the government sets forth facts pertinent to these factors.

15.   The government addresses each object of the Count One conspiracy and then addresses the Count Two conspiracy and Manafort's misconduct after his guilty pleas.

A.   Count One

i. The FARA Object

16.   This section first discusses Manafort's experience with the FARA statute. That history serves to distinguish Manafort from those who are unaware or unsure of FARA's parameters. It also exemplifies Manafort's boldness in choosing to disobey the law, as he committed his FARA. violations after being warned by the Department of Justice about the law's strictures and after resigning a Presidential appointment in connection with the Department of Justice review. Next, the three major prongs of Manafort's United States lobbying scheme for Ukraine are discussed. Finally, this section outlines Manafort's violations involving lying to the Justice Department in order to cover up his FARA crimes.

17. From 2006 until 2015, Manafort led a multi-million dollar lobbying campaign in the United States at the direction of Ukraine. Manafort did so without registering and providing the public disclosures required by law. Such disclosures would have revealed to the United States public, among other things, which United States government officials were being contacted by Ukraine, when such lobbying occurred, how much was being spent on the lobbying effort, and what public relations activities were undertaken by Ukraine (although appearing to emanate from independent sources). Secrecy was integral to the effectiveness of the foreign lobbying Manafort orchestrated for Ukraine to influence American leaders and the American public; compliance with FARA would have revealed the deceptive tactics Manafort and his Ukraine client were using to lobby in the United States. For instance, as set out in the Statement of the Offenses and Other Acts, Manafort orchestrated a scheme to smear surreptitiously a former senior Obama State Department official and then falsely blame the smear on an Obama rival, so that Ukraine could curry favor with the Obama Administration. Manafort also used secrecy to mislead Members of Congress, falsely using a Hapsburg member as a purported independent voice to advocate with Congress, while concealing that he was a paid Ukraine lobbyist.[1]

18. As part of the lobbying scheme, Manafort hired numerous firms and people to assist in his lobbying campaign in the United States. He hired the Hapsburg Group members, and Skadden, Arps, Slate, Meagher & Flom ("Skadden"), among others, to participate in what he described to President Yanukovych in writing as a global "Engage Ukraine" lobbying campaign which he devised and led. Leaving aside the money Manafort himself earned, these companies and law firm were paid the equivalent of over $11 million for their Ukraine work over a two-year period.

a. *Manafort's History With The FARA Statute*

19. Manafort had a lengthy history with the Department of Justice concerning the FARA statute. These interactions arose in connection with Manafort's lobbying in the mid-1980s when he was a principal at the firm Black, Manafort, Stone, and Kelly Public Affairs Company ("BMSK"). The Department of Justice inspected BMSK's files and provided BMSK its findings of deficiencies in both Manafort's and other BMSK FARA filings.

20. In or about the summer and fall of 1986, the Department of Justice Criminal Division (which then performed the functions now performed by the FARA Unit at the Department's National Security Division) conducted Section 5 inspections of Manafort and BMSK.

21. Manafort's position as both a lobbyist for foreign governments and a director of a federal agency—the Overseas Private Investment Corporation ("OPIC")—drew scrutiny from the Department of Justice, the White House, and the

press. Both then and now, public officials cannot be agents of foreign principals, sec 18 U.Q.C. § 219, and the White House had determined that it would not grant a certification under that statute to exempt Manafort from the law's requirements. Manafort had registered as an agent of the Saudi Arabian government from in or about June 1984 through June 1986." But Manafort did not register for other FARA work, Faced with the White House's decision not to grant him a waiver, Manafort contended to the Department of Justice that he did not run afoul of section 219 because he had not personally lobbied. He claimed that only his firm BMSK, and not he, had acted as a foreign agent. Manafort's argument was rejected by the Department of Justice. The language of section 219 mirrors FARA in applying to anyone who "is or acts as an agent of a foreign principal required to register under [FARA]," 18U.S.C. § 219(a). Even if there might be a theoretical case of "political consulting" that did not involve any personal contacts or other public-relations and lobbying conduct covered by PAR_A, Manafort's public-relations and lobbying services were determined not to fall within that limited type of consulting. Thus, Manafort had to either resign his appointment, or would have to cease all his activities on behalf of foreign principals. Manafort resigned his position as a director of °PIC on May 16, 1986.

22. In spite of these clear warnings and the personal ramifications to him for not adhering to the law, Manafort chose to violate the FARA. statute and to get others to as well. For instance, in 2007 he retained a large American lobbying firm, to assist in lobbying in Europe and the United States in connection with the Ukraine parliamentary elections in the fall of 2007. When sought to register under FARA, Manafort urged not to do so. After the Ukraine 2007 elections were over and was no longer working for Manafort and Ukraine, it belatedly registered in early 2008 under FARA.

b.   Ukraine's Lobbying Operation Through [REDACTED]

23. As he admitted as part of his plea, Manafort in 2005 began a lengthy relationship with foreign government actors, particularly in Ukraine. In 2012, Manafort spearheaded a major international lobbying operation for Ukraine, with a large focus on lobbying in the United States. It had three main aspects, which are discussed in turn.

24. First, Manafort retained two large Washington, D.C. lobbying firms, to engage from 2012 to 2014 in an extensive lobbying effort on behalf of Ukraine, without registering under FARA. Manafort arranged to pay the firms over $2.5 million from Ukraine funds funneled through his offshore accounts for the United States lobbying work for Ukraine. Those transfers also form the gravamen of one prong of the money laundering conspiracy.' Among other things, Manafort had the firms lobby dozens of Members of Congress, their staff, and White House and

State Department officials about Ukraine sanctions, the validity of Ukraine elections, and the propriety of imprisoning Yulia Tymoshenko.

25. One illustration of this aspect of the United States lobbying operation concerned its furtive activity in connection with the United States Senate's consideration of a resolution condemning Ukraine for President Yanukovych's locking up his political opponent Tymoshenko. The resolution was referred to as the Durbin resolution, after its main proponent United States Senator Richard Durbin. The imprisonment of Tymoshenko was a major sticking point in United States-Ukraine relations, as many in the executive and legislative branches thought her treatment demonstrated a lack of commitment to the rule of law. Manafort and President Yanukovych engaged in an all out effort to kill or at least delay the resolution. Thus, Manafort had his lobbying firms contact numerous Members of Congress, engaging in backroom lobbying using personal contacts and confidential Congressional information obtained secretly by from Congressional staff. A chart attached hereto in Attachment 0, which was provided to the Court and defense counsel in August 2018 as part of the Court's pretrial Order regarding trial exhibits, details the major aspects of this effort. None of this lobbying was reported under FARA, as required, so the public would be aware of what efforts this foreign government was making with Members of Congress and the Executive branch. The Durbin resolution is but one example of the lobbying campaign; the government has outlined in Attachment G, Exhibit 448, the principal legislative outreach efforts between 2012 to 2014 orchestrated by Manafort through [REDACTED]

26. Manafort was integrally involved in these lobbying efforts. He repeatedly communicated in person and in writing with President Yanukovych and his staff about the lobbying activities of [REDACTED]

27. He tasked the companies to prepare written reports on their work so he, in turn, could brief President Yanukovych. For instance, Manafort wrote President Yanukovych a memorandum dated April 8, 2012, in which he provided an update on the lobbying firms' activities "since the inception of the project a few weeks ago. It is my intention to provide you with a weekly update moving forward." In November 2012, Gates wrote to the firms that they needed to prepare an assessment of their past and prospective lobbying efforts so the "President" could be briefed by "Paul" "on what Ukraine has done well and what it can do better as we move into 2013." The resulting memorandum noted among other things that the "client" had not been as successful as hoped given that it had an Embassy in Washington.'

28. To appear to distance their United States lobbying work from Ukraine, and to avoid having to register as agents of Ukraine under FARA, Manafort, with others, arranged for [REDACTED] to be nominally engaged by a newly-formed Brussels entity called the European Centre for a Modern Ukraine (the Centre),

instead of directly by Ukraine. Manafort privately described the Centre as "the Brussels NGO that we have formed" to coordinate lobbying for Ukraine. The Centre was founded by a Ukraine Party of Regions member and Ukraine First Vice-Prime Minister. The head of its Board was another member of the Party of Regions, who became the Ukraine Foreign Minister. In spite of these ties to Ukraine, Manafort and others arranged for the Centre to represent falsely to FARA legal counsel that the Centre was not "directly or indirectly supervised, directed, [or] controlled" in whole or in major part by the Government of Ukraine or the Party of Regions (and thus did not need to register under FARA.'

29.   Despite the Centre's being the ostensible client of Manafort, they knew that the Centre did not direct or oversee their United States work. The firms received direction from Manafort and his subordinate Gates on behalf of Ukraine.

   c.   *Ukraine's Lobbying Operation Through The Skadden Report*

30.   As a second part of Ukraine's scheme to lobby in the United States illegally, in 2012 Manafort solicited Skadden, a prominent United States law firm, to write a report evaluating the trial of Tymoshenko. Manafort caused the Ukraine Ministry of Justice to hire the law firm. The goal was for the report to be used in the United States and elsewhere to defend the Tymoshenko criminal trial, specifically to argue that President Yanukovych and Ukraine had not engaged in selective prosecution. The selection of the lead attorney at Skadden [REDACTED] was made with the United States lobbying effort in mind. Although using an accurate report to lobby in the United States on behalf of Ukraine, without reporting under FARA, is itself illegal, Manafort's conduct was compounded by the fact that he knew the report was misleading and used to justify the political prosecution and jailing of a political opponent.

31.   Manafort also retained [REDACTED] a public relations firm, to prepare a media roll-out plan for the Skadden report. Manafort worked closely with to develop a detailed written lobbying plan in connection with what Manafort termed the selling of the report. This campaign included getting the Skadden report seeded to the press in the United States—that is, to leak the report ahead of its official release to a prominent United States newspaper and then use that initial article to influence reporting globally.

32.   A chart setting out a timeline of the major lobbying efforts orchestrated by Manafort to lobby in connection with the Skadden Report is attached hereto as Exhibit 444 of Attachment G. More than $4.6 million was paid to Skadden for its work. Manafort used one of his offshore accounts to funnel $4 million of that sum, Manafort used the same offshore accounts to pay the equivalent of more than $1 million.'

34.   Manafort was aware of various facts that were kept from the public Skadden report, because they would undermine the effectiveness of the report as a

lobbying tool. For instance, Manafort knew that the actual cost of the report and the true scope of the law firm's work would undermine the report's being perceived as independent. Although FARA would have required disclosure of the amount paid for the report (more than $4.6 million), Ukraine reported falsely that the report cost just $12,000. Further, Manafort knew that the report did not disclose facts that could be used to question Skadden's impartiality, namely that Skadden, in addition to being retained to write the report, was retained to represent Ukraine in connection with the Tymoshenko case itself and to provide training to the trial team. prosecuting Tymoshenko in another criminal case.

35.   Substantively, Manafort also knew the report was misleading. Manafort directed lobbyists to tout the report as showing that President Yanukovych had not selectively prosecuted Tymoshenko. But in November 2012—prior to the issuance of the report on December 13, 2012— Manafort had been told privately in writing by Skadden's lead partner that the evidence of Tymoshenko's criminal intent "is virtually non-existent" and that it was unclear even among legal experts that Tymoshenko did not possess the power to engage in the conduct at issue in the Ukraine criminal case. These facts were not disclosed to the public.

   d.   *Ukraine's Lobbying Operation Through The Hapsburg Group*

36.   Starting in 2011, Manafort secretly retained a group of four former European heads of state and senior officials (including a former Chancellor, Prime Minister, and President) to lobby in the United States and Europe on behalf of Ukraine. The former politicians, called the Hapsburg Group, appeared to be solely providing their independent assessments of the Government of Ukraine's policies, when in fact they were paid by Ukraine. Manafort explained in an "EYES ONLY" memorandum in or about June 2012 that his purpose: was to "assemble a small group of high-level European infuencial [sic] champions and politically credible friends who can act informally and without any visible relationship with the Government of Ukraine."

37.   In or about 2012 through 2014, Manafort directed more than the equivalent of $2.8 million to be wired from at least four of his offshore accounts to secretly pay the Hapsburg Group. To avoid European taxation, the contract with the Hapsburg Group falsely stated that none of its work would take place in Europe. And, in or about 2012 through 2013, Manafort directed more than the equivalent of $950,000 to be wired from at least three of his offshore accounts to the benefit of to secretly pay for its services, which entailed, among other things, interfacing with the Hapsburg Group for Manafort.

38.   All four Hapsburg Group members, at the direction and with the direct assistance of Manafort, advocated positions favorable to Ukraine in meetings with United States lawmakers, interviews with United States journalists, and ghostwritten op-eds in American publications. A chart setting out the payments to

the Hapsburg Group and a chart of the major lobbying efforts conducted by Manafort, including efforts conducted through the Hapsburg Group, are attached hereto as Exhibits 436 and 442, respectively."

39. One of the Hapsburg Group members, a former President, was also a representative of the European Parliament with oversight responsibility for Ukraine. Manafort solicited that official to secretly provide Manafort inside information about the European Parliament's views and potential actions toward Ukraine and to take actions favorable to Ukraine, Manafort also used this Hapsburg Group member's current European Parliament position to Ukraine's advantage in his lobbying efforts in the United States. As noted above, in the fall of 2012, the United States Senate was considering and ultimately passed the Durbin resolution, which was critical of President Yanukovych's treatment of former Prime Minister Tymoshenko. As noted above, Manafort engaged in an all-out campaign to try to kill or delay the passage of this resolution. Manafort told his lobbyists to stress to the United States Senators that the former President who was advocating against the resolution was currently a designated representative of the President of the European Parliament in order to give extra clout to his supposedly independent judgment against the proposed Senate resolution. Manafort never revealed to the American public, as required by FARA, that this representative (and his other lobbyists) were paid by Ukraine, thus violating a core purpose of the statute.

40. In another example, on May 16, 2013, amember of the Hapsburg Group lobbied [REDACTED] in the United States for Ukraine. The Hapsburg Group member accompanied his country's prime minister to the Oval Office and met with the then-President and Vice President of the United States, as well as senior United States officials in the executive and legislative branches. In written communications sent to Manafort, the Hapsburg Group member reported that the Hapsburg Group member delivered the desired message." FARA required Manafort to disclose such lobbying. Again, he did not.

41. In addition, [REDACTED], with the assistance of Manafort personally lobbied in the United States. He drafted and edited numerous ghostwritten op-eds for publication in United States newspapers.' He also personally met with a Member of Congress who was on a subcommittee that had Ukraine within its purview in March 2013 in Washington, D.C. After the meeting, Manafort prepared a report for President Yanukovych that the meeting "went well" and reported a series of positive developments for Ukraine from the meeting.

e. Manafort's Belated 2017 FARA Registration Statement

42. In June 2017, Manafort filed a retroactive FARA registration statement for the period 2012 through 2014. That filing was plainly deficient. Manafort entirely omitted the United States lobbying contacts noted above and in the

attached charts, all money (receipts and disbursements) related to the lobbying entities noted above, and a portion of the substantial compensation Manafort received from Ukraine.°

f. Manafort's False Statements To The Department of Justice

43. Manafort caused his attorney to submit two false and misleading letters to the Department of Justice when it inquired about Manafort's Ukraine work beginning in September 2016. The government has already briefed to this Court and to the Chief Judge the facts concerning Manafort's misconduct. The government supplements the record with the chart attached as Exhibit 438, which lists significant documents that Manafort had in his possession at the time that he had his FARA attorney (unwittingly) falsely represent to the Department of Justice that he had no documents concerning his Ukraine work because of a purported document retention policy.

ii. The Tax Arid Objects

44. The government has set forth the facts pertinent to this aspect of Manafort's crimes in a submission made in the EDVA, attached herein. The government relies on and incorporates that submission. The government notes that the FBAR crimes served to promote other crimes: the tax conspiracy herein as well as the FARA violations.

iii. The Money Laundering Object

45. Manafort participated in a money laundering scheme with multiple objects. For purposes of the money laundering object of Count One, it suffices to note that the money Manafort transferred from outside the United States into the United States served to promote FARA. crimes. For instance, as evidenced by Exhibits 434 (attached as part of Attachment 0), Manafort caused millions of dollars to be spent to further the FARA scheme.

B. Count Two

i. The Witness Tampering Conspiracy

46. The government has set forth the facts pertinent to Count Two in its filing with respect to bail, filed in June 2018, and more recently in the Statement of the Offenses and Other Acts." The Court is well acquainted with these facts; they are not repeated herein.'

47. Manafort's witness tampering is notable because it occurred after he had already sought to obstruct the government's FARA investigation by causing his lawyer to submit false statements to the Department of Justice on a host of topics. Then, after indictment and while on pretrial release from two courts, he again obstructed justice by repeatedly seeking to have witnesses lie for him, and getting another (Kilimnik) to participate in that obstruction.

C. Post-Plea Misconduct

48. Manafort's conduct after he pleaded guilty is pertinent to sentencing. It reflects a hardened adherence to committing crimes and lack of remorse. As the Court is fully familiar with this proof, we do not repeat the evidence herein.

49. Manafort voluntarily entered into a plea agreement that required that he cooperate "fully, truthfully, completely, and forthrightly" with the government. The plea agreement further provided that if the defendant failed "specifically to perform or to fulfill completely each and every one" of his obligations under the agreement, or "engages in any criminal activity prior to sentencing or during his cooperation," the defendant will be in breach of the agreement. The agreement further provided:

> "[s]hould it be judged by the Government in its sole discretion that the defendant has failed to cooperate fully, has intentionally given false, misleading or incomplete information or testimony, has committed or attempted to commit any further crimes, or has otherwise violated any provision of this agreement, the defendant will not be released from his pleas of guilty, but the Government will be released from its obligations under this agreement, including (a) not to oppose a downward adjustment of two levels for acceptance of responsibility described above... and (b) to file the motion for a downward departure for cooperation described above."

A breach leaves intact all the obligations of the defendant as well as his guilty plea, but relieves the government of its promises under the agreement.

49. The government relies on and incorporates herein its submissions on this issue. Based on the evidence provided to the Court, the government is not filing a motion for a reduction in sentence below the advisory Sentencing Guideline range or for a third point for acceptance of responsibility. Manafort is not entitled to such a motion under the terms of the plea agreement.

IV. Conclusion

50. For over a decade, Manafort repeatedly and brazenly violated the law. His crimes continued up through the time he was first indicted in October 2017 and remarkably went unabated even after indictment. Manafort engaged in witness tampering while on bail and, even after he was caught for engaging in that scheme,

Manafort committed the additional crimes of perjury and making false statements after he entered his guilty pleas herein. The sentence in this case must take into account the gravity of this conduct, and serve both to specifically deter Manafort and generally deter those who would commit a similar series of crimes.

51.   The Court has the discretion to run all or a portion of the sentence herein consecutive to that imposed in the EDVA criminal prosecution. As it is unknown what that sentence will be, we do not now take a position on the issue, but reserve our right to do so at sentencing herein.

Signed: Robert S. Mueller, III
Special Counsel

Prepared By: Andrew Weissmann, Jeannie S. Rhee & Greg D. Andres
Senior/Assistant Special Counsels

CHAPTER 15: MICHAEL COHEN'S TESTIMONY, FEB. 27, 2019

Public Testimony by MICHAEL COHEN to the Committee on Government Oversight & Reform, U.S. House of Representatives (as prepared in advance) - February 27, 2019

Chairman Cummings, Ranking Member Jordan, and Members of the Committee, thank you for inviting me here today.

I have asked this Committee to ensure that my family be protected from Presidential threats, and that the Committee be sensitive to the questions pertaining to ongoing investigations. Thank you for your help and for your understanding.

I am here under oath to correct the record, to answer the Committee's questions truthfully, and to offer the American people what I know about President Trump.

I recognize that some of you may doubt and attack me on my credibility. It is for this reason that I have incorporated into this opening statement documents that are irrefutable, and demonstrate that the information you will hear is accurate and truthful.

Never in a million years did I imagine, when I accepted a job in 2007 to work for Donald Trump, that he would one day run for President, launch a 2 campaign on a platform of hate and intolerance, and actually win. I regret the day I said "yes" to Mr. Trump. I regret all the help and support I gave him along the way.

I am ashamed of my own failings, and I publicly accepted responsibility for them by pleading guilty in the Southern District of New York.

I am ashamed of my weakness and misplaced loyalty – of the things I did for Mr. Trump in an effort to protect and promote him.

I am ashamed that I chose to take part in concealing Mr. Trump's illicit acts rather than listening to my own conscience.

I am ashamed because I know what Mr. Trump is.

He is a racist.

He is a conman.

He is a cheat.

He was a presidential candidate who knew that Roger Stone was talking with Julian Assange about a WikiLeaks drop of Democratic National Committee emails.

I will explain each in a few moments.

I am providing the Committee today with several documents. These include:

-A copy of a check Mr. Trump wrote from his personal bank account – after he became president - to reimburse me for the hush money payments I made to cover up his affair with an adult film star and prevent damage to his campaign;

-Copies of financial statements for 2011 – 2013 that he gave to such institutions as Deutsche Bank;

-A copy of an article with Mr. Trump's handwriting on it that reported on the auction of a portrait of himself – he arranged for the bidder ahead of time and then reimbursed the bidder from the account of his non-profit charitable foundation, with the picture now hanging in one of his country clubs; and

-Copies of letters I wrote at Mr. Trump's direction that threatened his high school, colleges, and the College Board not to release his grades or SAT scores.

I hope my appearance here today, my guilty plea, and my work with law enforcement agencies are steps along a path of redemption that will restore faith in me and help this country understand our president better.

Before going further, I want to apologize to each of you and to Congress as a whole.

The last time I appeared before Congress, I came to protect Mr. Trump. Today, I'm here to tell the truth about Mr. Trump.

I lied to Congress about when Mr. Trump stopped negotiating the Moscow Tower project in Russia. I stated that we stopped negotiating in January 2016. That was false – our negotiations continued for months later during the campaign.

Mr. Trump did not directly tell me to lie to Congress. That's not how he operates.

In conversations we had during the campaign, at the same time I was actively negotiating in Russia for him, he would look me in the eye and tell 5 me there's no business in Russia and then go out and lie to the American people by saying the same thing. In his way, he was telling me to lie.

There were at least a half-dozen times between the Iowa Caucus in January 2016 and the end of June when he would ask me "How's it going in Russia?" – referring to the Moscow Tower project.

You need to know that Mr. Trump's personal lawyers reviewed and edited my statement to Congress about the timing of the Moscow Tower negotiations before I gave it.

To be clear: Mr. Trump knew of and directed the Trump Moscow negotiations throughout the campaign and lied about it. He lied about it because he never expected to win the election. He also lied about it because he stood to make hundreds of millions of dollars on the Moscow real estate project.

And so I lied about it, too – because Mr. Trump had made clear to me, through his personal statements to me that we both knew were false and through his lies to the country, that he wanted me to lie. And he made it 6 clear to me because his personal attorneys reviewed my statement before I gave it to Congress.

Over the past two years, I have been smeared as "a rat" by the President of the United States. The truth is much different, and let me take a brief moment to introduce myself.

My name is Michael Dean Cohen. I am a blessed husband of 24 years and a father to an incredible daughter and son. When I married my wife, I promised her that I would love her, cherish her, and protect her. As my father said countless times throughout my childhood, "you my wife, and you my children, are the air that I breathe." To my Laura, my Sami, and my Jake, there is nothing I wouldn't do to protect you.

I have always tried to live a life of loyalty, friendship, generosity, and compassion – qualities my parents ingrained in my siblings and me since childhood. My father survived the Holocaust thanks to the compassion and selfless acts of others. He was helped by many who put themselves in harm's way to do what they knew was right.

That is why my first instinct has always been to help those in need. Mom and Dad...I am sorry that I let you down.

As many people that know me best would say, I am the person they would call at 3AM if they needed help. I proudly remember being the emergency contact for many of my children's friends when they were growing up because their parents knew that I would drop everything and care for them as if they were my own.

Yet, last fall I pled guilty in federal court to felonies for the benefit of, at the direction of, and in coordination with Individual #1.

For the record: Individual #1 is President Donald J. Trump.

It is painful to admit that I was motivated by ambition at times. It is even more painful to admit that many times I ignored my conscience and acted loyal to a man when I should not have. Sitting here today, it seems unbelievable that I was so mesmerized by Donald Trump that I was willing to do things for him that I knew were absolutely wrong.

For that reason, I have come here to apologize to my family, to the government, and to the American people.

Accordingly, let me now tell you about Mr. Trump.

I got to know him very well, working very closely with him for more than 10 years, as his Executive Vice President and Special Counsel and then personal attorney when he became President. When I first met Mr. Trump, he was a successful entrepreneur, a real estate giant, and an icon. Being around Mr. Trump was intoxicating. When you were in his presence, you felt like you were involved in something greater than yourself — that you were somehow changing the world.

I wound up touting the Trump narrative for over a decade. That was my job. Always stay on message. Always defend. It monopolized my life. At first, I worked mostly on real estate developments and other business transactions. Shortly thereafter, Mr. Trump brought me into his personal life and private dealings. Over time, I saw his true character revealed.

Mr. Trump is an enigma. He is complicated, as am I. He has both good and bad, as do we all. But the bad far outweighs the good, and since taking office, he has become the worst version of himself. He is capable of behaving kindly, but he is not kind. He is capable of committing acts of generosity, but he is not generous. He is capable of being loyal, but he is fundamentally disloyal.

Donald Trump is a man who ran for office to make his brand great, not to make our country great. He had no desire or intention to lead this nation – only to market himself and to build his wealth and power. Mr. Trump would often say, this campaign was going to be the "greatest infomercial in political history."

He never expected to win the primary. He never expected to win the general election. The campaign – for him – was always a marketing opportunity.

I knew early on in my work for Mr. Trump that he would direct me to lie to further his business interests. I am ashamed to say, that when it was for a real estate mogul in the private sector, I considered it trivial. As the President, I consider it significant and dangerous.

I knew early on in my work for Mr. Trump that he would direct me to lie to further his business interests. I am ashamed to say, that when it was for a real estate mogul in the private sector, I considered it trivial. As the President, I consider it significant and dangerous.

But in the mix, lying for Mr. Trump was normalized, and no one around him questioned it. In fairness, no one around him today questions it, either.

A lot of people have asked me about whether Mr. Trump knew about the release of the hacked Democratic National Committee emails ahead of time. The answer is yes.

As I earlier stated, Mr. Trump knew from Roger Stone in advance about the WikiLeaks drop of emails.

In July 2016, days before the Democratic convention, I was in Mr. Trump's office when his secretary announced that Roger Stone was on the phone. Mr. Trump put Mr. Stone on the speakerphone. Mr. Stone told Mr. Trump that he had just gotten off the phone with Julian Assange and that Mr. Assange told Mr. Stone that, within a couple of days, there would be a massive dump of emails that would damage Hillary Clinton's campaign.

Mr. Trump responded by stating to the effect of "wouldn't that be great."

Mr. Trump is a racist. The country has seen Mr. Trump court white supremacists and bigots. You have heard him call poorer countries "shitholes."

He once asked me if I could name a country run by a black person that wasn't a "shithole." This was when Barack Obama was President of the United States.

While we were once driving through a struggling neighborhood in Chicago, he commented that only black people could live that way.

And, he told me that black people would never vote for him because they were too stupid.

And yet I continued to work for him.

Mr. Trump is a cheat.

As previously stated, I'm giving the Committee today three years of President Trump's financial statements, from 2011-2013, which he gave to Deutsche Bank to inquire about a loan to buy the Buffalo Bills and to Forbes. These are Exhibits 1a, 1b, and 1c to my testimony.

It was my experience that Mr. Trump inflated his total assets when it served his purposes, such as trying to be listed among the wealthiest people in Forbes, and deflated his assets to reduce his real estate taxes.

I am sharing with you two newspaper articles, side by side, that are examples of Mr. Trump inflating and deflating his assets, as I said, to suit his financial interests. These are Exhibit 2 to my testimony.

As I noted, I'm giving the Committee today an article he wrote on, and sent me, that reported on an auction of a portrait of Mr. Trump. This is Exhibit 3A to my testimony.

Mr. Trump directed me to find a straw bidder to purchase a portrait of him that was being auctioned at an Art Hamptons Event. The objective was to ensure that his portrait, which was going to be auctioned last, would go for the highest price of any portrait that afternoon. The portrait was purchased by the fake bidder for $60,000. Mr. Trump directed the Trump Foundation, which is supposed to be a charitable organization, to repay the fake bidder, despite keeping the art for himself. Please see Exhibit 3B to my testimony.

And it should come as no surprise that one of my more common responsibilities was that Mr. Trump directed me to call business owners, many of whom were small businesses, that were owed money for their services and told them no payment or a reduced payment would be coming. When I advised Mr. Trump of my success, he actually reveled in it.

And yet, I continued to work for him.

Mr. Trump is a conman.

He asked me to pay off an adult film star with whom he had an affair, and to lie to his wife about it, which I did. Lying to the First Lady is one of my biggest regrets. She is a kind, good person. I respect her greatly – and she did not deserve that.

I am giving the Committee today a copy of the $130,000 wire transfer from me to Ms. Clifford's attorney during the closing days of the presidential campaign that was demanded by Ms. Clifford to maintain her silence about her affair with Mr. Trump. This is Exhibit 4 to my testimony.

Mr. Trump directed me to use my own personal funds from a Home Equity Line of Credit to avoid any money being traced back to him that could negatively impact his campaign. I did that, too – without bothering to consider whether that was improper, much less whether it was the right thing to do or how it would impact me, my family, or the public.

I am going to jail in part because of my decision to help Mr. Trump hide that payment from the American people before they voted a few days later.

As Exhibit 5 to my testimony shows, I am providing a copy of a $35,000 check that President Trump personally signed from his personal bank 14 account on August 1, 2017 – when he was President of the United States – pursuant to the cover-up, which was the basis of my guilty plea, to reimburse me – the word used by Mr. Trump's TV lawyer — for the illegal hush money I paid on his behalf. This $35,000 check was one of 11 check installments that was paid throughout the year – while he was President.

The President of the United States thus wrote a personal check for the payment of hush money as part of a criminal scheme to violate campaign finance laws. You can find the details of that scheme, directed by Mr. Trump, in the pleadings in the U.S. District Court for the Southern District of New York.

So picture this scene – in February 2017, one month into his presidency, I'm visiting President Trump in the Oval Office for the first time. It's truly awe-inspiring, he's showing me around and pointing to different paintings, and he says to me something to the effect of...Don't worry, Michael, your January and February reimbursement checks are coming. They were FedExed from New York and it takes a while for that to get through the White House system. As he promised, I received the first check for the reimbursement of $70,000 not long thereafter.

When I say conman, I'm talking about a man who declares himself brilliant but directed me to threaten his high school, his colleges, and the College Board to never release his grades or SAT scores.

As I mentioned, I'm giving the Committee today copies of a letter I sent at Mr. Trump's direction threatening these schools with civil and criminal actions if Mr. Trump's grades or SAT scores were ever disclosed without his permission. These are Exhibit 6.

The irony wasn't lost on me at the time that Mr. Trump in 2011 had strongly criticized President Obama for not releasing his grades. As you can see in Exhibit 7, Mr. Trump declared "Let him show his records" after calling President Obama "a terrible student."

The sad fact is that I never heard Mr. Trump say anything in private that led me to believe he loved our nation or wanted to make it better. In fact, he did the opposite.

When telling me in 2008 that he was cutting employees' salaries in half – including mine – he showed me what he claimed was a $10 million IRS tax refund, and he said that he could not believe how stupid the government was for giving "someone like him" that much money back.

During the campaign, Mr. Trump said he did not consider Vietnam Veteran, and Prisoner of War, Senator John McCain to be "a hero" because he likes people who weren't captured. At the same time, Mr. Trump tasked me to handle the negative press surrounding his medical deferment from the Vietnam draft.

Mr. Trump claimed it was because of a bone spur, but when I asked for medical records, he gave me none and said there was no surgery. He told me not to answer the specific questions by reporters but rather offer simply the fact that he received a medical deferment.

He finished the conversation with the following comment. "You think I'm stupid, I wasn't going to Vietnam."

I find it ironic, President Trump, that you are in Vietnam right now.

And yet, I continued to work for him.

Questions have been raised about whether I know of direct evidence that Mr. Trump or his campaign colluded with Russia. I do not. I want to be clear. But, I have my suspicions.

Sometime in the summer of 2017, I read all over the media that there had been a meeting in Trump Tower in June 2016 involving Don Jr. and others from the campaign with Russians, including a representative of the Russian government, and an email setting up the meeting with the subject line, "Dirt on Hillary Clinton." Something clicked in my mind. I remember being in the room with Mr. Trump, probably in early June 2016, when something peculiar happened. Don Jr. came into the room and walked behind his father's desk – which in itself was unusual. People didn't just walk behind Mr. Trump's desk to talk to him. I recalled Don Jr. leaning over to his father and speaking in a low voice, which I could clearly hear, and saying: "The meeting is all set." I remember Mr. Trump saying, "Ok good...let me know."

What struck me as I looked back and thought about that exchange between Don Jr. and his father was, first, that Mr. Trump had frequently told me and others that his son Don Jr. had the worst judgment of anyone in the world. And also, that

Don Jr. would never set up any meeting of any significance alone – and certainly not without checking with his father.

I also knew that nothing went on in Trump world, especially the campaign, without Mr. Trump's knowledge and approval. So, I concluded that Don Jr. was referring to that June 2016 Trump Tower meeting about dirt on Hillary with the Russian representative when he walked behind his dad's desk that day — and that Mr. Trump knew that was the meeting Don Jr. was talking about when he said, "That's good...let me know."

Over the past year or so, I have done some real soul searching. I see now that my ambition and the intoxication of Trump power had much to do with the bad decisions I made.

To you, Chairman Cummings, Ranking Member Jordan, the other members of this Committee, and the other members of the House and Senate, I am sorry for my lies and for lying to Congress.

To our nation, I am sorry for actively working to hide from you the truth about Mr. Trump when you needed it most.

For those who question my motives for being here today, I understand. I have lied, but I am not a liar. I have done bad things, but I am not a bad man. I have fixed things, but I am no longer your "fixer," Mr. Trump.

I am going to prison and have shattered the safety and security that I tried so hard to provide for my family. My testimony certainly does not diminish the pain I caused my family and friends – nothing can do that. And I have never asked for, nor would I accept, a pardon from President Trump.

And, by coming today, I have caused my family to be the target of personal, scurrilous attacks by the President and his lawyer – trying to intimidate me from appearing before this panel. Mr. Trump called me a "rat" for choosing to tell the truth – much like a mobster would do when one of his men decides to cooperate with the government.

As Exhibit 8 shows, I have provided the Committee with copies of Tweets that Mr. Trump posted, attacking me and my family – only someone burying his head in the sand would not recognize them for what they are: encouragement to someone to do harm to me and my family.

I never imagined that he would engage in vicious, false attacks on my family – and unleash his TV-lawyer to do the same. I hope this committee and all members of Congress on both sides of the aisle will make it clear: As a nation, we should not tolerate attempts to intimidate witnesses before congress and attacks on family are out of bounds and not acceptable.

I wish to especially thank Speaker Pelosi for her statements in Exhibit 9 to protect this institution and me, and the Chairman of the House Permanent Select Committee on Intelligence Adam Schiff and Chairman Cummings for likewise defending this institution and my family against the attacks by Mr. Trump, and also the many Republicans who have admonished the President as well.

I am not a perfect man. I have done things I am not proud of, and I will live with the consequences of my actions for the rest of my life.

But today, I get to decide the example I set for my children and how I attempt to change how history will remember me. I may not be able to change the past, but I can do right by the American people here today.

Thank you for your attention. I am happy to answer the Committee's questions.